D0209768

CREATIVE STRATEGY

Creative Strategy

A Guide for Innovation

William Duggan

Columbia Business School
Publishing

Columbia University Press
Publishers Since 1893
New York Chichester, West Sussex
cup.columbia.edu

Library of Congress Cataloging-in-Publication Data

Duggan, William R.
Creative strategy : a handbook for innovation / William Duggan.
p. cm.
Includes bibliographical references and index.
ISBN 978-0-231-16052-0 (cloth : alk. paper) —
ISBN 978-0-231-53146-7 (ebook : alk. paper)
1. Creative ability in business. 2. Creative thinking. 3. Diffusion of innovations.
4. Strategic planning. I. Title.

HD53.D843 2013
658.4'012—dc23

2012036053

Columbia University Press books are printed on permanent and durable acid-free paper.
This book is printed on paper with recycled content.
Printed in the United States of America

c 10 9 8 7 6 5 4 3 2

Cover design: Alexandrine Koegel Lambert
Cover image: Shutterstock

For Lynn and Emmaline

CONTENTS

CREATIVE STRATEGY

Introduction

This book is a practical guide to a big idea about innovation. It's an idea with roots in modern neuroscience, classical military strategy, and Asian philosophy, and it's played a part in countless cases of creative innovation in business and other fields. Over the past decade, I've explained the idea in a series of books and articles, and I've taught the idea to thousands of graduate students and executives in courses at Columbia Business School and in sessions at companies around the world. This book offers a method to apply the idea, in a form that any innovator can learn and use, without any advanced training in business or economics or any other technical field. All you need is a passion for ideas and a desire to put them into action for personal and professional fulfillment. You can use this method as an individual, in a team, or throughout your organization.

The idea is *creative strategy*. It solves the problem of innovation, not just for designing new products but for coming up with creative ideas for strategy at any level: the overall company, a division, a team, or just yourself. It applies to businesses, government agencies, nonprofits, and your own career and personal development. In all kinds of strategy, you always need a creative idea to some degree because the world around you is always changing, so the future is never exactly the same as the past. Your strategy must change to keep up with the times. But how should it change, exactly?

There are two kinds of traditional methods that claim to yield creative ideas for strategy: methods of creativity and methods of strategy. You will see that neither set of traditional methods actually solves the problem. Methods of strategy show you how to analyze your strategic situation, but that's where they stop. They don't give you the next step, how to get a creative idea for what to do. Methods of creativity show you how to come up with lots of creative ideas, but they don't connect those ideas to your strategy. So you end up doing lots of strategic analysis first, and then go into a room to brainstorm creative ideas. There is no connection between the two methods.

This common sequence—formal analysis, then creative brainstorming—actually comes from an old theory of how the brain works. You've probably heard this: the left side of the brain is analytical, and the right side is creative. So first you do your analysis (left side) and then let your creativity (right side) take over. Unfortunately, this is not how the brain really works. In the past ten years, neuroscience has overturned that old model of the brain. We now know that analysis and creativity are not two different functions on two different sides of the brain. In the new model—called *learning-and-memory*—analysis and creativity work together in all modes of thought. You cannot have an idea without both.

The new science of learning-and-memory reveals at last how creative ideas form in the mind. When you do something yourself or learn what someone else did, those details go into your memory. When you face a new situation, your brain breaks down the problem into pieces and then searches through your brain for memories that fit each piece. It then makes a new combination from those pieces of memory. The combination is new, but the elements are not. These three steps—break it down, search, combine—are very different from the two conventional steps of analyze and brainstorm. Creative strategy puts the three steps of learning-and-memory for new situations into a practical method that fits how the human brain actually works.

Part I of this book offers a step-by-step guide to the practice of creative strategy. It begins with a picture of how the brain puts creative ideas together, and then shows how that translates into a formal method for innovation. As you proceed through Part I, you will see that each creative strategy step differs in key ways from traditional methods of strategy, creativity, and innovation. At various points I pause to explain the differences to keep the distinctions clear.

Part II goes into these traditional methods in greater depth to help you alter or depart from them to make room for creative strategy. For example, perhaps you currently use Porter's Five Forces or Blue Ocean Strategy, Six Thinking Hats, the Balanced Scorecard, Design Thinking, Design for Six Sigma, brainstorming sessions of various kinds, or the like. Your aim is to make them work with creative strategy, not against it, and Part II shows you how.

Part III offers miscellaneous materials that provide more background for you to refer to according to your interest or need. It includes a brief summary of the creative strategy method and a review of key sources that led me to the main ideas of this book. As it turns out, I used creative strategy to create creative strategy, and this section shows where the ideas came from that made up the new combination.

As you go through this guide, try to look at creative strategy with a "beginner's mind," as they say in Zen—itself a key source for creative strategy. Try to clear your mind of other methods and allow it space to consider this new idea. At the end, when you've gone through it all, you can decide whether to toss the book away or try to apply its methods, at least in part. Of course I hope, if you've read this far, you're willing to give it a chance.

I

Creative Strategy from the Inside

Part I of this book immerses you in the method of creative strategy. It shows step-by-step how to use creative strategy for innovation problems of various kinds. By the end you become an insider—you know how it works, what makes it tick, and all the moving parts.

Each step in creative strategy has its own complexity and calls for different skills to master. Here I present a much simplified version, which will fit no situation exactly. But it does fit all kinds of situations to some degree. Whenever you face a complex problem that you don't see a way to solve, you need an innovation. But you might not realize that's what you need. You were hired because you know the answers, and it's hard to admit that you don't, that instead you need something new.

Normal planning methods often hide the need for innovation. You lay out your goals and initiatives and timetables for marketing, operations, product development, or your overall strategy. You know how to plan, so that's what you do. But for every goal you set, every initiative you design, there might be a better one just beyond your grasp—an innovation you don't yet see. Creative strategy helps you see it.

1

From Mind to Method

This chapter shows how the human mind creates solutions to new problems and then translates that mental method into a series of formal steps that an individual or group can use for innovation of any kind. The mental method is "strategic intuition," and my previous book *Strategic Intuition* explains it in detail. "Creative strategy" is the set of formal steps you can use to apply strategic intuition.

Strategic Intuition

To start, we must go back to three key milestones in the recent history of the science of the mind. The first came in 1981, when Roger Sperry won the Nobel Prize in Physiology or Medicine for his work on the two sides of the brain. Sperry concluded from his experiments that one side of the brain is rational and analytical but lacks imagination and that the other side of the brain is creative and intuitive but irrational. This conclusion fit the much older idea that human thought is sometimes rational and sometimes irrational. Sperry located these two kinds of thinking in two different parts of the brain.

Traditional views of innovation all conform in some way to this dual model of the human brain. They all involve some "hard/soft" sequence, such as deductive plus inductive reasoning, analysis plus creativity, art plus science, critical thinking plus gut instinct, logic plus feeling, and so on. Some versions add iteration: first analysis, then creativity, then analysis again, then creativity, and so on.

Unfortunately, our second key milestone overturned this dual model of the mind. In the early 1990s, Seiji Ogawa figured out how to use magnetic resonance imaging (MRI) scans to show how ideas emerge in the human brain. Ogawa has been on the short list for the Nobel Prize for some years now. His work let scientists see which parts of the brain different mental tasks actually use. From Ogawa's first MRIs, it was immediately clear that there are not two kinds of thinking that operate on two different sides of the brain.

Although Ogawa's work overturned Sperry's dual model, it took science another decade to arrive at a new model to replace it. Our third key milestone came in 2000, when Eric Kandel won the same Nobel Prize as Sperry for his work on this new model. Kandel called it "learning-and-memory," where the whole brain takes in and stores information through sensation and analysis and retrieves it through conscious and unconscious search and combination. In this model, analysis and intuition are not two different kinds of thought, in two different locations, but rather two key inputs into a single mode of thought that operates throughout the brain. Some thought has more analysis, some has more intuition, but all thought requires both.

Learning-and-memory gives a very different picture of how innovation works. Let's start with analysis. We commonly say analysis is a rational or logical process, but it can never be purely so except in mathematics. We can break down the number 20 into factors of 10 and 2 or 5 and 4. Mathematics is a closed system, so we know we are right. It's logical. But now let's analyze something that is not pure math: the performance of your company or organization over the past decade. What do I include in my analysis, and what do I leave out? For example, the weather: Should we gather data on temperature and plot that against a measure of unit performance? If I say yes and you say no, which one of us is right? And what is our measure of unit performance? What if you and I have different ones? Which one is right?

There is no logical answer for any of these questions. In all cases, we do our best to make an educated guess. You use your judgment, and I use mine. If we disagree, we argue using "logical" arguments, but that does not mean our educated guesses came to us through logic. And our arguments are not purely logical at all, of course, regardless of what we might claim. So how did our educated guesses arrive? Why did I say we should collect weather data, and why did you say we should not? If not by logic, then by what?

Learning-and-memory gives us a clue. You and I have different information in our memories, which we acquired by learning different things. Although we face the same question—the performance of your company or organization over the past decade—we draw on different memories to analyze it. And we do so in two distinct ways: "expert intuition" and "strategic intuition." These are the two main mechanisms the brain uses to apply memories to current and future situations.

Let's start with expert intuition. Herbert Simon won the Nobel Prize in Economics in 1978 partially for his research on how experts think, and in the 1990s Gary Klein took to the field to study experts in action, such as firefighters, emergency room nurses, and soldiers in battle. In the past decade, expert intuition has become a significant field of study in its own right. Malcolm Gladwell's popular book *Blink* gives a recent summary of that research.

We now know that expert intuition is the rapid recall and application of thoughts and actions from direct experience in similar situations. The more experience, the better and faster your expert intuition. So a nurse can walk across the emergency room floor, glance at a child, and rush over to save the child's life. How did she do it? She noticed something she had seen before—in the child's eyes, how the child was sitting, and so forth. Expert intuition happens so fast that experts can seldom explain how they did it, but Klein developed an interview method that pins down to a surprising degree exactly what they recall from their prior experience.

We develop and use expert intuition every day, in all kinds of skills and tasks. Most professional training increases expert intuition. But expert intuition can be the enemy of innovation. We see a new situation and quickly see what's familiar within it and act accordingly. But if the situation is different enough, we've just made a big mistake. Expert intuition cannot solve a strategic or creative problem, which by definition is a new situation. What if our nurse's emergency room is dirty, crowded, and losing money—and she's never experienced that before? She can't just walk across the floor and recall the answer from her past experience. Expert intuition won't work.

She needs strategic intuition instead. This is a particular form of learning-and-memory that has strong roots both in the science of how ideas form in the mind and in empirical cases of successful strategy. The brain selects a set of elements from memory, combines them in a new way, and projects that new combination into the future as a course of action to follow. Strategic intuition typically occurs as one or a series of flashes of insight when the mind is relaxed. The past elements come from both direct experience and the experience of others that you learned through reading, hearing, or seeing.

Once we understand how learning-and-memory creates new ideas, we can go back to some classics of strategy and see elements of strategic intuition within them, in particular Sun Zi's *Art of War* and *On War* by Carl von Clausewitz. Modern brain research shows that Sun Zi's Dao philosophy promotes a state of mind conducive to flashes of insight. Modern Asian martial arts feature the same mental discipline: the *do* in *judo*, *aikido*, and *taekwando*, and the like means "Dao." And Clausewitz gives four keys to strategic intuition that produce innovation in any field of endeavor: examples from history, presence of mind, *coup d'oeil*, and resolution.

These four steps of Clausewitz offer a useful bridge from the science of strategic intuition to the method of creative strategy. They help us see how you can make conscious use of your unconscious learning-and-memory, at least in part. Let's look at each step in turn to see how.

In the first step, "examples from history," you learn, retain, and recall in memory the elements of what others did to succeed in a previous situation. This happens naturally, because we're human. It's how you learned most things in life, from walking and talking to sports and calculus. But it can happen actively as well through study. And here we meet Clausewitz's main example: Napoleon. By studying what Napoleon himself described as the "eighty-three campaigns" of the "great captains whose high deeds history has transmitted to us," he had an arsenal of elements to combine in each new situation he faced.

The second step, "presence of mind," has a direct parallel in the Dao philosophy of Sun Zi and Asian martial arts. You must free your mind of all expectations. You "expect the unexpected," as Clausewitz puts it. This is actually very difficult to do. The two biggest obstacles to presence of mind are excessive focus and negative emotions. Excessive focus means you can't let go of your current understanding of the problem, your goals, your timeline, options you've already listed, and so on. You must free your mind of all of that in order for your brain to make new connections. And all kinds of negative emotions—anger, frustration, worry, fear—flood the brain with the hormone cortisol, which blocks recall. You literally cannot think creatively.

The third step, *coup d'oeil*—or "glance" in French—is the term Clausewitz uses for a flash of insight. Modern brain science shows how presence of mind fosters flashes of insight. When your mind is clear, selected examples from your memory combine in a new way to show you what course of action to take. The result is a strategy, but not a complete one—just key elements that show you the way. It may be one big *coup d'oeil*—the famous "Eureka!" in the bath—or a series of smaller ones that you hardly feel as discrete cognitive events. But the mental mechanism is the same for epiphanies large and small.

Last comes "resolution," that is, resolve, determination, will. The flash of insight sparks a conviction that this is the right path despite the obstacles and resistance you will face, especially from others around you who did not have the idea. Of course, it is hard to distinguish good resolution for a good *coup d'oeil* from stubborn persistence for a bad idea. But examples from history offer help. If these examples that made up the *coup d'oeil* are solid and in sum cover the new situation, then it's likely a good idea.

We can now look at how innovation really works. Let's go back to the question of your company's performance over the past decade. You look at the situation and come up with a set of measures and data that you compile from memory of similar situations. If these parallels come quickly, from only your own direct experience, that's expert intuition. If it takes more time, and you draw from situations you know about but are not from your direct experience, that's strategic intuition. In practice you typically draw from both and don't sort out which is which. But the strength of your resolution—how hard you argue your case and how firmly you believe the idea will work—depends on how strong those parallels seem to you, regardless of whether you are conscious of them and able to explain them to others.

It is unlikely that anyone on earth has had enough of the right direct experience to understand every aspect of your company's performance over the past decade solely through expert intuition. Situations where expert intuition alone won't suffice are "strategic," so you need strategic intuition to find a solution. If the situation is within your direct experience, that's a "tactical" situation, and expert intuition can work. Innovation as strategic intuition is thus the search for the right combination of parallels within and beyond your own experience to apply to a new situation.

In the same way that learning-and-memory applies to understanding your situation, it helps you decide what action to take in the face of the situation. Quite literally, an idea comes together in your mind. Here we can apply the same distinction between expert and strategic intuition: Do the elements of your idea come just from your own experience (expert) or also from the experience of others (strategic)? What course of action your company should pursue in the future is clearly a strategic question, where no one person has enough direct experience to give a good answer solely from that source. Expert intuition won't work. You need strategic intuition instead.

Creative Strategy

In ordinary practice, innovators are seldom conscious of the precise examples from history that make up their flashes of insight. But in team situations, it helps greatly to make your examples explicit. Once he was in charge, Napoleon never had to explain his *coup d'oeil*. In modern organizations, we do. The solution is to convert the four elements of Clausewitz into a more formal method of innovation for teams. The result is "creative strategy," where you apply strategic intuition in a systematic way to find a creative solution to a strategic problem.

The rest of this chapter summarizes the creative strategy method and shows how it follows the four elements of Clausewitz. The next few chapters go through the steps of the method in greater detail.

The method of creative strategy follows three phases that draw from three diverse sources beyond those I've cited so far: "rapid appraisal" in international economic development, a "what-works scan" from social policy research, and "creative combination" from General Electric's corporate university in the late 1990s. Together, these three sources give us a team method that matches what a single brain does in the flash of insight that comes from strategic intuition.

All three phases—rapid appraisal, the what-works scan, and creative combination—use an "insight matrix" to organize examples from history that the rapid appraisal and what-works scan discover. Figure 1.1 shows the basic matrix before you start. At the top of the matrix, your team writes down your current understanding of the situation or problem, always as a provisional draft, because the problem might change as you proceed to solve it. This kind of shift is normal in innovation: sometimes that flash of insight you have at night or in the shower is a realization that the problem is actually different from what you first thought.

Once you have a preliminary problem statement, analysis comes next: you break down the problem into smaller pieces. You list these in rows,

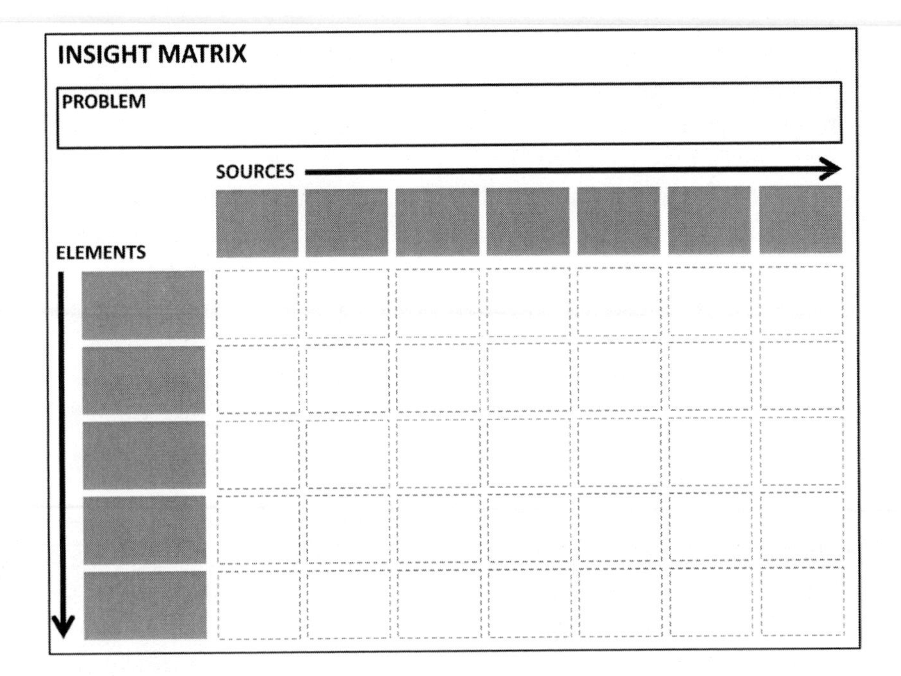

Figure 1.1
Insight matrix.

also in draft, because they too might change as you proceed. We call these problem pieces "elements," as in chemistry, where different chemical compounds are made up of elements in various combinations. After all, the term *analysis* itself comes from chemistry, where you break down a compound into its elements.

These first two parts of creative strategy—stating the problem and its elements—need not take much time, but you must do them well and with the right people. This is where rapid appraisal comes in. It's a set of iterative interview and research techniques that gain insight into a complex problem. The interviewees must include the leaders who will ultimately decide what innovation to pursue in addition to the leaders who will take the lead in pursuing it. These are sometimes the same person, sometimes two people, sometimes more. In complex situations and organizations, you often must conduct one quick round of interviews just to find out who these people are. If you then change the problem or its elements as you proceed, you must go back to that key group to get their understanding and approval and perhaps add to the group because of the shift of focus.

Next you move to the second phase of creative strategy: the what-works scan. You ask the most important question you can ever ask to solve any problem of any kind: Has anyone else in the world ever made progress on any piece of this puzzle? Across the top of the matrix, as columns, you list sources to search for answers to this question. Again your list is in draft form, because you might add or delete sources as you proceed. Once you have a few sources on the list, the team starts a treasure hunt: the what-works scan. You search the sources for "examples from history" that might apply to each element on the list of problem pieces. An example from history is anything that existed before you find it: something that happened a century ago and something that happened this morning are both examples from history.

We will call examples from history "precedents." In the what-works scan, every source has several potential precedents that might or might not fit your problem. You never use the whole source as your precedent. For example, if "branding" is a problem element, Starbucks might be a source for you. You might say you want to brand "like Starbucks," but you're not going to imitate everything Starbucks does to build its brand. You study what Starbucks has done and you choose from within that study something you find useful for your problem element, for example, how Starbucks owns rather than franchises its stores to keep greater control of the store experience. That's a precedent you might want to use yourself.

Finding relevant precedents is not easy, because outside of physical science we lack statistical "proof" that one set of actions works best to yield a particular effect. Because of this, the what-works scan has its own specialized methods and techniques to arrive at a set of precedents that fit the problem at hand. This scan is a key difference between creative strategy and most other innovation methods, which spend most of their time and effort on research about the problem. In contrast, creative strategy comes after the key leaders in charge of the problem have already done their homework in that regard by whatever method they think best. Once they understand the problem to some degree and decide to try to solve it, creative strategy spends most of its time and effort on searching for solutions through a what-works scan.

The what-works scan should take as much time as you have to devote to it. In urgent situations, that might be one day. For longer-term problems, it can take a week, a month, or a year. In principle, a what-works scan can go on forever, as there are always more corners of human experience to investigate. In the old days of gold mining, if you had infinite time and money, you would dig a hole everywhere on earth as deep as possible. The less time and money you have, the fewer and more shallow the holes—so too with a what-works scan. Yet you don't dig just anywhere—you look for sources where someone else found gold for problems related to yours.

One byproduct of the what-works scan is learning, which lets you build up an inventory of precedents to apply in the future to other problems. And the scan can be fun, a voyage of discovery where you're never sure what you'll find. But it can make some people anxious, especially if they search for days or weeks and do not find what they need. This brings us back to "presence of mind," where you need the mental discipline to face the unknown with a calm, open mind. Otherwise you revert to expert intuition and fill the matrix with what you already know.

When you run out of time, or when you judge that you have found enough promising precedents, you move to the next phase: creative combination. You select and combine precedents to make a solution. There is no precise formula for creative combination because it matches the flash of insight in a single brain, when precedents come together in your mind. You connect the dots, but not all the dots. The what-works scan yields a set of worthy precedents, but if you combine them all you will just have a giant mess. You see how one, and another, and yet another together make an innovation that fits your situation and solves your problem.

Last, but not least, the creative combination produces "resolution": the will to pursue the idea you see. It's a fact of human nature that people have greatest resolution for their own ideas; that's why so many consulting reports gather dust on office shelves—the consultants had the idea, not the client. Creative strategy solves this problem by including key leaders at two decisive points: the rapid appraisal and creative combination. You bring them the precedents you found that fit the elements of the problem they understood and agreed to in rapid appraisal, and you lead them to select and combine a subset of them in creative combination. They literally see the answer, and that makes all the difference.

That, in brief, is how you can translate the brain's mechanism for creating new ideas—strategic intuition—into a formal method for innovation: creative strategy.

2
Precedents

Precedents are the heart of creative strategy. Rapid appraisal tells you what kind of precedents you want, the what-works scan searches for them, and creative combination selects and combines them to create an innovation. Part of the discipline of presence of mind is the ability to see all human activity as potential precedents for later use. That doesn't mean you put everything you ever see, hear, or read on the shelves of your brain—if you did that, your head would explode. But it does mean that everything is a candidate to go on the shelf. You must consider all things, even if you select very few.

Here's an example that illustrates how an innovator picks out specific precedents from a wide set of activities to arrive at a creative idea.

It's 1997, and Reed Hasting has just sold a successful software company, founded ten years before when he was just out of college. He's living in San Jose, California, and goes to the video store to return the movie *Apollo 13*. It's woefully late, so he pays a $40 late fee. He's dismayed and embarrassed. How will he tell his wife? Hmm . . . does he have to tell her?

> *Oh, great! Now I'm thinking about lying to my wife about a late fee and the sanctity of my marriage.*

He drives from the video store to his gym club. On the way there something strikes him:

Whoa! Video stores could operate like a gym, with a flat membership fee . . . I wonder why nobody's done that before?

Here we have two precedents coming together from two very different sources. The first is American video stores, which at the time were big boxes filled with racks of videocassettes that customers browsed through to rent and pay for one at a time. Blockbuster was the largest chain in the country. The second precedent is gym clubs, which were open spaces with lots of machines that members used freely. If you list all the elements of Blockbuster, and all the elements of a gym, you could imagine dozens or even hundreds of possible combinations. Hastings selects a particular subset of elements from Blockbuster as one precedent and a particular subset of elements from the gym club as another precedent.

For his Blockbuster precedent, Hastings takes the whole operation minus the payment system. For his gym club precedent, Hastings takes only the payment system. Such imbalance is typical: some precedents combine many elements from a source, and other precedents combine very few. There is no way to know ahead of time whether a particular source will yield a multi- or single-element precedent. And as we see from this example, a single-element precedent can be just as important as a precedent with many elements.

In taking the Blockbuster precedent, Hastings assumes that the elements work. There were many Blockbuster stores at the time, and they seemed full of stock and customers. Afterward he checks to make sure video rental is a big enough business to sustain his idea, but for the moment he knows enough to judge that the elements that form his precedent contribute to Blockbuster's success. Same with the gym club precedent: Hastings sees the flat fee for members as a successful part of the gym club formula. And gyms at the time seemed like a thriving industry. Again he can check the numbers afterward, but he knew enough to judge that the precedent he picked was a worthy one. Even when he does check the numbers, it's impossible to pin down precisely the dollar contribution of any particular element, like a flat fee, to the overall success of a company or industry.

In combining these two precedents, Hastings displayed tremendous presence of mind. One moment he saw his gym club as a place to exercise, and the next moment he broke down its elements and found a precedent to apply to a completely different industry. This is exactly the kind of presence of mind you need for a what-works scan.

After combining these two precedents, Hastings keeps going. Amazon was two years old at the time, and already served as a source of precedents for many new online business ideas. Amazon pioneered many of the features of e-commerce that we now take for granted, including safe payment with credit cards. Hastings takes many e-commerce features from Amazon to add to his new combination. He strips his Blockbuster precedent of its physical form and uses an Amazon mail-order precedent to go online instead.

For this switch to e-commerce, Hastings needs one more precedent. A friend tells him about a new technology for movies that just reached the American market from Japan: the digital video disc, or DVD. It's far lighter and smaller than Blockbuster's videocassettes. That makes it much easier to mail.

> *I ran down to Tower [Records] and bought a bunch and mailed them to myself and then I waited . . . And I opened them up. And they were fine. And I thought, "Oh my God. This is gonna work!"*

You probably recognize the company by now: Netflix. Hastings combined precedents from Blockbuster, gym clubs, Amazon, and the new DVD technology to create his innovation. Every precedent was partial, even the DVDs; they made recording movies easier too, but Hastings did not take that part for his precedent. Some filmmakers did, and that led to other innovations.

Note that the combination Hastings came up with had little to do with his own past experience or software expertise. Certainly thousands of people knew enough about Blockbuster, Amazon, gym clubs, and DVDs to have the same idea. His knowledge of software probably helped him implement his idea, although the idea itself included no actual software innovations. Thousands of software experts knew how to do what Hastings did to make his Netflix website. Perhaps his software expertise helped give him confidence in the idea—resolution—because he knew he had the technical skill to do it. But none of the precedents that made up his idea came from his own software experience.

This Netflix story comes from a 2006 interview with Hastings by Lesley Stahl for CBS News. It does not tell us everything about what went on in Hastings's mind, but we learn enough to see that he used strategic intuition

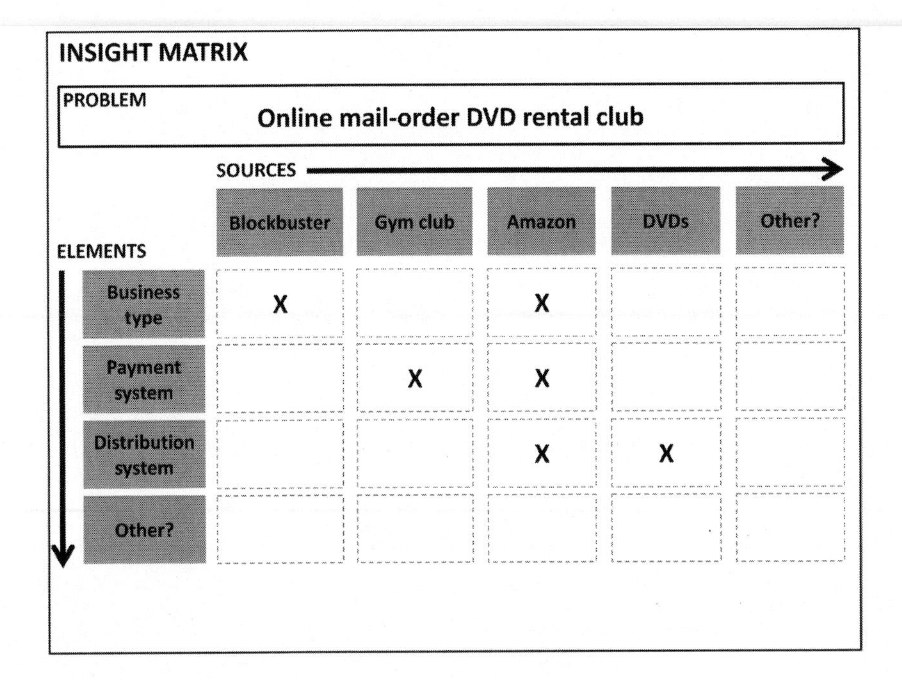

Figure 2.1
Netflix precedents.

to arrive at his big idea, that is, he combined precedents, but without using the insight matrix or any other formal tool. If an innovation strikes you in the same way, all the better. But companies also need a method to innovate as part of their normal routine, or at least to make sure that their normal routines do not inhibit innovation. For that they need to know how to translate what happened in the single mind of Reed Hastings into a formal method for a group to follow. So let's translate Hastings's strategic intuition into the steps of creative strategy.

Figure 2.1 is an insight matrix, after the fact, for the Netflix idea. We know that the problem statement changed each time Hastings brought in another precedent. This version shows only the elements and sources Hastings mentioned in his interview. Certainly there were others, so we leave space for them in the matrix. And of course Netflix continued to change; for example, it streams videos now too, which again Hastings did not invent but took as a precedent from elsewhere.

This Netflix example illustrates how to translate strategic intuition into creative strategy. In Hastings's mind, strategic intuition selected and

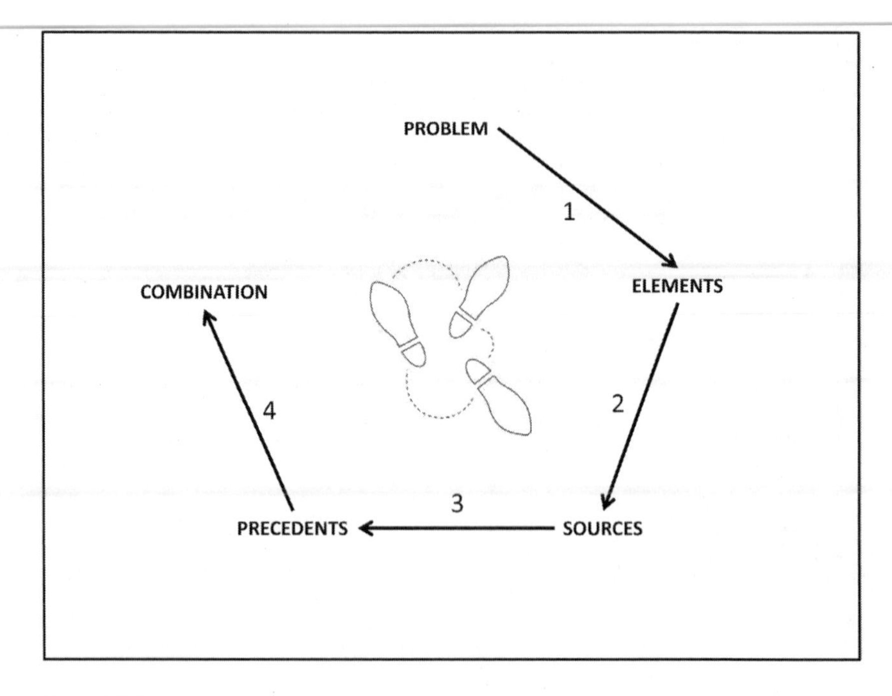

Figure 2.2
Creative strategy: basic steps.

combined a subset of precedents from four sources to solve different elements of a problem. The problem and elements changed along the way. For creative strategy, we usually work backwards: first we identify the problem, then break it down into elements, and then search for precedents to select and combine. The problem and elements might change along the way.

The exact sequence of steps will vary in each case. Figure 2.2 shows the simplest form. We recognize Steps 1 and 2 as rapid appraisal, Steps 3 and 4 as the what-works scan, and Step 5 as creative combination. In most cases Steps 3 and 4 will take the most time. Yet this simple sequence is rare. You will likely do at least one iteration, where you go back to an earlier step and pick up again from there. The most common example is to add sources after you start to find precedents. Or you might add an element or alter the problem during the what-works scan.

Figure 2.3 shows the sequence of steps for Netflix, according to the CBS interview. We see right away that even this simple case looks more complicated when we follow it step by step. Each time you do creative strategy, you will find that you stray from the basic sequence at some point in the

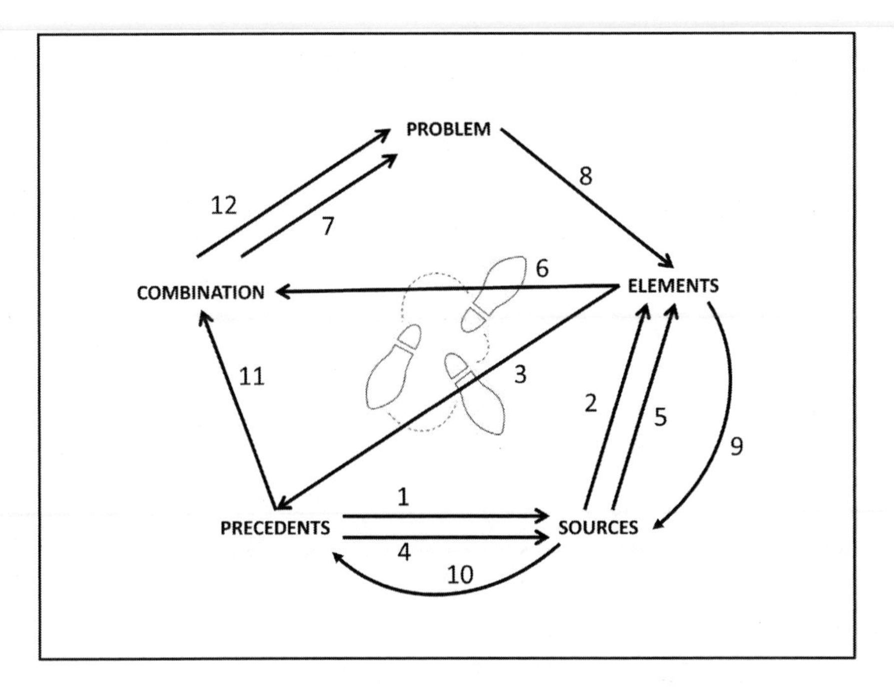

Figure 2.3
Creative strategy: Netflix steps.

method. Your precise sequence will depend on the problem, how you break it down, the sources you find, the precedents you discover, and who participates in rapid appraisal, the what-works scan, and creative combination. You will never do it exactly the same way twice.

Because your sequence of steps changes along the way, as discoveries steer you one way and then another, you can't plan out all the steps ahead of time. Or if you do plan them out, be ready to change them as needed. It's better to plan out only the phases, for example, one week for rapid appraisal, eight weeks for the what-works scan, and one week for creative combination. Beyond that, plan as you go, day by day and week by week as you see each step unfold.

Creative strategy is the closest we can come to a formal method for the mental mechanism of strategic intuition. We dare go no farther. Even with the insight matrix, the three phases and the steps within and between, your innovation idea depends on presence of mind and flashes of insight to find, select, and combine precedents. There is simply no other way to do it.

3

What's the Problem?

The first phase of creative strategy, rapid appraisal, identifies what problem your innovation needs to solve and breaks the problem down into elements. It includes interviews with key leaders and a quick study of documents and data about the problem. For simple problems and a few key leaders, rapid appraisal might take less than a day. For complex problems in big organizations, it can take more than a week. Discoveries in the second phase, the what-works scan, can lead you to go back and repeat parts of the rapid appraisal to revise the problem and its elements.

Not all problems, of course, call for an innovation. Perhaps what you're already doing is fine and still works for the situation you will face in the foreseeable future. In that case you don't need creative strategy. But those cases are rare. The business world changes fast, so if you think your current strategy needs no changes at all next year, or the next, or the year after that, you're probably prey to wishful thinking.

Most companies recognize this. They might not think they need an innovation, but they still look to the future in a variety of ways. They might ask for an evaluation, a feasibility study, a marketing report, a strategic analysis, a benchmarking study, or some other systematic review before they begin formal planning for all or part of their enterprise. In these cases, you can propose creative strategy as the method for the study they want.

You don't have to say up front that your aim is innovation. As long as the company agrees to the three key phases of rapid appraisal, the what-works scan, and creative combination, you can proceed.

But often the company does know that they need an innovation: they recognize that they have a problem they don't know how to solve. They are not always able to state the problem clearly, though, and sometimes they pick the wrong problem. The first phase of creative strategy is rapid appraisal, and the first step of rapid appraisal is stating the problem; if the company already has a clear notion of where they need to innovate, this first step need not take much time. But if the problem does not seem clear, you might need a full round of interviews just for this step.

The question of where you need to innovate is not always easy to answer. Ideally, you want an innovation that increases your performance by an infinite amount and reduces your costs to zero. But you know that's impossible. And even if you choose a smaller target—increase performance and decrease costs by 20 percent, let's say—that does not identify a creative problem. If you can meet these targets by working harder or hiring more people or expanding to new territory, then you don't need an innovation. You just do more of what you're already doing.

Yet many organizations use targets routinely as the first step for strategy. The board or top executives announce performance targets and then tell their divisions to propose budgets and activities to meet them. It's no surprise that the divisions simply propose doing more of what they're already doing. By definition, that's not innovation. Instead, even if headquarters sends out performance targets, they should then tell each division to pause and look for a problem that doesn't yet have a solution but that would have a big payoff if they found one. This missing step is much harder than increasing current activities by a certain percent to reach a target increase. It's not automatic what the division should do. First they have to think.

Research can help you think. For this you can find many traditional strategy methods that collect data on your industry and your competitors, your customers, the economy as a whole, or on your own strengths and weaknesses. These methods give you lots of information but no conclusion. There is no formal, logical way to go from an analysis of your situation to a statement of your problem. Here's what happens in practice: an idea of the problem forms in the mind of whoever does the studies or analysis. From learning-and-memory, we know that ideas come from similar situations in your memory. Because everyone's memory is different, we all draw somewhat different conclusions from the same analysis.

Some managers or consultants organize a brainstorming meeting to go from analysis to a problem statement. That can work, as long as the meeting does not try to come up with solutions too. This is a very important distinction, because brainstorming cannot solve innovation problems. It can solve ordinary problems, where the collective experience of everyone in the room will suffice. An innovation problem, by definition, is something you don't see a way to solve. If you can solve a problem by brainstorming, it's not an innovation.

Often, an innovation problem arises not through formal research and analysis, but naturally in the normal flow of business and life. You study your annual results and see a number that's much too high or much too low, or there's a big market or source of funds that you repeatedly fail to tap. This natural method for identifying a problem is often just as valid as more formal methods of research and analysis.

Whatever the problem you settle on, it has to be worth trying to solve. You're going to spend time and effort figuring out a creative answer, and if you succeed you'll spend time and money putting the creative idea into practice. So you want something big enough to matter. And it has to be something you think no one else has figured out, at least not exactly in your situation. You need an innovation, not a lesson you take and apply wholesale from someone else.

Here's an example where the first problem statement did not call for an innovation. An executive came to me and said, "I have a great project idea but I've never sought funding before—I'm going to use creative strategy to find out how to fund it." Well, not necessarily. There is plenty of existing expertise about project funding. This executive might simply need to find someone who has that expertise, or read up on the subject, in order to solve the problem, and you don't need creative strategy for that. But, if it's such an unusual project that there is no precedent for ever funding something like it, you need an innovation. That's where creative strategy comes in. You would identify the unusual characteristics of the project—call them X, Y, and Z—and then state your innovation problem like this: "Innovate in funding a project with the unusual characteristics of X, Y, and Z."

Here's another example. Two executives came to see me from a big financial services company. It had grown successfully in its home market, Japan, and then spread into the rest of East Asia, also successfully. Now it aimed to expand further, to Europe and the rest of Asia. At first glance, this is not an innovation problem: your expansion to East Asia worked, now do the same thing in the next regions you target. What's the problem?

When I asked that question, the executives shook their heads. They replied, "Our company has a strong Japanese business culture. Across East Asia, the business culture is similar. In the rest of the world, it's not." So far they were able to expand organically—set up a local office with some headquarters staff and then hire locals too. And they could expand through acquisition as well—buy a local firm and add some headquarters staff. The cultural fit made that possible because the local staff understood how the business operated within the local business culture. When they tried to set up a local office beyond East Asia, their headquarters staff did not know enough about the local business culture to fit in. And locals did not want to work for a Japanese company for cultural reasons, including lower pay. They tried acquiring a local company instead, but the existing local staff of that company threatened to quit, for the same cultural reasons.

They were stuck. "We've already missed our three-year targets."

Now we're talking. They need an innovation.

First, let's take a step back. Where did their three-year target come from? They made the classic mistake of doing strategic planning without first having a strategic idea. If you start your strategy with setting financial targets, you're really saying, "Our strategic idea is to do what we're already doing, just more of it." So Step 1 for them is: throw out the three-year targets. Before setting targets, you need an idea.

Their problem statement is something like this: "Expand quickly into global markets while keeping key parts of Japanese business culture intact in each office." For this they need an innovation. They're ready to proceed with creative strategy. If they end up with a good idea, they can then estimate what targets they will hit, and at what pace. Setting three-year targets before they have an idea is putting the cart before the horse.

Now I'll give you an example that we'll follow in more detail. It comes from General Electric (GE) in the late 1990s. At that time the company was widely hailed as a smashing success, with a decade and a half of steady growth in revenue, net income, and stock price. They accomplished all this without one main business leading the way: they had 24 different companies in 24 different industries. Their CEO, Jack Welch, gave each of those companies no overall GE strategy other than to succeed against their competitors in their particular industry. Although he did not give them a strategy to follow, he gave them a method to find their own strategy for their particular situation. That method used creative strategy as its guiding force.

GE executives learned the method at GE's corporate university in Crotonville, New York, some fifty miles from headquarters in Fairfield,

Connecticut. Groups of executives came to Crotonville for two-week programs of leadership training and briefings about the other GE companies. GE grew fast partly through acquisitions—a company per day at one point—which meant that many of the Crotonville participants were new to GE. Other participants were newly promoted, and thus also new to Crotonville.

At the start of the program, GE gave the group a real strategic problem from one of their companies to work on during their free time over the two weeks. At the end of the program, the group gave their answer to a panel of top GE executives, including one or more top leaders from the particular industry concerned. This was a real exercise, not a simulation. If the group came up with a worthy idea, the GE panel decided whether or not to pursue it further.

Let's walk through the Crotonville method in some detail. The group begins by stating the problem in exactly the terms of creative strategy: Where do we need to innovate most? Here's one answer, from a real GE case: online retail for appliances. In the late 1990s, e-commerce was just taking off, with Amazon leading the way. GE sold appliances to big stores, who sold them to consumers. If GE offered appliances for sale to customers online, the big stores would revolt, and buy appliances from someone else. So GE needed an idea for how to sell appliances online, without killing their big-store business.

If we're the Crotonville group, we take a sheet of paper or a whiteboard or a flip chart and write the problem statement at the top: "Wholesale to e-commerce in appliances." We leave it in draft, because the problem might change as we get further into it. This happens all the time in real life: you start into a project and realize at some point that you're working on the wrong problem. The real problem is something else. So you switch to that, or at least you try to. If your boss or client tells you, "Stick to the original problem," you've got an even bigger problem.

That's why it's very important to leave the problem in draft, until you see a way to solve it. Premature goal setting is one of the biggest mistakes in corporate strategy around the world—like our Japanese friends who set three-year targets without any idea how to reach them. First, figure out both a goal and a course of action to reach it. That gives you a strategy. Only then are you ready to plan, and you set that goal as your target.

So in our GE example, we don't yet have a goal. There is no good term in English for what we do have. It's a "goal we will recommend that GE set if we can figure out a good course of action to reach it." As a single word, *hypothesis* comes close, but that implies that what we do next is conduct an experiment. And that's not so. Perhaps the best we can do is "possible goal." Because what we do next is try to figure out a possible course of action to reach it. Only when we find both, and they fit, do we consider actually setting the goal.

Once we have our draft problem statement, analysis comes next. We break the problem down into parts. That's what analysis means: to examine something to determine its elements. This component analysis is very different from the kind of industry, market, or competitor analysis you find in most conventional strategy methods in the business world. That traditional kind of analysis comes before your statement of "possible goal." For example, GE might have done some analysis of the new online commerce industry to see which part of it already served the appliance market, before setting the possible goal of e-commerce in appliances. That's fine. But once we have our problem statement, our problem analysis takes a very different form: we break down the problem into a list of puzzles we need to solve to reach the goal.

Our list can take the form of obstacles or solutions. They're two sides of the same coin. So in the GE case, we can break down "from wholesale to ecommerce into appliances" into something like this:

- Identify customers
- Retain customers
- Customer credit
- Retain wholesalers
- Customer service

Again, the list is in draft, for the same reason as before: as we proceed, it might change. If we realize we left something out, that's fine, we just add it to the list. Or we realize that one item is trivial or really part of another item, and that's fine, we delete it. On a different scale, we might realize that one item on the list is really the big problem to solve. Then we elevate that to the overall "possible goal" and start over. Now we break that down into parts. From the GE case, we might have thought that "retain wholesalers" was really the big problem, so that would go up top. Instead we decided to keep it as a major part of the larger problem.

How long a list should we make? Logically we can break down complex problems into dozens, even hundreds of parts. But each of us will have to keep all the pieces in our mind at once, and there's a human limit to that. Once we go over ten, it's nearly impossible for the normal brain to consider all elements at once. Our previous GE list does a good job covering the major categories. It's better to start with a short list, and then add more elements as they arise.

Above all, we don't want to spend too much time at this stage. Most executives in business are good at analysis, and can spend hours and hours happily doing it. Resist that temptation! We want to spend our time on searching for solutions, not studying the problem. In many cases, we won't have to spend more than an hour or so figuring out our starting list. That's because we picked a possible goal that comes from good knowledge of the field or industry we're in, so that same knowledge allows us to break it down quickly.

These two items, the problem and its elements, start us on our insight matrix. Figure 3.1 shows how the matrix looks for our GE example at this point. Now we begin our what-works scan: we search widely for sources that solve one or more pieces of the puzzle.

Our GE example shows the first phase of creative strategy, rapid appraisal, in its simplest form, where the team gets a clear draft problem statement from someone else and works on its own to break it down. But sometimes rapid appraisal before the scan takes much more time and effort. Often the leaders who have the problem are not yet clear on exactly what the problem is—like our Japanese example—and so rapid appraisal takes much more time and effort.

Some of the techniques of rapid appraisal are common to conventional consulting methods, and some are specific to creative strategy. Rapid appraisal comes from a qualitative research method developed in the 1980s for streamlining economic research in poor countries. There, the kinds of elaborate economic surveys you find in richer countries didn't work: in the difficult conditions of poor countries, such surveys cost too much, took too long, and produced unreliable data that the statistical models imported from richer countries could not use. In rapid appraisal, a quick series of iterative semi-structured interviews with a widening circle of key informants can yield better information much faster and at a much lower cost than conventional surveys. The interviews point you to specific documents and data that already exist, to help you fill out the picture.

Many consulting firms have adopted rapid appraisal methods to some degree. My conversation with the Japanese executives was a form of rapid appraisal that led them through the steps of stating the problem and starting to break it down. In its fullest version, rapid appraisal involves many interviews back and forth that continue to revise the problem and its elements.

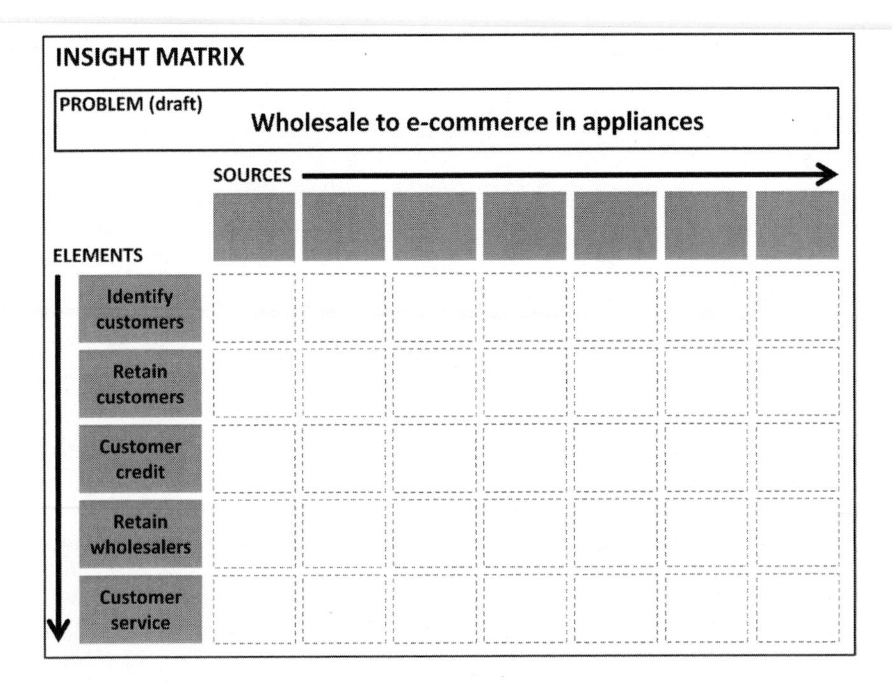

Figure 3.1
Insight matrix: rapid appraisal.

Each round of interviews sends you to key documents and data that the interviewees mention as relevant to their understanding of the problem. You do not create new documents or collect new data yourself.

Rapid appraisal can replace the weeks or even months of costly research that conventional methods of strategy typically start with: customer surveys, industry analysis, and so on. Rapid appraisal makes key leaders active participants in analyzing the problem, and that helps them understand the solution and commit to it later on. In creative strategy, you trust that the leaders know enough about their problem to get started on solving it. But they do not always know what they know: your interviews together make up a picture that the leaders could not have drawn themselves.

Rapid appraisal leads to a preliminary problem statement and breakdown of elements. It can also lead to a first round of sources for the what-works scan. Sometimes one or more leaders you interview has extensive knowledge of not just the problem but also of potential parts of the solution: they know examples of partial success inside and outside their industry that bear some relation to some element of the problem. You want to find these additional key informants and mine their brains for these examples. You never know beforehand if the person you are about to talk to can become a key informant. The only way to find out is to ask during the interview: "Have you seen something somewhere that does that element well?" It's not a typical question, so they might not tell you without you asking first. Or if they don't know, they might know who does: "Do you know someone who might know what worked somewhere for that element?"

In its simplest form, rapid appraisal is a discrete phase that ends when the key leaders agree to a preliminary problem statement and breakdown of elements. But if the problem is especially large or complex, the problem statement and the list of elements might change several times or shift dramatically. Or your key informants might be willing to give you more leads and contacts as you proceed. In these cases, your rapid appraisal might continue well into the search phase.

It's common in consulting to propose back to the client at an early stage a restatement of the problem that's different from their original version. So too for creative strategy. For example, "Improve our marketing" is too vague. "Shorten delivery times" is too specific. "Become the leader in our industry" is too grand. In each case, rapid appraisal can draw out from key leaders what problems they see in their current marketing, or what problems they think shorter delivery times will help solve, or what problems they think prevent them from rising in their industry ranks.

It's possible during rapid appraisal that you end up with more than one good candidate to put at the top of the insight matrix. For example, I think we should seek an innovation in marketing, and you think we should seek an innovation in financing. In that case, do both, separately: one matrix for marketing and another one for financing. If only one leads to a creative combination, that's the one you do. If both do, you have to decide between them, or see if you can do them both, at least in part.

Because creative strategy will likely be new to the key leaders, make sure to explain in early interviews how rapid appraisal works. Show your informants your draft insight matrix. Ask them to help you craft the problem statement up top and fill in the element rows—always in draft. Make sure they understand the iterative nature of your rapid appraisal and the what-works scan to come.

One of the key results of the rapid appraisal is a list of key people who would implement the innovation that creative strategy comes up with. Sometimes the list is obvious: it's a division or department or the top executive group. But changes in the problem and its breakdown can alter who will implement the idea. You need to add these new people to your list and interview them. For each new name, you or a key leader must inform them ahead of time about the steps of creative strategy and the timetable you foresee. The final list is the core of the group you invite to the final workshop to arrive at the creative combination. There is no set number of people to invite: for big companies with big, complex problems, the list could be fifty or more.

In simple cases, there is a clear line between the end of rapid appraisal and the what-works scan. For complex problems, you might start searching a bit during the rapid appraisal, as a way to confirm your list of the elements. Find a few precedents to bring to one or more key informants, and ask if they fit the elements you listed. You're not looking for a perfect match at this stage, so don't spend too much time on this step. You want to devote as much time as you can to the full-blown what-works scan.

4

Where Do We Look?

The second phase of creative strategy, the what-works scan, scours the world for companies and organizations that have solved different elements of your problem in different situations. You find out exactly what worked for each element, why, and how you might adapt it to your own problem.

The techniques of a what-works scan range from simple interviews to statistical analysis. The social sciences pioneered formal methods of the what-works scan for social policy, where success is much harder to measure than in the business world. The most formal of the social science methods is meta-analysis: take all the evaluations of a set of programs and develop common measures across them to see which programs stand out against their peers. Even in a meta-analysis, statistics can take you only so far. Each element of a problem has a different measure of success, and not all programs include all elements, so each program needs a unique set of measures. At some point you need to go beyond the statistics and use your judgment to determine what works.

The what-works scan does not search for sources that solved the whole problem. If some source did solve the whole problem, you would probably know it, and you have the option of copying that solution. That's not innovation, but often it's the best path to take. In our GE case, there was no successful online appliance retailer yet. So no one had solved the whole problem.

Instead, the what-works scan searches for sources that solved pieces of the problem. In our GE case, let's start with the first element: Has anyone figured out how to identify customers online, in any industry at all, not just appliances? And so on through our list. Our aim is to find a precedent here, a precedent there, on through the list until we find a combination that works for our specific problem.

As we proceed, we might find new sources and add them to our list. We can't know ahead of time where the search will lead. We might find answers within our industry, but we might also find them outside. Henry Ford is a famous example. He invented the moving assembly line, which now accounts for virtually all of modern manufacturing. Where did he get the idea?

Ford started out not by innovating, but by imitating others within his industry. He did not invent the internal combustion engine: the Belgian Etienne Lenoir did that. Ford did not invent the automobile: that was the German Karl Benz. Ford did not even invent the automobile assembly line: that was his fellow American Ransom Olds. The first cheap mass-produced car was the Oldsmobile Runabout, not a Ford. Henry Ford imitated the Oldsmobile factory exactly to make his first cars. That was not an innovation. He just copied what Olds did. Olds in turn took the idea from bicycle and horse carriage assembly lines that preceded cars. And so on, back through time.

Then Ford got a further idea, and that came from outside the auto industry. In the Olds factory, they lined up the cars in a long row and each team moved along the line: the motor team put in the motors, the electric team put in the wiring, and so on. The stationary assembly line was actually an old factory technique from the early days of the industrial revolution. But in the Chicago stockyards, they used a moving assembly line. The animal came into the slaughterhouse, and a worker killed it and hung it on a rack. The worker stayed put, while the carcass moved along the rack. At the next station, another worker pulled off the hide. The carcass moved again along the rack. The next worker scooped out the guts. And so on down the line. It was a moving *dis*-assembly line. Ford and his engineers said, "Let's do it the other way. Let's make it a moving assembly line, where the workers stay still and the car moves past them." And thus, modern manufacturing was born.

So where should we look for possible elements to combine? Everywhere.

We have to open our minds to everything we've seen and read and heard of, and seek out sources completely new to us. But where do we start, and where do we end? It's impossible to look everywhere, especially when we look back into the past. That would take forever, to look at all possible past and present sources, and none of us has that much time. But if we fail to look at a source, perhaps that's the very source we need. How can we know?

We can't. There is no formula for where to look. The best we can do is take each element on the list and try to find at least one precedent somewhere. Then we find another. And so on until we hit pay dirt. It helps to have a team with diverse backgrounds, expertise, and interests, so that everyone looks in a different place. But we do not have to have experts on the team. You find experts outside the team, as you search.

Ideally, we want as much time and scope as possible because it's often quite hard to figure out what works. We look for empirical evidence, especially numbers, but cause and effect are not always clear, especially for parts of a whole. For example, someone dealing with large numbers of walk-in clients for a low-cost service in New York City, with huge differences between slow and peak times, contacted European ferry operators to see how they handled a similar problem. The result was good ideas and lots of numbers, but even so there was no way to demonstrate precisely what contribution a certain procedure made to the total efficiency of the ferry system. So you put whatever numbers and other evidence you find in the scan, and explain why and to what degree you find it convincing enough to select a precedent for your own situation.

The what-works scan makes explicit that creative strategy is both an art and a science. Of course, any good scientist will tell you that the practice of science is partly an art, and any good artist will tell you that the practice of art is partly a science. You cannot possibly have training in all or even many of the fields you must scan, but still you must understand and make judgments about the science—the numbers and other evidence—that you encounter in each field. As with any art or science, you get better at making such judgments the more you do them. You don't become an expert in ferries or any of the other fields you mine, but you can become an expert in the what-works scan.

The key to a good scan is to recognize that you're not an expert in the field you're scanning. Of course your knowledge will vary for each field you encounter, but even for fields you know very well your attitude must be that you are not an expert. That's because you expect an expert to know what works. For a what-works scan, you must look at each field with fresh eyes. What experts really know is what works for them now in certain situations, not what works across all cases, across all time, in endless variations. In this wider sense, not even experts know what works without a what-works scan.

If you have enough time to do a deep scan, the first place to look is the scientific and professional literature, starting with journals and reports in relevant industries and fields. Sometimes you need someone with advanced training or experience to understand these sources, so if you don't have that training yourself you should find someone to guide you. It's best if this helper is on your core scan team to provide ongoing expertise, because your judgment of what works changes as you encounter other sources in the scan. You will find few results that meet a gold standard of scientific validity, so you must develop a "good-enough" ranking of your own in each field you encounter. It's a rolling evaluation of everything you find, not a one-time assessment of each source in turn.

The scientific and professional articles you find point you to experts who did some of the studies you uncover. Because the review and publication of scientific research takes time, most of the results you find will be several years or more out of date. So contact the authors of the more useful studies and ask them their views on what works today. Beware the reply that their published work is the last word on the subject, or that a particular solution is best for all situations. That's the kind of expert you don't need. A more open-minded expert will be glad you're interested and will be willing to discuss the latest results in the field, other sources to consult, and other experts and practitioners to talk to. All this improves your judgment for your "good-enough" ranking: you will likely find that most of the elements that rank high do not have conclusive statistics to support them.

Especially for complex or rare elements, statistics alone cannot tell you what works. That's especially true for the overall subject of this book: methods of innovation, creativity, and strategy. No one has figured out a way to run a valid scientific test of one method versus another. That's because there are far too many variables, each with its own data problems: size, location, industry, and composition of the company; degree, quality, and consistency in using the method; inputs other than the method itself that affect results; consistency in measures of results across cases; and so on. For a flavor of how hard it is to get a scientific measure of what works for any management practice—let alone methods that combine practices, like creative strategy or its competitors—see a recent research paper by Ichniowski and Shaw in the bibliography of this book.

Although statistics cannot tell us what method of innovation, creativity, and strategy to choose, a what-works scan can help. That's what I did some years ago, and the result was creative strategy. I searched for evidence about what works for coming up with creative ideas for strategy. The scan covered several fields, including neuroscience, military strategy, and business history, where I found countless examples of how successful innovators actually came up with their creative ideas. A section on sources at the end of this book gives a brief overview of my own what-works scan and how it led to the method I offer you here.

It is also important to distinguish the what-works scan from "benchmarking," which is a popular method in business today. A good definition of benchmarking comes from Bain & Company, a leading strategy consulting firm:

> Benchmarking improves performance by identifying and applying best demonstrated practices to operations and sales. Managers compare the performance of their products or processes externally with those of competitors and best-in-class companies and internally with other operations within their own firms that perform similar activities.

As defined here, benchmarking is clearly a good idea. It's a fine way to improve operations. But that's not innovation. Let's go back to Henry Ford. First, he benchmarked "competitors and best-in-class companies," and that led him to pick Olds to imitate. But his big innovation came from outside the automobile industry, in the Chicago stockyards. Does that mean we should benchmark related industries too? If so, how related? You never know where the innovation will come from, so you must benchmark every industry in the world. But that's impossible. No one has time for all that.

So our first step is far lighter than benchmarking: a wide search for some part of some company activity in some industry that strikes us as relevant to our problem. That's how we start the treasure hunt. We could call this step "rapid preliminary benchmark search but not just in our industry." Then once we find something we think might be promising, we look closer to understand how it works. Even then we don't do a full benchmark analysis because we don't know yet if we're actually going to use that element. Instead, we make a short description: what is the element we found, how does it work, what makes us think it succeeds for that source, and how we might apply it to our current problem. There will be some numbers in there, but it's not a full-blown analysis. We could call this step "quick-and-dirty benchmarking."

Sometimes we think a source is promising but we don't quite see at first which part of it we might use for our own problem. So we take an extra step: we break down the source, in the same way we broke down the problem. We make a short list of the key precedents that we think make the source work. If that doesn't do it, we make a short description for each precedent: how it works, why it succeeds, and how we might apply it. That will help us determine better which of its precedents, if any, we might actually want to use.

As we can see, the what-works scan is a lot of work. If we add formal, detailed benchmarking at every step, we will spend all our time crunching numbers instead of searching and thinking. Formal benchmarking can come at a later stage, after we've found the elements we know we want. Then we benchmark them. Detailed benchmarking during the what-works scan is a woeful waste of time.

If someone else has already done benchmarking, we can use what they did as a reference. But beware: in a what-works scan we look for (A) one or two examples of an element that works in a particular situation, rather than (B) an element that works most of the time in a large number of situations. The B element is known as "best practice," and ordinary benchmarking can capture that. The A element is the unusual one, the needle in a haystack, that just might apply to your particular situation. By definition, the A's are "outliers" in a statistical sense, and they often end up on the cutting-room floor of scientific articles and reports. That's why we want to talk to the experts and practitioners directly, to find and understand those more unusual results.

Let's return to our GE example to see how the Crotonville group did their scan. The team had only two weeks, so they could not do a deep search. Yet GE had a rare advantage: twenty-four different companies in twenty-four different industries around the world. They had ready access to experts, studies, and other documents within the company. GE also looked externally: for example, their quality program, Six Sigma, came from Motorola. But twenty-four different global industries is a wonderful place to start a what-works scan.

Figure 4.1 shows how the matrix looks for the GE example at this point. The X's indicate promising precedents that the team found for that element row. The column sources are the various GE companies by industry: Finance, Plastics, NBC TV, and so forth. We quickly ran out of space, but the actual matrix included all twenty-four GE companies. There is no limit to the number of sources you search, and you add and delete sources as you proceed.

INSIGHT MATRIX

PROBLEM (draft): **Wholesale to e-commerce in appliances**

SOURCES →

ELEMENTS ↓

	Fin.	Plast.	NBC	Med.	Power	Mort.	Appl.
Identify Customers				X	X		
Retain Customers			X				X
Customer Credit				X		X	
Retain Wholesalers		X					
Customer Service			X			X	

Figure 4.1
Insight matrix: what-works scan.

This GE matrix shows that the team found two promising precedents for customer retention: at GE's appliance company and at the NBC television station. And they found two promising precedents for customer credit and customer service, at GE's mortgage company. Right away we see that it's fine to find more than one precedent at the same source, and more than once source for the same element. Along the way we find other things, but reject them. We're being very selective, looking for precedents that might especially apply to our particular problem, rather than to a common problem across the industry. Behind the X's are the short descriptions of each precedent we select: what it is, how it works, why we think it succeeds for that source, and how we might apply it to our problem.

We can now see clearly how the what-works scan differs from conventional strategy methods, which typically feature a research phase where you analyze the problem in depth. The what-works scan might take just as long, but instead of spending all that effort studying the problem, creative strategy spends it on finding solutions.

In some cases, you might hit on a key informant midway through the scan. Or you encounter something you think an earlier key informant can help you understand and assess. Or your discoveries lead you to change the problem and its elements, and for that you need to go back to the key leaders for agreement. In this way, your rapid appraisal overlaps more or less with your what-works scan, according to what you discover. New sources, new informants, new documents, new elements, new precedents, a new problem statement—each can send you back on another iteration of your rapid appraisal or what-works scan. One thing leads to another, one person leads to another. You're a detective seeking leads and evidence wherever you can find them.

5

Creative Combination

The third phase of creative strategy, creative combination, selects and combines a subset of precedents from the what-works scan to arrive at an innovation. If you can, do this phase in a workshop with key initiative leaders, to increase their commitment to the solution. The creative combination includes a preliminary plan to implement the idea, based on the activities of each precedent you chose.

Once again, the line between phases is not always clear: How do you know when to stop the what-works scan and move on to creative combination? One answer might be that you run out of time. In the GE example, the group had two weeks. At Crotonville, it was perfectly fine to report at the end that you searched and searched but found no solution. After all, you can't solve every problem in two weeks. Some problems you can't solve at all. That's the whole point of a search: you don't know what you'll find, when, or whether you'll ever find anything at all. So you search as long as you can, given the scale of the problem and your own personal or company timetable: it might be two days, it might be two weeks, it might be two years.

Figure 4.1 showed us the GE matrix toward the end of our what-works scan. We saw the problem, the elements of the problem, the sources to search, and promising precedents from specific sources. Note that there was no solution yet. Everything was still in draft, on paper and in our minds, including the X's. Our group can edit or delete anything at any time. For example, we might decide that one of the pieces of the puzzle is really the big problem, and then we put that on the top and break it down into elements. Or we could decide that the problem on top is really part of a bigger problem, so we drag the current problem down to the list of pieces and put the bigger problem on top.

As our what-works scan proceeds, we continue to fill matrix cells, and alter the problem and the lists of sources and elements if needed. Our search might fill all the cells, but that doesn't mean we're done. We can always add another source, and another and another. As we noted before, there is no end to this: we can always seek out more sources, across the world and back into the past. So how do we know when we find a solution?

The answer: when we see it—when a combination of elements solves a list of elements of a problem that we think it is worthwhile and possible to solve. A flash of insight connects the dots in our minds. Even in a team that works very closely, this can happen only in one mind first. One of us sees it, and then explains it to the others. They see it too, because they have the same elements in their minds. You connect the dots in your head, and then you connect the dots in theirs. There's no other way it can happen. That's how strategic ideas form in the human brain.

In our GE example, one last element did the trick. GE's finance company was offering one of their products online just to employees, as a benefit. This goes under the element "identify customers." Our appliance team said, "very interesting." There were 300,000 GE employees at the time. With family, call it a million. What if we offer appliances online just to GE employees and their families, as a benefit? The big stores can't get mad because it's just an internal program, part of human resources. But it's a million customers, and they all buy appliances. This is a wonderful way to get started in online appliances. GE can work out all the details with this large, internal market, and decide later whether and how to open it up to the public.

Note that the problem changed, from "wholesale to e-commerce in appliances" to "get started in online appliances." The team did not solve the whole problem. They solved a piece of it, how to get started. Now GE has a strong proposal to accept or reject. In this case GE did accept and implement the idea. As it turns out, they were lucky that they did not set out to solve the whole problem and go big time into online appliance retail, because the dot-com crash came soon after. It was fortunate that they only

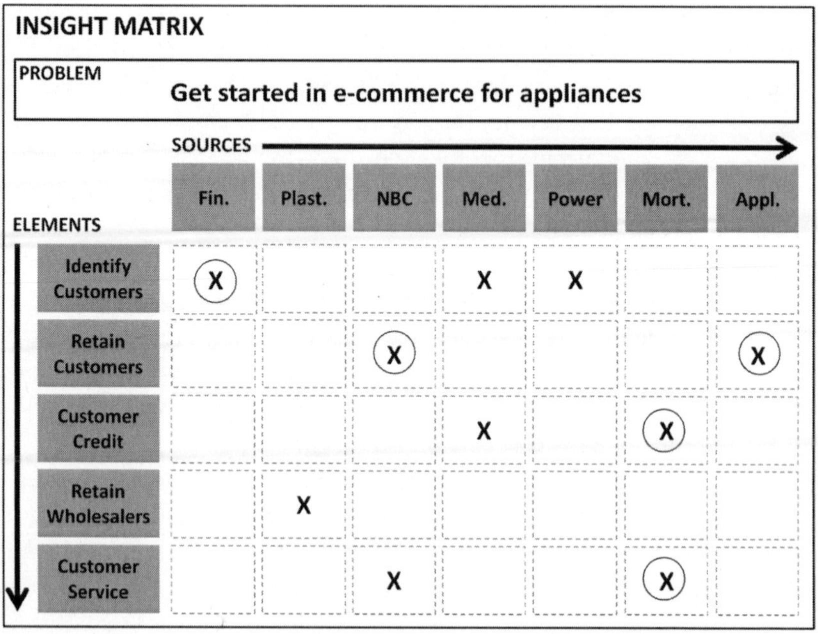

INSIGHT MATRIX

PROBLEM: **Get started in e-commerce for appliances**

SOURCES →

ELEMENTS ↓

ELEMENTS	Fin.	Plast.	NBC	Med.	Power	Mort.	Appl.
Identify Customers	(X)			X	X		
Retain Customers			(X)				(X)
Customer Credit				X		(X)	
Retain Wholesalers		X					
Customer Service			X			(X)	

Figure 5.1
Insight matrix: creative combination.

bit off that one piece. And it worked: the program continues today, more than a decade later.

Figure 5.1 shows the final insight matrix for this GE example. We see that the most important element turned out to be "identify customers," and the most important source was "finance." It's impossible to predict which elements and sources will matter most; you discover that in the what-works scan. In this case, once they had that one big insight, they could take more conventional elements of e-commerce—still from real sources—to complete the picture. The circled elements show the final selection and combination. That's your innovation.

You can also organize this third phase, creative combination, as a formal workshop. You declare an end to the what-works scan and pull the team together to select and combine from the large number of precedents you found. This makes most sense when your team and the problem are both big, so you have lots of X's in a very big matrix. A workshop is also best when the team that does the what-works scan is not the same as the team that will implement the innovation.

There are many possible variations on a creative combination workshop. Here I present one version from beginning to end, for illustration. In this version there are three sets of participants in the workshop: the team that did the rapid appraisal and the what-works scan, the key executives who will decide whether to do the innovation and lead its implementation, and other key staff who will implement it. We'll call these three groups the creative strategy team, the innovation leaders, and the innovation staff. The creative strategy team interviewed all the innovation leaders during rapid appraisal. If you plan a creative combination workshop at the end, tell the innovation leaders that when you interview them. These leaders in turn select and invite the innovation staff to the workshop.

Within the creative strategy team, the more senior members might do most of the rapid appraisal and the junior members do most of the what-works scan. The whole team facilitates the creative combination workshop. Schedule the workshop at least a month in advance, because everyone is so busy. When you get closer to the workshop date, confirm the invitation and send out a brief write-up of the problem, the elements, and the sources, as well as up to a page on each precedent you found for the matrix cells. Ask the participants to read through these items before the workshop.

The workshop takes a day and a half. You start the workshop itself with a full group session. As in any workshop, you introduce everyone, review the purpose and agenda, and ask the most senior executive present to affirm that the company wants to go ahead with whatever proposal the group comes up with. Of course that's no guarantee that the company will in fact approve the proposal. Make it clear what the next approval step will be after the workshop.

Also at this stage, make it very clear that the group is not there to brainstorm new ideas. This is very important, because that's the norm, and what they likely will expect, no matter what you said in the invitation. It's just part of corporate culture these days: you bring people together in a workshop, and they think they're supposed to brainstorm solutions.

Next, the creative strategy team presents what they've done so far. Briefly review what you sent out to participants: the matrix with the problem, elements and sources filled in, and the pages of precedents for the matrix cells. At this point, you have many options for how to get the group to discuss, select, and combine the precedents. Small groups are best, with reports back to the full group. The simplest breakdown for the precedents is by the list of element rows: if you have four elements, you might have a series of four breakout sessions where each small group gets a chance to work on the precedents for each element in turn.

The small groups need strong facilitators or strong self-policing to keep reminding the group that they are not there to brainstorm solutions to the problem. If someone does insist on offering a solution that's not one of the precedents in the workshop materials, write it on a side sheet—a parking lot—for later study. Whoever suggested it then has to research whether the solution actually worked somewhere for someone, at some time, and only then it can come out of the parking lot and onto the main list as a precedent. This discipline is very important; otherwise, the breakouts end up as typical brainstorming sessions.

Ask each small group to write on a flip chart which precedents they selected, why they chose each one, and any preliminary ideas they might have for combining them. Post these in the main room, and review them as a full group at the end of the workshop day. In the previous scenario, of four sessions for four elements, each small group would post four sets of flip charts, one for each element they worked on. There will likely be quite a lot of overlap among what the groups selected. The more overlap, the better.

That evening, relax. Let everyone unwind, but on-site. Have an informal full-group dinner or some other social event that lets everyone talk informally and get to know each other a bit better. Meanwhile, the consultants take the flip chart reports and produce a matrix with only a few cells filled in, plus one-page reports on each chosen element. To do that, they look for the elements that the small groups together favored most. They make copies for all participants.

The next morning, distribute the draft document. Small groups discuss it and propose additions, subtractions, or other changes, including further insights anyone had overnight. They report these proposed edits back to the full group. The consultants just make a record—there is not enough time to change the document itself right then. Back to breakouts: each small group takes an element of the problem and the precedents the group chose to match that piece. Their job is to start a draft action plan—who does what next, and when. They post and discuss these in the full group.

That's it. You conclude with a recap of what you did and what are the next approval steps. Let everyone know that the creative strategy team will write everything up and send it to the participants.

Note: In this workshop version of creative combination, who gets the idea? Whoever decides on and implements the idea. If the creative strategy team is a set of internal or external consultants, we can see how this method differs from the common practice where consultants do the analysis and make a recommendation about what to do. That's why so many consultant reports sit on the shelf—because it wasn't the client's idea. It's a fact of human nature that people are more committed and work harder for their own ideas versus someone else's. Clausewitz called this "resolution"—that commitment you feel from the flash of insight where you see a creative combination.

Creative strategy is also very different from the usual form of participatory strategic planning, where facilitators lead the group to reach consensus on mission, vision, goals, activities to reach the goals, and so on. In that kind of session, the participants toss out their own ideas. In the creative strategy workshop, they select and combine precedents from the past successes of others. The other advantage of creative strategy is that it gets a head start on planning: the list of chosen precedents are the key activities of your plan. Participants leave the workshop excited because they see what to do, how to do it, and how it solves a major strategic problem before them.

This description of the concluding workshop for creative combination leaves out the magic. It's hard to describe if you haven't seen it. I say that people "select" or "choose" or "combine." What they really do is "see." They might see a parallel between a precedent from the matrix and their own situation. Or they see a way to connect precedents to make a solution. Their brains connect the dots, and they feel it as a flash of insight: the proverbial light bulb goes off in their heads. Of course it's not really magic, but it can seem like it at the time. Although science has come very far in explaining how flashes of insight work, a part of it will always remain mysterious. You never know what you will see, until you see it. One moment you don't see it, and the next you do. That's how creative strategy works.

6

Resolution

The resolution phase of creative strategy—after you have your creative combination—can take days, weeks, months, or years, depending on the idea itself and the obstacles you encounter. The idea can succeed or fail. Creative strategy does not guarantee success; it increases your chances of success by giving you a strong idea that's worth the effort of trying to implement.

Once you have a creative combination, your next step is to plan. We saw that in the final workshop you end with the start of a plan. You have a goal: your final problem statement. And you have some activities to reach the goal: the precedents you found and selected from the sources. These precedents come with some numbers: costs, revenue, staffing, and timing. Of course you need to adjust them for your situation, but these numbers give you a solid start.

Note that only now do you have an idea of how long your plan will take. In the GE example, their solution was probably a nine-month project. For many innovations, the implementation period is much greater. Whatever the length of time, that's how long you can plan. If you plan in detail beyond that period, you're in fantasyland. You have no basis for what you put down in your plan beyond the idea your creative combination gave you. If we go back to our Japanese company seeking to expand beyond Asia, only when they find a good idea—when they have a matrix that works—can they know what period their idea will span and what timeline to set out.

Of course there are some big items you might need to plan for beyond the idea that creative strategy gives you. But if you think carefully, these are few and far between. For example, perhaps factories in your industry take five years to build, or your product takes seven years to design and make. Don't you need five- or seven-year plans? If you decide on a factory that takes five years to build, of course you need a five-year plan to build the factory. Same with the product: you need a seven-year plan to design and make it. But those are just pieces of a bigger, longer-term strategy, or at least let's hope so. That overall strategy comes out of your matrix, including an overall timeline, and the factory and product are pieces of that. Don't plan in detail for your factory or your product until you have a good idea for your overall strategy, which will come with its own span of time.

It's entirely possible, even likely, that some part of your idea will call for people or knowledge you don't possess at the moment. So part of your plan is how to acquire those missing pieces. Innovations usually go beyond your current abilities—that's one thing that makes them innovations. The farther your sources reach beyond your own industry, the greater the innovation, and the more you need to learn beyond what you already know. This is why strategy should not follow your "core competencies," because that can and should change. Once you innovate successfully, you have a new core competencies.

On the other hand, if you are currently capable of doing none of the elements from your matrix, it might not be a good idea to proceed. This is a question that bridges the flash of insight that gives you the creative combination and the start of your plan: It's a good idea, but can we do it? Sometimes you have to start planning in order to judge. You work out the plan and take another look: Is this too expensive, will it take too long, is it too risky? You now enter the realm of your usual methods of decision making. It's perfectly normal to turn down a plan.

But on what grounds? Beware the tyranny of projections. It's common practice to project costs and revenues into the future, subtract one from the other, and call that future profit. If the future profit is high enough, you accept the plan. If the future profit is low or negative, you reject the plan. If you have to decide between two plans, you pick the one with the higher future profit.

Unfortunately, this method of selecting projects is a big mistake. Your projections of cost and revenue are not real. You made them up. You have no hard numbers on future costs and revenue; there are no data about the future. You make an educated guess about what the future costs and revenue might be, so your future profit is a guess as well. Perhaps you based your projections on past numbers. That's fine. Those past numbers are facts. To turn them into projections, you make up a percentage increase or decrease. When you take a real number and multiply it by a made-up number, the result is a made-up number. Perhaps you got your percentage increase or decrease from past numbers too. Let's say revenues increased by 8 percent every year over the past six years. If I now say revenue will be another 8 percent higher next year, I have just made up a new number. You might look at the same past numbers and conclude that revenue next year will go up 9 percent. I say 8 percent. You say 9 percent. Someone else says 15 percent. Which one of us is right?

You know the answer: whichever one of us has more power in the organization. Their projections win. Let's admit that. We have to accept it. But that doesn't mean we have to pretend the projections are real.

Projections are not and cannot be a scientific measure of the value of a strategic idea. They are an expression of your faith, or lack of it, in that idea. If your planning projections show high future profit, that means you have a lot of faith in the strategic idea that the plan aims to implement. If your planning projections are low or negative, it means you lack faith in that same strategic idea. Unfortunately, in business we often get two sets of numbers for two competing proposals and decide between them by comparing the two sets of projections. This makes no sense. You made up the number for Proposal A, and you made up the number for Proposal B, and now you note that the B number is higher than the A number, so you go with B. But of course B is higher—you made it that way. The numbers are not real.

Of course, often you have two different teams presenting two different proposals. So one team makes up one set of numbers and the other team makes up another set of numbers. When that happens, both show high profit projections. Now how do we choose? Not by the numbers, that's for sure. Arguing whose made-up numbers are better makes no sense.

We do need to make projections as part of planning to implement a strategic idea, but projections are not a good basis for deciding whether or not to do the idea in the first place. So how do you decide? The steps of creative strategy give us the answer. The strength of a strategic idea depends on the strength of the past elements you combined to make the idea in the first place. If I can show you that each of five elements I combined for an idea was key to someone's success in some way, and the elements together solve pieces of a puzzle that well match our current problem, then I have a strong idea. If I can show that for only three of the five elements, or if the pieces poorly match our current problem, then you should have less faith in my idea.

But if you do approve the idea, the same numbers I used to make my case from past elements are the start of the numbers for the plan. Now we project costs and revenues, staffing, profits, and so on, as far into the future as the idea takes us. We do the best we can to fill in these numbers, remembering at all times that we're making them up. That means we need to revise them often, as the true numbers appear each week, each month, and each year that we proceed.

Once you start implementing your creative combination, the real hard work begins. Thomas Edison once said, "Genius is 1 percent inspiration and 99 percent perspiration." I think he's exactly right. He's telling us two things. Any idea worth doing calls for a tremendous amount of effort to implement—that's the perspiration. But he's also telling us, you need a good idea. That's the inspiration. Perspiration without inspiration is a waste of time. Creative strategy gives you that 1 percent. Next comes the 99 percent, when you put your idea into action.

But even during that 99 percent, you will run into problems where you need a creative solution. The problem might be too small, or you might not have enough time to do all the steps of creative strategy. You can always do a mini-treasure hunt instead, by yourself or with others. However little time you have, ask yourself this: If you don't use creative strategy, what's the alternative? How else do you solve a problem?

Well, let's take a look. There are five common methods for problem solving during implementation: benchmarking, call in an expert, quality control, research, and brainstorming. In chapter 4, we saw that benchmarking cannot give you a creative idea beyond the usual sources in your industry, and you can't spend the time benchmarking every company in every industry around the world. Often the problem does call for the kind of ordinary solution that benchmarking can give. That's fine. But if you want to innovate, try a mini-treasure hunt also or instead.

Call in an expert. This is a form of benchmarking, where one person or a team of experts gives you best practices from your industry. Again, that's fine for many problems. The same with quality control. You have a process that works, and when defects arise you go back through the system to look for deviations from the process that might have caused the problem. Again, these methods solve many ordinary problems but do not lead to innovation.

Research—this is good, depending how you do it. "Let's do some research," is a common response to a difficult problem. Unfortunately, there are dozens of ways to research a problem without doing a treasure hunt. Sometimes there's a partial treasure hunt, usually mixed in with all sorts of other material like customer feedback and industry trends. Unless you clearly mark out the treasure hunt as a separate method beforehand and as separate results to report, you will never find a creative combination that solves your problem.

Brainstorming—this is the most common method by far. A problem comes up and someone says, "Let's meet tomorrow morning to brainstorm a solution." We will look at brainstorming more closely in chapter 9. For now, the main point is this: brainstorming is a good way to put together, fast, what everyone in the room has on the top of their heads from direct experience. Once again, many ordinary problems in business can be solved this way. But again, that's not innovation. A treasure hunt goes beyond the direct experience of people in the room to the experience of others not in the room. Henry Ford's engineers can brainstorm forever, but unless someone in the room once worked in a slaughterhouse, they will never think of the moving assembly line.

The discipline of creative strategy to solve problems works for unforeseen opportunity too. Sometimes you discover something that doesn't solve a problem but rather improves what you're doing in some new way. An example of this comes from the early days of Apple Computer. Steve Jobs and his partner, Steve Wozniak, had their first success with the Apple II, the world's first cheap, small, easy-to-use computer. It had a green screen, like all computers those days. Xerox invested some money in Apple, and that made Jobs part of the Xerox family, so he was able to visit their research center. Apple was already hard at work on the Apple III, so when they went to Xerox, they were already in the implementation phase. But Xerox showed Jobs a big computer with a mouse and a graphical user interface (GUI). Jobs immediately changed direction: he went back to the drawing board to combine Xerox's mouse and GUI with a small Apple machine. The result was the Mac, and the next phase of the computer revolution.

Jobs did not go to Xerox to solve a problem. What he saw there solved a problem he did not even know he had: how to make his small computer more visual. Jobs was not an engineer; it was Wozniak who built their early machines. Instead, Jobs stayed on a permanent treasure hunt, looking for elements for his next creative combination. That was his job, and for many years he did it very well.

Here's another example of creative strategy during implementation, or, rather, the lack of it.

In 2001, Donald Washkewicz became CEO of Parker Hannifin, a major producer of parts for complex industrial machines and equipment. He had worked at Parker since 1972. Now as CEO, he took a tour of its factories—they had 225, in 115 divisions. In one of them, he had an "epiphany": Parker should act like a retailer. Up to now they priced their parts by calculating the cost of making them and adding a flat percentage. Instead, they should charge different percentages, according to what the market would bear—just like retail. This is a classic flash of insight, very similar to Jobs at Xerox or Henry Ford and the slaughterhouse: take an element from there and use it here. If it's big enough, and important enough, you feel it as an epiphany. Washkewicz had clear parallels in mind: airlines and sports teams that raise prices for seats at times of most demand.

This is a common way for creative combination to happen in business—as a flash of insight rather than through the formal steps of creative strategy. Both are valid. One you can plan, the other you can't. But even when the creative combination happens unplanned as a flash of insight, you should still do the other steps of creative strategy. The Parker example shows why.

After Washkewicz had his idea, he unveiled it to the staff in October 2001. It included a new vice president for pricing and a big team of outside consultants to do all the repricing work. Right away, the staff hated the idea. Washkewicz heard so many objections that he made a list of the 50 most common reasons the staff gave him for why the idea would fail. If you had a new objection, he would listen. If it was already on the list, he didn't want to hear it again.

In 2003, the first divisions rolled out their new prices. Parker's customers were parts distributors, who in turn sold to equipment manufacturers. And the distributors howled. How could they raise prices to their own customers when the cost of making the part didn't change? The protest grew so strong that in 2005, Parker started workshops to explain to distributors how to pitch the different parts and prices to the manufacturers.

The story has a happy ending. As of 2007, Parker's operating income, net income, and return on capital all rose far faster than for industry peers. Yet this success disguises a problem. If these financial returns had been poorer, perhaps Washkewicz would have thought twice and fixed the problem. Instead, the problem lies in wait, ready to strike at a moment of weakness.

So what's the problem?

Let's start with Washkewicz's list of fifty objections. Is that a good way to handle dissent? From the view of creative strategy, there's no doubt that he had a very good idea. Unfortunately, it seems that Washkewicz was not looking for further ideas to make his original idea even better. The list of fifty doesn't exactly stifle dissent, it just channels it into a holding ground where it can't do any damage. But here's another way to look at that list: as problems Parker needs to solve. Washkewicz's idea was a radical change of strategy for Parker. There were countless details to work out. Washkewicz should have responded to each item on the list of fifty by saying "You're right. That's a problem. Any ideas how to fix it?"

Each problem, then, becomes the subject of its own insight matrix. Or you could do one for the whole idea and the problems are the list of pieces in the left-hand column. In either case, you want a treasure hunt that looks widely for elements elsewhere. And Washkewicz already had a wealth of sources to search: retailers who used demand pricing. He would quickly find that retail in general and demand-price retail in particular has myriad successful tricks of the trade for Parker to learn from and borrow.

For example, surely one problem on the list of fifty was "the distributors will hate it." That's correct, it's a real problem. Now how do we solve it? That's the right response. Instead, Parker waited four years, from 2001 to 2005, before explaining the strategy to customers, who probably spent those years looking for other suppliers. If Parker had done a matrix in 2001, it would have immediately found ways to work on the customer problem much sooner. After all, the minute you declare a retail strategy, the most important person in the world is your customer. Washkewicz didn't think of that. He can't think of everything, of course, so he should have looked for ideas from his staff. If you know the distributors will be a problem, ask your staff to search for elements to solve it.

We can't know if Parker would have had even better results if Washkewicz had followed through on his good idea with more creative combinations. In strategy, alas, we can't rerun experiments. But from the view of creative strategy, Washkewicz stopped innovating the moment after he had his good idea. That's too bad, because if he had continued seeking innovations along the way, his result might have been even better.

So in the end, perhaps inspiration is 2 percent of a good idea: 1 percent at the start and another 1 percent as you solve problems along the way.

7

Get Organized

Over the past decade or so, more and more companies have turned their attention to innovation. Their efforts take various organizational forms. You find chief innovation officers, innovation councils, innovation funds, incubators, greenhouses, and many other new structures or procedures to stimulate or support new product or business ideas. Many of these are good when they serve as a hub for ideas to come together from various sources or bring attention, endorsement, and concrete support to innovation as a key activity of business. Just add creative strategy—to help people get ideas in the first place—and it can be a winning combination. Without creative strategy, these innovation structures and procedures can waste time at best and suppress innovation at worst.

A specialized consulting firm, Innovation Point, offers a typical range of structures and procedures that they help companies adopt. Let's look at their list:

Venture boards: Top-level company-wide panels of internal and external executives who review and recommend major new initiatives

Innovation councils: Committees of top managers from each division who meet on a regular schedule to coordinate innovation across units and develop joint incentives and procedures for innovation

Cross-group solution teams: Experts from different units join together for specific innovation projects

Thought leader resource networks: External experts that the company draws on formally or informally, as needed or in regular seminars of conferences

Open innovation networks: Formal or informal partnerships with external individuals or organizations to work on specific innovation projects.

Communities of practice: Formal or informal communication networks of internal and external individuals across fields and units who exchange ideas about a topic of mutual interest

Incubators: Separate divisions, or separate units within divisions, whose sole job is to develop innovations and hand them off to the operating divisions or units

This Innovation Point list organizes ideas nicely at different levels of the company. You can easily imagine an idea arising in one format on the list, handed up or over to another one, further refined or approved, and then moving through another to actual implementation. But beware—don't get too organized. Innovation Point itself makes a common mistake in its guidance at each formal level—develop "metrics" beforehand to judge which ideas to pursue or approve.

You cannot predict what metrics to use because the best innovations surprise you and make you recast your ideas about which metrics matter. If you say ideas must "bring in at least $5 million in new revenue," what do you do with an innovation that cuts costs dramatically with no change in revenue? So you add that as another metric: "cut costs by at least 20 percent." But does that mean an idea must meet both metrics, or just one, or a combination of both? For example, if the idea increases revenue by $4 million and decreases cost by 10 percent, does it pass? And what if the idea simply increases customer satisfaction by 20 percent, without increasing revenue or decreasing cost? So now you add that, and you have three metrics. And so on, until the judges spent all their time debating metrics rather than the idea.

And remember, all the metrics are false to some degree. They are based on projections of what you think the idea will do in the future, which has no metrics. You can't measure the future. So-called "metrics" about innovation ideas are really just educated guesses dressed up as real numbers. Instead, make sure that whoever proposes the idea tells you the sources that inspired it. The innovation proposal should follow the format of the insight matrix, which tells you the strength of the sources and how well they fit your situation. That's the best way to judge a creative idea.

That leads us back to another common mistake that Innovation Point makes, despite the excellence of its list. Once you have all those organizational structures and procedures in place, how do people actually come up with creative ideas? Innovation Point tells you to brainstorm, as usual. This is not to single out Innovation Point for this mistake; it's nearly universal in the innovation world, as we know. Innovation Point deserves praise for a terrific summary of good practices on the organizational side. But when it comes to coming up with the idea itself, use creative strategy.

And when you put in any of these innovation structures, the devil is in the details. There are ways to do it well, and ways to do it badly. No two companies are the exactly the same, so you need to adapt any and all of these structures to your own situation. To do that, use creative strategy. Start with rapid appraisal: What problem, exactly, do you think these structures will solve? If your problem is as general as "we don't innovate enough," you want the rapid appraisal to list as elements what obstacles prevent you from innovating now. Then comes your what-works scan, starting with sources that have tried versions of what structures you think you need. Be careful to look for evidence of success; just because someone else uses a structure, that doesn't mean it works.

There is one common organizational form that's not on the Innovation Point list: acquisitions. Many big companies innovate by buying up smaller innovative companies. That's often a good idea. But what happens next? In many cases, the big company develops formal procedures and routines for the new product or service that stifle creativity. That might not matter. When the market dries up for that innovation, the big company simply looks for a new company to acquire. But other times, it doesn't work out. Many entrepreneurs and their staff value creativity highly, and they leave en masse once they feel the new procedures tighten around them. That throws the acquirer into crisis, because it can't yet replace the original crew.

All this means that acquisition should not be your only method of innovation. Tell the entrepreneur you're acquiring what your formal procedures are for further innovation after the acquisition. If you don't have any yet, perhaps that entrepreneur can help develop some, especially if you don't have a very entrepreneurial culture already.

And there is a feature of your organization that is far more important than these formal structures: how you treat each other's ideas. If for some reason you can't use creative strategy to innovate or solve problems, you must at least have a culture that welcomes new ideas. And that doesn't mean regular brainstorming sessions. It means when you rush into the boss's office Monday morning to gush about an idea that struck you over the weekend, the boss doesn't tell you it's a bad idea, get back to work. As we know, most flashes of insight strike at odd moments when your mind is relaxed. Does your company have a way to capture those ideas? Of course you don't want everyone bursting into the boss's office all day.

Try this: reverse brainstorming. That's a regular meeting—weekly is best—where everyone just listens to ideas people had since the previous meeting. The purpose of the meeting is just to listen and ask for more explanation. You don't rank, vote, critique, or decide on ideas. And the ideas can be about anything, even what you're not working on. That's one feature of innovation: it's different from what you're doing now. The meeting need not last long. After, anyone who finds something interesting can follow up with the person who brought the idea. For example, the boss might ask you to write up your idea as a formal proposal. But don't ask for anything written before the reverse brainstorming meeting; speech is creative, and often people need to talk about an idea before they can explain it on paper.

Outside of a reverse-brainstorming meeting, how do you talk about ideas? The culture of innovation in any organization starts with the informal exchange of ideas in hallways, over coffee, or dropping into someone's office for a quick chat. At those occasions, it's common to hear that you should "build on each other's ideas"—but how, exactly? If you tell me an idea for a product, and I tell you to put wings on it and paint it pink, should you do it? If you reject my idea—no wings, no pink—does that mean you're not open to the ideas of others? If I'm your boss, do you feel you have to put on the wings and paint it pink or else I won't approve it?

And what if I see a problem with your idea, do I tell you? But then you'll think I rejected your idea, especially if I'm the boss. And that's not building, it's critiquing.

At this atomic level—two coworkers discussing an idea—many possible innovations meet an early death. Some people know how to build on each other's ideas, and some don't. The right way to do it follows the steps of creative strategy, but informally. You ask what problem the idea is solving. That's the top of the matrix. If you see a problem with the idea, that's an element row. These are the steps of rapid appraisal. If you add to the idea—wings, pink—explain the source. That's a matrix column.

If there is no source, wings and pink are probably bad suggestions. You might even grab a piece of paper and sketch out the matrix, to make it clear what you're doing.

Many people follow this method exactly when they build on each other's ideas. After all, creative strategy is just a formal version of how creative ideas form in the human brain. But this kind of deep discussion doesn't happen casually, with strangers. A new field of "network research" shows that you tend to discuss creative ideas with people you trust, and that in turn depends on triangulation. You trust someone more if you both know a third person in common. Mass methods like online discussion boards, where anyone can comment on any idea, do not build personal trust. Instead, encourage joint projects and regular meetings to learn about each other's work and achievements so that everyone can build their own dense network of trust.

General Electric took this internal networking a step further; at the time they used an earlier version of the insight matrix at their Crotonville campus. Each unit reported each year what they were best at and where they needed help. Crotonville helped match them up. If you were good at something, someone bad at that came to visit you, and vice versa. Your performance appraisal included mention of what you learned from another unit and what you taught another unit over the past year. This system made what-works scans far easier, thanks to a record of who did what best. And it fostered a host of dense, personal networks you could trust to discuss your creative ideas.

Another good example comes from Boeing, which over the past decade has expanded a program of employee innovation teams across its sprawling production system. A recent *Wall Street Journal* article reports that "Boeing's employee teams are composed of workers with varying backgrounds—from mechanics to engineers—and tend to focus on a specific part of a jet, such as the galleys. Teams meet as often as once a week and typically have seven to 10 members." This fits "cross-group solution teams" from the Innovation Point list. Rather than strangers submitting lots of ideas, team members form close ties working together and come up with fewer, better ideas. Boeing's innovation teams save lots of money and time—for example, canvas wheel covers protect airplane tires as the body moves down the assembly line. That saves Boeing $250,000 year in new tires at one plant alone. But how did the innovation team get that idea? It came from one of its members, Jay Dohrmann: "The idea, in place for about a year, occurred to Mr. Dohrmann as the avid sports fan watched a motorcycle race and noticed crews used special covers to warm up tires so they got a better grip on the track."

We recognize creative strategy: a key precedent from another source solves a key element of your problem. Innovation is a social sport, so you should organize your company to help everyone find teammates of various kinds. But the quality of the ties is more important than the quantity. And however you organize innovation, make sure everyone understands creative strategy, to help guide them to creative combinations from wide and many sources.

8

Kinds of Innovation

Creative strategy offers a method for innovation, but you will never follow the method exactly the same way twice. That's because every situation is different to some degree, and so is every innovation. But there are some big categories of innovations that we can group together, where the method will stay roughly the same within each category. This chapter explains some different ways of applying creative strategy to five different types of innovation problems.

Products, Services, and Functions

The most common kind of innovation in business is a new product or service—that's what most companies mean by "innovation." To pursue this kind of innovation, you can use the simplest form of creative strategy. Your problem statement is the category of product or service you're looking for, and the pieces of the puzzle are a general list of its characteristics. Then you scour the world for existing products or services that match the pieces in part.

If you have no idea what kind of product or service you're looking for, just put your industry at the top. For example, if you're a paper company, you put down "new product or service in the paper industry." And then put nothing in the left column. That is, don't break it down into pieces. Your sources are basically two: within the paper industry, and outside it. That is, you scan very widely. When you find something promising, you make that source more specific, and you now fill in the piece of the problem in the left column that your discovery solves. Then you find something else. Eventually you find enough elements that solve enough pieces that together make a new product or service.

Because creative strategy mirrors how innovation really happens, it's no surprise that we find versions of it among current existing practices for finding new products and services. Many product designers especially often use the basic method of creative strategy—search and combine—without giving it a formal name. Unfortunately, it's more common to find methods of product or service innovation that promise to invent something completely new. But successful innovations don't happen that way. We will take a closer look at some of these misguided methods in the next chapter.

Functional innovations are similar to new products or services. The basic functions are marketing, manufacturing, distribution, finance, research and development, and so on. You can also innovate in more specific domains, like reaching a particular customer group. As with product or service innovations, your problem statement is simply to "innovate in that function." Be careful of straight benchmarking. That's a way to copy industry leaders in that function, but it's not a path to innovation. Looking as widely as possible outside your industry is the key to functional innovation.

Business Models

The second kind of innovation in business generates a new product or service that is so different from what you're doing now that it calls for big changes in your organization. This is "business model innovation." These bigger innovations often bring bigger payoffs than product and service innovations, but they are more complex and harder to do. The hardest part is not the idea itself, once you understand and practice creative strategy. No, the hardest part is what happens next: putting your idea into practice. Especially in big, successful companies, a new business model means that most everyone has to change what they're doing to some degree. This is a major problem of organizational change, as we saw in the Parker example in the last chapter. Creative strategy can help you solve creative problems along the way—which Washkewicz neglected—but otherwise the job of putting a new business model into action mostly calls for good management and leadership, not more creative ideas.

You might want to consider the following method for business model innovation, which allows for the kind of ongoing innovation that Parker's "one idea" lacked. This method comes from Christian Majgaard, who led Lego into the computer age as head of innovation. In the 1990s, the company was conservative in two ways: its success was in a single product that dominated the market for decades, and the culture of its headquarters reflected its location in a remote, religious, rural part of Denmark. Majgaard put innovation in the hands of small mixed teams, each composed of older established insiders who knew Lego and younger flamboyant outsiders who knew the new world of computers.

The insiders thought computers did not belong in the hands of children, and the outsiders saw Lego as hopelessly out of date. Only a mixed team could bridge the gap. Majgaard freed the teams of most existing bureaucracy, insisting only that they stay within the budget he gave them. Now that you understand creative strategy, it won't surprise you that the innovations that resulted were all hybrids from these two worlds that met in the mixed teams. The economic downturn of the early 2000s nearly crippled Lego, but the company bounced back on the strength of its new products that fit the digital age.

Many companies have adopted versions of Majgaard's method—mixed inside/outside innovation teams that you give more freedom—but the Lego story gives us the added angle of starkly conflicting corporate cultures. Is your company big and successful? If so, even if it's not based in Danish farm country, you likely have a Lego problem. The main part of your firm has an execution culture, where you know exactly what to do and exactly how to do it. For innovation, you need to allow small teams to have a creative culture instead, where they don't know what to do or how to do it—yet. You have to recognize that these are two different cultures, one dominant but both necessary. Like Majgaard, you must protect the creative pipsqueak from the execution bully until it can show results.

Another example comes from IBM. In the mid-1990s a new CEO, Lou Gerstner, transformed the IBM business model from a proprietary hardware company to an integrated services company—using creative strategy, by the way, but that's another story. Yet the struggle never ends. In the early 2000s, Gerstner read in a monthly report that a unit cut a promising new business idea because it hurt its quarterly results. This is a common and age-old problem: the more the innovation changes your business model, the more money it drains before it turns a profit. So Gerstner created a new unit, the Emerging Business Organization, with its own budget and senior staff to lead each innovation. That gave new ideas more time and support to develop and grow.

There are many examples, like Lego and IBM, where leaders used new organizational forms to protect business model innovations from the normal bureaucratic and financial demands of execution. And then some companies have the opposite problem. They let a thousand flowers bloom, and bloom, and bloom, and they don't know when to pull the plug. This happened to Google, whose revenue grew rapidly in the 2000s because of its original product, search ads. The company encouraged employees to work on new projects of their choosing, and they did. In December 2008, the *Wall Street Journal* reported that Google found the results of this practice very disappointing and planned to cut back new projects dramatically.

How long should you let an innovation go on before it turns a profit? Unfortunately, there is no set answer to this. But creative strategy offers some help—a clearer view on what's a good innovation in the first place. Ask this: Is the innovation based on a creative combination? That's a very high standard. It will result in far fewer innovations worth trying out, but more that succeed in the end.

Entrepreneurial

A third kind of innovation is "entrepreneurial." This means that you start a new company to implement the idea. It's the flip side of business model innovation; changing business models is so hard for big companies that it's usually easier to start a new company instead. Financing, hiring, operations—all go faster when you start from scratch. On the other hand, the risks are greater. Failure usually means the company dies too, and the entrepreneur is out of a job.

Beyond these differences of implementation, creative strategy is very similar for business model innovation and entrepreneurial innovation. If you want to start a new business, creative strategy can help. But very often an entrepreneurial idea happens by accident, as a classic flash of insight. Sometimes the entrepreneur is already working for a larger company and tries to convince the boss to adopt the idea. When that doesn't work, you quit and start your own business.

We see a good example of this in how Starbucks began. It was a chain of six high-quality coffee bean stores in the Seattle area when its marketing director, Howard Schultz, went to a housewares trade show in Milan, Italy. There Schultz wandered into one of the city's many coffee bars and had an "epiphany," as he called it: "It was so immediate and physical I was shaking." Starbucks should become a chain of coffee bars, not coffee bean stores, on the Italian model. When Schultz got back to Seattle, his boss said no. Schultz ended up leaving to start his own company, and then bought Starbucks when the boss retired.

That day in Milan, the idea came to Schultz over several hours, as he went in and out of Milan's coffee bars. If we plot out his thinking as creative strategy, we see that first two elements came together in his mind—Seattle high-quality coffee bean chain, Italian coffee bar—and then he filled in the rest of the matrix from there. That's usually how entrepreneurial ideas happen. You don't start out by saying, "Let me create an entrepreneurial idea." The key lesson here is that creative strategy gives you not just a method but also a state of mind: stay open to everything you see, read, and hear to consider as possible elements to combine.

On the other hand, there are countless innovations that don't see the light of day because they are incomplete. Someone gets a new business idea but doesn't act, because they're not certain it will work. Often they beat themselves up: "I'm too risk-averse," or "I don't have the nerve," or "I don't have a strong enough will." That might be so, but more likely the problem is this: you don't have a complete idea. We might call this a partial flash of insight. Two or three elements come together in your mind, and you see a new business. But you immediately see as well three or four big problems you don't know how to solve. You are probably right, but instead of struggling to screw up the courage to take the leap anyway, try creative strategy. Do the matrix, with the problems you foresee as matrix rows. In the search you might uncover someone who not only knows how to solve some of the problems, but wants to join you. Maybe you need a partner who brings elements into the combination that make your idea even better.

Social Enterprise

Yet another kind of innovation solves social problems, usually by government agencies or nongovernmental organizations (NGOs), but sometimes by for-profit businesses too. We call this "social innovation." Very often these arise as entrepreneurial ideas that create new organizations. For example, Muhammad Yunus in Bangladesh had a classic flash of insight that started Grameen Bank, the world's first major microfinance lender. As for innovation in existing organizations, here's an example from government, where innovation is often hardest of all.

As in most big cities, New York City's government is a sprawling maze of overlapping bureaucracies built up over decades by a succession of different administrations. The city's three-term mayor from the business world, Michael Bloomberg, explicitly set out to foster innovation within the various city agencies. An example of creative strategy comes from Kevin Kelly, Deputy Commissioner of the Business Development Division at the city's Department of Small Business Services. In the mid-2000s, New York City set out to streamline the many steps businesses must take to start, operate, and expand legally. In many cases businesses had to go to up to a dozen different agencies and fill out many different forms. Kelly broke down the problem into elements and looked for precedents to solve it.

His first source for precedents was online commerce. Putting everything online cut out the need for businesses to visit multiple government office locations. And, by then, many government agencies around the world had already started putting their procedures online, from downloading forms to applying and paying for licenses. One big precedent was the "wizard" you find on many sites, for example, eBay's Tools Wizard for sellers. Kelly set up a "Requirements Wizard" with easy-to-understand questions whose answers assemble a customized list of government requirements that fit exactly the specific situation of each business, so that each business can know exactly what it needs to do to be in compliance.

Next, Kelly turned to the problem element of multiple applications to multiple agencies for the same business. There his source was college applications, and the main precedent was the Common Application, where nearly 500 colleges allow applicants to fill out about 80 percent of the application only once, and the data go to all the colleges they apply to. Each college then asks its own questions for the other 20 percent. For Kelly, that meant a business only had to fill out its basic information once, and that information would go into each agency's application.

Another problem element was that individual agency applications usually covered all possible use cases, so the form took a long time for any single business to fill out, even if the answer to most questions was "Not applicable." For this, Kelly used the precedent of Turbo Tax, which asks questions up front so you only have to see those portions of the form relevant to you, in order to make the NYC Business Express Common Intake application more user friendly.

One of the biggest problem elements was the underlying technology, and the fact that agencies had their own, separate databases, using different hardware and software of different ages and with different degrees of connectivity among them. Conventional wisdom—and some technology experts—said that all of these separate databases should be replaced with a single new one. Kelly knew that would take far too much time, be far too complex, and require much more money than he had to spend.

Then one day he was getting cash from an ATM. He stopped and stared at the screen. He looked at all the options it gave him. He knew that his bank was now very big, after a series of mergers among smaller banks. And he knew that each of those merged banks still had their own separate systems and databases. His checking account was in one system, his savings account in another, his IRA in a third, and his CD in another. There was no single database that contained all of the information for all of his accounts and services. The ATM screen was simply a portal to and from each system.

That was it! NYC Business Express would do the same thing—interact with each city agency database like an ATM interacts with multiple bank databases behind it. When you applied for and paid a fee for a license or a permit on the screen, it would send the record and the money to that agency only. Note that this was a change not in the overall problem but in a single problem element: from "harmonize databases" to "interact with databases." But that one change made a big difference in the solution. As we see in Kelly's case, a change of element often comes when you find a good precedent, not before. You can see the result of Kelly's work at www.nyc.gov/BusinessExpress.

In this case, the innovation did not disrupt what the several government agencies were already doing. Kelly knew that was the only practical way to proceed. But sometimes an innovation does, or should, disrupt what social agencies are doing. A recent example comes from the field of juvenile justice, also from the mid-2000s, when a family foundation in Florida asked Lynn Ellsworth to evaluate the program they funded in aftercare, that is, social work to help kids who come out of jail reintegrate into society and, most of all, not get arrested again. The recidivism rate—how many kids go back to jail—is the key measure of success in this field.

Ellsworth did a rapid appraisal and what-works scan, and found a disturbing result. Aftercare simply did not work. The nonprofit agencies worked hard, but kids kept going back to jail. In her search, though,

Ellsworth found programs in the field of juvenile justice that had very low recidivism rates, at much lower costs, without aftercare. More than 90 percent of kids go to jail in the United States for nonviolent offenses, and for those the successful programs "diverted" the kids to therapy, restitution, and rehabilitation that kept them out of jail. The kids "served their time," but not in jail. And they stayed out of trouble afterward. Ellsworth did not present one creative combination at the end, but rather listed the programs that worked so that different agencies could choose their own combination to suit their situation.

The family foundation that sponsored the aftercare review showed great courage; they accepted the switch. They turned from funding aftercare to promoting diversion instead. But for the field of juvenile justice, this is a long, hard road. Aftercare agencies work with kids who need help. That's a good thing, right? After all, many people choose the social sector precisely to help other people. Creative strategy's hard-nosed view of innovation is often more foreign to many social agencies than Majgaard's young computer whizzes were to Lego's rural Denmark.

Yet another difference between innovation in the business and social sectors is how to measure what works. In business, the market rewards what works and punishes what doesn't, but in the social sector a program can continue to receive plentiful funding even if it doesn't work. So the social sector relies heavily on formal evaluations to identify success. A what-works scan for social innovation starts with evaluations in fields that touch on the elements of your problem.

Some fields have meta-evaluations that review a full set of evaluations in a field, and that's an extra help. But beware of meta-evaluations that rely heavily on statistics; once you aggregate many social programs, their local factors are so different that most statistics that summarize them miss important elements of each. Evaluations and meta-evaluations steer you to programs worth considering as sources, for further study through the normal means of the what-works scan.

Personal Strategy

Our last type of innovation is personal. Sometimes you need to innovate in your personal life. Most likely you won't come up with an innovation that's completely new to the world, but the combination that fits your life will indeed be unique in some way. Just as no two companies ever have identical characteristics or face exactly the same circumstances, you too must find a strategy that fits only you, now. That's how creative strategy works; you find a particular strategy for a particular situation at a particular point in time.

Innovation in personal strategy is the most difficult of all, precisely because it's personal. There are myriad emotional barriers to seeing your problem clearly, calmly breaking it down, identifying sources, and searching for elements to combine. At each point, human nature tells you the fault is someone else's personality or animus, circumstances beyond your control, or some past event that you cannot change. Often, these obstacles are partly true. But perhaps there's something you can do. It takes great presence of mind to follow the steps of creative strategy despite the feeling that it's hopeless even to try.

Once you do set out on the steps, the hardest one is finding sources. It's likely that the parts of your problem are not unique, and that someone else somewhere has faced the same thing. For personal problems, it's very hard to find out who that is. The Internet and social media have made this much, much easier. Remember as you search, you're not after opinion or sympathy, you're after success. You want to find someone who solved that part of the problem you're trying to solve yourself.

In a way, all innovations are personal. Committing to a new idea will always change your life to some degree. It will change where you fit in your organization and how others view you. Not everyone will want you to succeed. Jealousy and competition come with every innovation. The potential conflict that new ideas might bring contributes to the mental blocks that prevent people from creative thinking in the first place. "Don't stick your neck out" starts with "don't stick your mind out"—where you're not even looking for new ideas.

In this way, the most important skill for personal innovation is mental. Creative thinking is the key discipline for innovations of all kinds, and you must have the right mind for it—meaning not the right-hand side of the brain, but the correct method of thinking. You constantly study what works in whatever you read, see, hear, and do, even if you have no particular problem you're working on at the moment. You file the example on the shelves of your brain. You let your brain make new combinations of elements that you consider acting on but don't seem strong enough to inspire you to do them. And then one does, and you're on your way.

When you encounter something that doesn't work, you study why, but don't spend too much time on it. You can study a million examples of what doesn't work, but that still doesn't tell you what does work. Instead, try to figure out what element of the failure made the most difference. Did they do one piece wrong, was a key piece missing, should they have left one piece out? See if you can come up with a combination that might have worked better. Of course it's not a true test—you can't repeat the experiment—but it's good practice for the right way of thinking. Train your mind to constantly look for elements and combinations that succeeded in some way.

This way of thinking has an added advantage. It's good for your health, both mental and physical, especially if you're in a demographic group where stress-related diseases are the biggest killers. If you have a professional job, in any country, studies show that means you. Modern medicine, nutrition, and sanitation will keep you free of most diseases, except for those you bring on yourself through overwork and worry.

Creative strategy as a mental discipline reduces stress. That's because all stress has two components: pressure and anxiety. Both produce hormones in your brain. Pressure releases adrenalin, which is good; your heart rate goes up, you have more energy, you can work faster. Too much, of course, for too long, causes harm. But in normal doses, adrenalin is good. Anxiety releases cortisol. That's bad. Too much cortisol ruins your health and actually blocks recall, making it harder to think through your problems, because your brain can't draw as quickly or as well from all the elements you've put on the shelves. Creative strategy reduces cortisol by reducing stress. That's good.

All negative emotions are a form of anxiety—not getting what you want, in the past or the future. Something happened in the past that upsets you, or you foresee something in the future that will upset you. You might think you're worried about "now," not the future; for example, you're unhappy in your current job. But think again. You're really unhappy about what you foresee about your job in the next hour, or next day, or next week, or next year, or ten years from now. That's the future. If you foresee a future problem, or regret the past, worrying about it does no good at all and harms your health. Try creative strategy instead.

When you feel a negative emotion, ask yourself: What's the problem? As we saw for corporate innovation, this is not always easy to answer. But trying to figure it out means you're thinking, not worrying, and it immediately reduces stress. Once you decide what the problem is, you can go through the matrix to try to solve it. That mental exercise reduces stress as well. It's entirely possible that in the end you do not find a good solution. In that case, you get to the toughest step of all: let it go. Stop worrying about it. You did your best to figure it out. Accept that there's nothing you can do.

Sometimes it's not so clear-cut—you don't find a good solution, but the future you fear is so far ahead you have time to keep searching. So close your formal search but keep open an informal one. Let your mind continue to take in new elements and new combinations that might solve the problem to some degree. The key is to turn worry into either search or acceptance.

The right mind is the hardest kind of innovation to practice yourself and to promote within an organization. It takes individual desire and willpower to achieve. It's not something a boss can order the staff to do. But as a boss, you can create less anxiety and better thinking among your staff by never inflicting your own negative emotions upon them. Instead, lead them through the steps above. It's the same among peers, or managing up. The right mind disciplines your emotions at work for everyone's benefit. It's a key source of good ideas, good health, and a good life for all.

II

Creative Strategy from the Outside

Part I of this book gave the inside story of creative strategy, and now Part II looks at creative strategy from the outside. Most likely your company already has methods for strategy, planning, creativity, and innovation. In that case, creative strategy is an outsider. To bring it inside, you must adapt it to your existing methods. That's not always easy to do.

Your existing procedures are both formal and informal: all the habits, routines, frameworks, spreadsheets, meetings, and other forms of practice that guide how you, your team, and your company develop ideas for action. Part I mentioned a few of these other methods and showed briefly how creative strategy differs from them. Part II delves into the main ones in greater detail, to show how they might accommodate all or part of creative strategy.

As you move from section to section within Part II, you will see that many different methods call for similar adjustments to make way for creative strategy. Because of this repetition, you might want to treat Part II as a guidebook. Read through once quickly now and then later in depth for particular sections when you need them. There are many details, and you can't possible remember them all. Use Part II as a reference guide when you come up against a particular method that you want to adapt to creative strategy.

9

Brainstorming

The most common mistake in methods of innovation, creativity, and strategy is to rely on some type of formal or informal brainstorming to fill the gap between analysis and planning. Even ordinary problem solving often follows the same three steps: first, you do some kind of analysis; second, you brainstorm solutions; and third, you turn what you brainstorm into a plan. Many methods do not state this formally, but rather leave a blank between analysis and planning that people fall back on brainstorming to fill.

Brainstorming depends on spontaneous creativity on the right side of the brain. For many years, science seemed to support this notion. We saw that Roger Sperry won the Nobel Prize in 1981 for his work on the two-sided brain: the right side is creative, artistic, and intuitive; the left side is logical, rational, and analytical. This idea became very popular throughout the business world and in organizations of every kind. In almost any situation, you get a group together and ask them to turn off their logical left brains and turn on their creative right brains—otherwise known as brainstorming.

Today brainstorming is probably the world's most widely used method for problem solving. There are countless variations for how exactly you run a brainstorming session: how long to spend on the problem, how many ideas to throw out, and how to sort them, or combine them, or vote on them.

Unfortunately, all these versions are wrong. The problem is brainstorming itself. As a method, it's massively misconceived.

First, the science. As we noted before, since the year 2000 neuroscientists no longer think there are two sides of the brain that work in two different ways, thanks to Eric Kandel's Nobel Prize-winning work on "learning-and-memory"—how the whole brain takes in information, organizes it, stores it, and recombines it as thoughts of all kinds: analytical, creative, even emotional. There is no left side, there is no right side, and analysis and intuition are not two separate modes of thought.

Think too of your own experience. Where do you get your best ideas? Most people answer: the shower, falling asleep, waking up, exercising, walking, driving, or at some other random moment when your brain is relaxed. The work of Kandel and others now gives us the science behind it: when your brain doesn't have a usual combination to put together, it does a slow, thorough search through your memory to make new combinations. But even if we don't know about the science, we all know that we don't get our best ideas in brainstorming sessions. Yet still we brainstorm, week after week after week.

If we all know it's wrong, why do we keep doing it?

The first reason is inertia. Most of your procedures fit the basic sequence of analyze, brainstorm, and plan. You schedule X amount of time to analyze, then schedule a brainstorming meeting on Y date, and then you have Z number of days to plan. It's all built into your corporate routine. You can't simply wait for ideas to hit you in the shower. Random insights at random times do not fit your company's schedule. That's true, but the formal method of creative strategy offers a solution: you spend X amount of time on the treasure hunt, you schedule the combination session on Y date, and then you have Z number of days to complete the plan you started. But notice, you have to change all three steps of the sequence. If you still analyze the same way, and plan the same way, you have no time left for creative strategy. To generate ideas, all you have time for is brainstorming.

The second reason brainstorming is so popular is because it fosters teamwork. It's an organized way to get people to listen to each other's ideas. Lots of people are too busy, too impatient, or too egocentric to want to listen with an open mind to the unformed thoughts of their coworkers. At the very least, brainstorming sessions force you to listen, but not all the time. It's just a few hours. At the very best, you actually build on each other's ideas. All that is good for teamwork. But is it creative? If you toss out ideas off the top of your head in a scheduled meeting, you're not giving your "best" ideas. Those happen at other more random moments, elsewhere. But you're probably tossing out "good" ideas, and for most business problems that's good enough. But it's not innovation.

You might think there's an easy answer to this: simply ask people to bring to the meeting ideas they've had beforehand, at those random moments when their brains are relaxed. That's better, for sure. If you do that, tell them the idea can be on anything, not just the problem you're working on. That's because a common mistake of brainstorming sessions is the rule to "stick to the topic"—but an innovation is usually off topic. The greater the innovation, the farther off topic it is.

But this meeting to collect ideas still relies on random moments and no clear guidance on where ideas come from. So give people help. Tell them to keep their eyes open for elements elsewhere that solve some piece of the problem you're working on or cause you to rethink the whole problem. Once you tell them that, you're very close to creative strategy. You've told them to do the treasure hunt. Just add the insight matrix, and you're on your way. And as long as you've gone that far, why not lead your team through the whole creative strategy method?

The third reason brainstorming is so popular is agreement. After you toss out ideas, the group decides which ones to use, and how. In the end, they agree on a plan. In principle, if you're part of deciding something you have more commitment to it. That's often true. Especially when it's really brainstorming for planning, not innovation, the ideas are less controversial and it's very efficient to work out the plan together in a room. For example, if you brainstorm on "rolling out our new product," this is not a call for innovation. A brainstorming meeting is an efficient way to get each person to figure out what actions to take and how that fits what others will do, and then to commit as a group to that joint plan.

But if it's brainstorming for innovation, forced agreement can backfire. The facilitator tells you to toss out lots of wild ideas. By definition, your wild idea is not realistic and others won't like it. Whatever idea wins the vote, many people in the room think it's not a good idea. Once the meeting is over, despite the agreement, most people are not really committed to the idea. So it dies a slow or even quick death from lack of any real follow-up.

Even worse, brainstorming sometimes promotes group consensus when instead a single individual should make the decision. Who's in charge? The group. That's a recipe for conservative action—groupthink—not innovation. Big organizations especially have complex matrix arrangements, for example, country divisions, product divisions, and company-wide corporate departments like human resources, all at the same time. So when a problem touches more than one division, a group comes together and brainstorms. You get group agreement. But unless an individual is clearly in charge, you won't get innovation. Remember Majgaard of Lego. He put together mixed teams for innovation, but in the end, he was in charge.

Last but not least, brainstorming is so popular because of a common misconception that the more ideas, the better. For example, here's what the famous scientist Linus Pauling said: "The best way to have a good idea is to have a lot of ideas." But if you think about it, the actual sequence of "a lot ideas" is you first get one idea, then another idea, then another, and so on. But let's pause and ask: How do you get the first idea? Pauling doesn't tell us. Instead, let's look at his own success. Pauling won a Nobel Prize for something called "orbital hybridization," where he combined the valence-bond work of Heitler and London with the new wave results from deBroglie and Slater in quantum physics. Pauling's innovation in "hybridization" was literally a hybrid of previous work by others—otherwise known as creative strategy.

10

Top Ten

Bain & Company, a leading strategy consulting firm, does an annual survey of management tools in use among businesses "across industries and around the globe." So that's where we'll start. Below is their latest top ten, from 2011. My purpose here is to explain how and why creative strategy is better for innovation than each of these ten popular methods. This is not a criticism of Bain. Quite the contrary; they have done a wonderful job of finding out and summarizing what businesses actually do. Here's the list:

Benchmarking
Strategic planning
Mission and vision statements
Customer relationship management
Outsourcing
Balanced scorecard
Change management programs
Core competencies
Strategic alliances
Customer segmentation

We can see right away that "creativity" and "innovation" do not appear on the list. Yet we know that most big companies consistently claim that creativity and innovation rank high among their top priorities. For example, the Boston Consulting Group's 2010 global innovation survey reported that innovation was a "top-three priority" for 72 percent of the companies they interviewed. Then why does innovation fail to appear on the Bain list? There are two simple answers. First, most companies see creativity and innovation as a function of specialized departments, such as research and development or product design, rather than methods for the whole company to use. Second, they try to be creative within the Bain list, so that strategic planning, for example, leads to innovation.

Unfortunately, both answers lead to trouble. If you make creativity and innovation the job of certain departments and not others, you have three problems. First, you miss out on bigger innovations that can change the course of the whole company. Second, you miss innovations in other departments that need them, such as operations or finance. Third, you leave that creative department—R&D or product design—on its own to come up with its own innovation methods, which, as we see elsewhere in this book, are often deeply flawed.

The second method—expecting innovation to happen within the methods on the Bain list—is wishful thinking. These methods can hinder innovation as much as they foster it. Let's go through the list one by one to see why.

Benchmarking

We saw in chapter 4 that formal benchmarking is part of implementation, not creation. It helps keep you generally competitive in your field. For innovation, once you have your creative idea, you can benchmark to make sure you're up to date on operational techniques to put the idea into practice. The treasure hunt of creative strategy calls for a wide scan within and beyond your industry. If you do formal benchmarking for each source, you would spend all your time crunching numbers and none of it searching and thinking. The core idea of benchmarking, to look elsewhere for solutions, is excellent. The way to do it creatively, strategically, is to use the insight matrix instead.

Strategic Planning

Bain tells us that strategic planning "helps companies decide where to focus, where to compete and how to allocate resources." When Bain helps clients do this, they take special care to help them "incorporate a long-term perspective into their strategies, while focusing on the biggest issues they currently face and on the best way to get results." These are very general guidelines, and as such they do not conflict with creative strategy. The problem usually arises when the company turns to its "biggest issues" and "the best way to get results": how exactly do you go from one to the other?

The "issue" is a problem, and the "result" is the solution. Within the field of strategic planning, there are myriad ways to go from issue to result. Most, unfortunately, do not involve creative strategy.

The most popular methods of strategic planning start with some framework of strategic analysis. The key here is that analysis does not give you an idea for strategy. It helps you understand your current situation and arrive at your "issue." But how do you move to the next step? How do you get an idea for what you should do to solve that problem? The usual answer is to brainstorm. A group gets in the room and throws out ideas. The frameworks of strategic analysis themselves do not give you an idea for what to do.

There is nothing wrong with frameworks of strategic analysis that help you understand your problem, but if you spend too much effort on that phase you won't have time to do the creative strategy treasure hunt. That's what should follow your analysis, not brainstorming.

Most popular methods of strategic planning end with some kind of resource planning. That is, once you have your idea, you need to plan out how to do it. But how you do resource planning also matters. Recall that creative strategy gives you the start of a plan: the elements you found and combined. If you don't start with those, where do you start? Unfortunately, most resource planning simply uses templates from previous years or the judgment of the planners, which typically comes from their own direct experience rather than a wider search. If your strategic idea is very similar to what you've done before, then this kind of resource planning can work. But if your idea is an innovation, these sources are likely far too narrow.

In sum, creative strategy is itself a method of strategic planning. To use it, you have to abandon or at least modify your current methods of strategic analysis, brainstorming, and resource planning. Use the insight matrix as early as possible in your strategic planning routine.

Mission and Vision Statements

Bain gives a good definition of this tool: "The mission and vision statement is a company's proclamation to its employees and other stakeholders about its business goals and aspirations as an organization." Then they add: "Creating a sound mission and vision statement is the first step in building strategies that help clients to reach their full potential." That sequence is a common mistake. In reality, you cannot have a mission and vision without first some idea of a strategy to get there. Otherwise your mission and vision are unrealistic, or so vague as to be meaningless.

First, creative strategy shows you what to do. Then the longer-term implications of that become your mission and vision, which you then "proclaim" to employees and other stakeholders in a statement. The statement itself is not the start of strategy.

Let's take a closer look at this mistake. At any particular moment, a company typically already has a mission and vision. When it comes time to develop a strategy, most methods take the mission and vision as given. There are two problems with this. First, if your strategy method results in a big idea for innovation, that might alter the mission and vision of the company. For example, in the early 1990s, IBM had a clear mission and vision as a proprietary hardware company. But Louis Gerstner altered both dramatically by switching to integrated services. It wasn't easy to make the switch, of course. And changes that dramatic seldom happen. But you have to stay open to the possibility, always, at the start of your strategy method.

The second problem with taking mission and vision as givens is forgetting where they came from in the first place. Back in time, someone had a good business idea, and that idea became the mission and vision of the company. For example, Gerstner had seen a small example of IBM as an integrated service provider when he was at American Express, and in his first weeks on the job at IBM, he found a small unit there operating that way. These were the sources of his new mission and vision for the company.

It is important to look back and recognize what led to your current mission and vision. Someone, at some time, probably put together a creative combination. You want to ask whether the parallels are still valid for the present situation. If so, the mission and vision do not need to change. If they are no longer valid—if the current situation is too different—then you have a problem. That problem becomes the start of creative strategy.

On the other hand, sometimes the mission and vision statements don't matter. They are general and vague enough that even radical innovations would fit them. For example, if IBM's pre-Gerstner mission statement was "be the world leader in business technology," that would allow both the strategy Gerstner inherited and the one he developed. In that case, you can accept the mission and vision and go on to creative strategy.

Often business units develop their strategy after headquarters hands down a mission and vision. The business unit takes them as given, because headquarters tells them to do so. As noted before, if the statements handed down are vague enough, there's no problem. If they are specific, however, headquarters should tell the unit that they can propose a strategy for themselves that changes the mission and vision of the overall company. Headquarters might reject it, but the unit must have the freedom to propose it. Otherwise, headquarters stifles possible innovations.

In practice, creative strategy rarely changes the mission and vision of a company. But even if it does so only 1 percent of the time, at the start of your strategic planning you do not know if this will be one of those times. That's why it is an error to start strategic planning with mission and vision statements.

Customer Relationship Management

Bain tells us that customer relationship management (CRM) is "a process companies use to understand their customer groups and respond quickly—at times, instantly—to shifting customer desires." CRM gives you a useful data stream from and about customers. How you use it varies according to what you aim to achieve. CRM is not a method for innovation. It helps you adjust your current strategy for your current customers. It doesn't give you a new strategy, or new customers. You gather constant feedback from your current customers about your current products and services, and then adjust your current strategy accordingly.

For innovation, or other big changes to your strategy, CRM can sometimes lead you astray. Customer focus groups, for example, work well for variations on existing products and services but badly for wholly new products and services. If something is too different from what customers are used to, they can't understand it quickly. Instead, they need time to try it out. So customer trials work better for innovations.

Another trap is thinking that your CRM system will lead to innovation because customers will tell you what innovation they need. Most innovations are things the customers didn't know they needed until they saw them. CRM is fine for improving your current strategy, but not for innovation.

Outsourcing

For the most part, outsourcing has nothing to do with innovation. It's a way to cut costs. Once you know what your strategy is, you decide what to outsource. At first companies outsourced operations, but now all functions are candidates, including research and development, human resources, and marketing. If you innovate, your strategy changes, and you rethink what you outsource. So outsourcing does not conflict with creative strategy.

There is one thing to watch out for: the common claim that you should not outsource your "core competencies." The problem is that it is very hard to know exactly what your core competencies are and should be at any particular time. Outsourcing puts functions outside your core, while mergers and acquisitions—and sometimes just hiring—bring them in. You can, and should, change your core competencies according to your strategy, and therefore your outsourcing, mergers, and acquisitions change too. Rigid thinking on any of these domains can hinder innovation. We will return to this problem under the discussion of core competencies.

Balanced Scorecard

Balanced Scorecard is a popular book by Robert Kaplan and David Norton that tells you to monitor not just financial numbers but also figures for customer relations, internal operations, and learning and development. You set targets and measure progress in all four areas. Like CRM and outsourcing, this is clearly a method for performance improvement, not innovation. Again, that makes it compatible with creative strategy, as long as you don't try to make the balanced scorecard produce innovations.

On the other hand, there is one step where creative strategy can help the balanced scorecard. For each of the four areas of the scorecard, you perform four tasks in sequence: set objectives, identify measures to track those objectives, set intermediate targets that use those methods on the way to the objectives, and then design initiatives to reach those targets. We can recognize these four tasks as a typical cycle of strategic planning. When we get to the fourth task, design an initiative, we face our usual problem: How do we get an idea for the initiative?

Kaplan and Norton tell us that "formulating" initiatives is "largely a creative process." We are back to the old model of the left-right brain: detailed analysis (left brain) and then the magic of creativity (right brain). In practice, the balanced scorecard relies on brainstorming: a group gets together and throws out ideas. Instead, try the insight matrix. You might not have time for a long treasure hunt, but even a short one is better than brainstorming.

Change Management

Change management goes hand in hand with innovation. The bigger the innovation, the more change management you need to move lots of people from doing what they did before to doing something new. There are many different methods of change management, and Bain includes them all as part of its count for the top ten. Elsewhere on its website, Bain gives its own method for change management. Despite some differences, almost all popular versions of change management, including Bain's, have the same basic elements. These come from John Kotter's classic 1996 book *Leading Change*. We'll look at Kotter's original method here, but our conclusions apply to other popular methods as well.

Here are Kotter's steps:

1. Establish a sense of urgency
2. Form a powerful guiding coalition
3. Create a vision
4. Communicate that vision
5. Empower others to act on that vision
6. Plan for and create short-term wins
7. Consolidate improvements and keep the momentum for change moving
8. Institutionalize the new approaches

What's wrong with this picture? Look at Step 3: create a vision. How exactly do you do that? From the view of creative strategy, you need a good idea about what you want to become. Otherwise, people might resist change for a very good reason—that the status quo is better than your idea. So how do you come up with a "vision" that's worth the effort? Kotter is silent on that. His whole method is about implementing a vision, and skips the key step of coming up with that vision in the first place. In principle, then, change management can be quite compatible with creative strategy; creative strategy first comes up with the idea, and then change management implements it.

When we look at the details, though, Kotter's sequence conflicts at key points with creative strategy. Let's start with Step 1. Does a "sense of urgency" help you come up with a creative idea? It depends. If executives need to direct others to innovate, then a sense of urgency can help win their attention. But if those executives know they need to innovate and set out to do so, immediately communicating that same sense of urgency throughout the organization can be premature. If you don't have a good solution ready, getting everyone upset about a problem might only make things worse. A sense of urgency works best when you have specific actions you want people to take. For example, if you want them to participate in innovation, a sense of urgency plus clear instructions can help. And those instructions are the steps of creative strategy.

Kotter's next two steps are in the wrong order. Step 2 and Step 3 should switch. Forming a powerful coalition before you create a vision is a recipe for groupthink. Powerful coalitions tend to protect their interests, not generate creative ideas that might change the strategy and thereby threaten the interests of those around the table. Innovation by definition means that new ideas supplant old ones, and you need a new coalition to put them into action. Once you get your new idea (Step 3), then you know what coalition you need (Step 2).

Kotter makes this mistake because his method is a product of its time: the mid-1990s. Then, top executives knew what change they wanted, and many of their people did resist it: computerization. The computer revolution sent companies scrambling to streamline operations and cut costs through internal information technology. Michael Hammer and James Champy fueled the trend with their 1994 book *Reengineering the Corporation: A Manifesto for Business Revolution.*

Kotter noticed that companies treated reengineering as a mechanical exercise rather than an overall cultural change for the organization. For reengineering, Kotter's method can work because the answer is essentially the same for every company and you know what it is ahead of time.

For innovation—where the answer is unforeseen and different for every company—Kotter's method needs reengineering. First you need creative strategy, and then comes all the rest.

Core Competencies

Advances in information technology led to this item on the Bain list too. Companies found they could outsource some of their activities to cheaper economies through electronic communication. The growth of outsourcing in the early 1990s led companies to wonder how to determine which activities to perform themselves and which ones to contract out. Gary Hamel and C. K. Prahalad gave an answer in their 1994 book *Competing for the Future*. Their advice is to hold onto your "core" competencies. These are the unique strengths that make you better than your competitors, versus the functions where you're similar to them. Strategy scholars call it the "resource-based view" of the firm. More recent versions of the idea ask the same question—Which functions belong in the core?—for headquarters versus divisions or other operational units.

This question is important for strategic analysis: you study which functions take place in your industry, and where, both among your competitors and in your own operations. Core competencies can help organize a large company into units of common strength. As such, core competencies are is not a method for arriving at a strategic idea. For that you need creative strategy. Then once you have your strategic idea, you ask the "core" question again as part of planning: Which functions go in the core and which go elsewhere? So the idea of core competencies can be quite compatible with creative strategy.

But beware, the misuse of core competencies can stifle innovation. If you think that you should always stick to your core competencies, you will ignore possible innovations that call for you to change your core competencies. Remember Gerstner—when he arrived at the company, IBM had an overwhelming core competency in proprietary hardware, and a tiny, peripheral competency in integrated services. Gerstner drastically transformed the core competencies of IBM.

There are many ways to change your core competencies: through outsourcing, strategic alliances, mergers and acquisitions, hiring, or training. Above all, you should understand that your strategic advantage comes not from your core competencies but from a combination of elements that fits your situation. In each element separately you might be no better than your competitors. It's the combination that counts. As you proceed through the steps of creative strategy, you keep an open mind about what your core competencies should be. They follow your strategy, they don't lead it.

Strategic Alliances

This item on the Bain list reflects globalization to a great degree; instead of starting your own operation in a new country, make a strategic alliance with a local firm. Of course the practice of strategic alliances long predates the recent globalization boom; they are simply agreements among firms to join together in some way for a specific purpose. Like outsourcing, a strategic alliance is one of many tactics you consider as part of your strategy. They might be a good idea or a bad idea for you in a particular situation. Strategic alliances are not an innovation method in and of themselves. So strategic alliances are sources to look at when you do your insight matrix. As such, there is no conflict between strategic alliances and creative strategy.

As with outsourcing, though, watch out for claims that your strategic alliances should complement rather than replace your "core competencies." Your core competencies are subject to change, like everything else in your strategy. You can inhibit innovation if you determine ahead of time—before you get your idea—what you keep as your core and what you might pursue as a strategic alliance. Better to get the idea first, and then decide what you keep as your core and where you might need a strategic alliance.

Customer Segmentation

This item on the Bain list falls neatly under strategic analysis. You study your customers not as a single group but broken down by segment, so that you can devise a somewhat different strategy for each segment. This is a very good way to break down your market. But as usual with strategic analysis, this method does not yield a strategy or an innovation. After analysis comes creative strategy. You might want a different problem statement, and therefore a different matrix, for each customer segment. Remember too that innovation can change the landscape. You might have to redo your customer segmentation when your strategy changes.

So ends this review of Bain's top ten management methods in use today. With some adjustment and caveats we can make them all compatible with creative strategy. Without those adjustments and caveats, they can inhibit innovation. And none of them produces innovation. They are methods of analysis or implementation. They do not produce the idea for innovation itself. They cannot substitute for creative strategy.

11
Creative

The Bain top ten is a good place to start our review of other methods that might compete with creative strategy, but of course dozens more are common throughout the world of business. I will look at just a few of them here, in two main categories: "creative" and "strategy." That is, some methods promise to help you come up with creative ideas. Other methods tell you how to decide on a strategy.

This chapter takes on "creative" methods. The next chapter takes on "strategy." In both cases you will see patterns repeat, as the various methods make the same few omissions or mistakes over and over again. Some of these creative methods aim to make you a more creative person, while others lead you step-by-step to design an innovation. I will compare both kinds of creative methods to creative strategy.

Art

Go on the Internet and find the TED talks. These are video speeches of exquisite quality from TED conferences around the globe. Find the one by Sir Ken Robinson. You will hear a compelling case for teaching more of the arts in schools, and less math and science, to make children more creative.

Unfortunately, Sir Ken makes a common mistake: he confuses "artistic" and "creative." They are not at all the same thing.

Certainly there are many good reasons to study or practice art. None of them has to do with innovation directly. Art can make you a better person, and it can make the world a better place. But artists are not better at innovation than non-artists. They're better at art. For creative strategy, art is simply another field—like sports or medicine or shipping—where you might search for elements to apply to your current problem.

Math and science, on the other hand, are more than fields to search for elements to combine. Math helps you understand your strategic situation, the elements you find in your treasure hunt, and how they might go together. Art does not help in that way. Of course the numbers alone cannot give you a creative combination. But neither can art. As for science, we have an even stronger case for innovation. Science teaches you to analyze things by breaking them down into elements, to understand how the elements work, and to search out what other scientists have done—all steps of creative strategy.

Sir Ken's depiction of art versus math and science is an old and common mistake. Sometimes the mistake takes the form of a clash of cultures too. For example, you might hear that Americans are better at innovation because they teach their children to express themselves through art and humanities, while Asians are worse at innovation because their schools teach math and science but not creativity. Yet acquiring knowledge (Asia) and practice in free thinking (America) are both good for innovation. The first gives you things to combine, and the second helps you combine them. The best schools in Asia and America do both. And Asians are not worse at innovation that Americans. Certainly Asian companies are copying American firms right now, but that's a sensible stage in economic development, not a cultural defect. Americans copied Europeans in the nineteenth century in exactly the same way.

But Sir Ken asks the right question—how to teach creativity—even if his answer falls short. Artistic and creative are not the same thing. The trend is declining now, but for years you saw company workshops where employees "drew on the right side of the brain," or made collages, or threw paint on walls to make them more creative. That doesn't work. But a creative spirit, that's worth teaching to counter the narrow outlook that many people develop over time through habit and routine. Art can play its part in that, to show all the diverse styles of artistic expression across the world and through the ages, and to let you try them out yourself as freely as you wish.

To search widely beyond your usual boundaries, to try combinations that don't yet exist, that's a healthy blend of art and science that's vital to learn, hard to teach, but worth the effort to seek.

Sir Ken also says that standardized testing, like SATs or IQ tests, cannot measure your most important ability: to come up with creative ideas in the face of novel situations and real-world problems. He's right about that. Unfortunately, this ability defies measure, standardized or otherwise. There is no test of creativity. Standardizing tests solve a very different problem: how to provide a low-cost, universal measure for selecting students for limited places at academic institutions. These tests do not measure your innate abilities or your intelligence. They simply satisfy a particular practical need better than anything else at the same cost. Sir Ken himself does not offer an alternative.

At one point, Sir Ken does come close to recognizing creative strategy. In his popular book *The Element*, he recounts the career paths of various creative people and observes: "Growth comes through analogy, through seeing how things connect rather than only seeing how they might be different. Certainly, the epiphany stories in this book indicate that many of the moments when things suddenly become clear happen from seeing new connections between events, ideas, and circumstances." This comes very close to the flash of insight from creative combination. Thank you, Sir Ken.

Collaboration

The Internet has led to a boom in "crowdsourcing" for innovation. The notion is that lots of people working on a problem can solve it better than only one person, and the Internet makes that easier than ever before. We can see several versions of this idea in a number of popular books on the subject.

Where Good Ideas Come From by Steven Johnson tells us that innovation comes from collaborative environments like big cities and the Internet, rather than as "Eureka!" moments by lone inventors. *The Wisdom of Crowds* by James Surowiecki tells us that the average answers of large groups of people do better than experts for predictions of various kinds, such as stock prices or election results. And *Open Innovation* by Henry Chesbrough tells companies to shift from closed research-and-development departments to more open networks that draw on different kinds of expertise outside your own company. On the academic side, some sociologists follow Thomas Kuhn's classic 1962 study *The Structure of Scientific*

Revolutions to show how recent scientific advances come from groups of scientists embracing a new paradigm rather than a single scientist achieving a solitary breakthrough.

At first glance, the point seems obvious: two heads are better than one. And ten are better than two, and so on. So far, we have no conflict with creative strategy. But just putting people together and telling them to collaborate is not enough. What if they use the wrong method? If your collaboration is essentially one big brainstorming session, that's a mistake. Instead, ask lots of people to contribute elements that work elsewhere to your insight matrix. Of course the management of that exercise might prove more difficult than it's worth.

Johnson is right that collaborative environments foster innovation. But he's wrong to oppose that to flashes of insight. Take Steve Jobs and the Macintosh. He invented none of its components, but he had the idea to put together Wozniak's small machine and Xerox's graphical user interface and mouse. A flash of insight typically combines elements from others. It's the core mechanism for how many people contribute to a single innovation. Kuhn's *Structure of Scientific Revolutions* shows exactly that for the key breakthroughs that other scientists then build on as the next paradigm.

It's a similar story for Surowiecki's "wisdom of crowds" and Chesbrough's "open innovation." If there is a central intelligence—an individual or a team—selecting and combining elements that worked elsewhere from the mass of material the crowd contributes, these notions hold. Creative strategy thrives on the widest scan, across space and back through time, of the experience of other people. You don't want their ideas, you want elements that worked for them. And the team that does the scan is a unit of collaboration as well.

In sum, collaboration and creative strategy are friends, not enemies. Creative strategy offers a method to make collaboration actually pay off and produce innovation.

Competitions

In an innovation competition, you invite large numbers of people to submit lots of ideas that other people then judge. You might call it a "suggestion box"—or some other name. The judges might be top executives, a panel of experts, an online crowd, or the participants at a big conference who walk from flip chart to flip chart voting for their favorites. This kind of competition can get people interested and even excited about innovation, which is good. But it's not a good venue for creative strategy.

Think of your own work: if you have a pile of a hundred reports or proposals or some other mound of paperwork to go through in a very short period of time, you would hardly call that "creative" work. You don't have time for much real thinking about each item you judge. That means you use your expert intuition. If it makes sense from your own experience, you like it. If it's beyond what you know, it seems strange and unrealistic, so you don't like it. Competitions and suggestion boxes work best for small ideas, which face less misunderstanding and opposition from the many people who judge them.

Dragon's Den

Some companies have formal methods to rip apart new ideas. You might go before a panel of top executives who pummel you with tough questions; these meetings sometimes have names like the "Lion's Den" or "Hot Seat" or "Dragon's Den." Or the panel meets privately to "tear into" a set of proposals. Other times the method is informal; the company culture encourages everyone to poke holes in any new idea. The theory here is simple: the survival of the fittest. Harsh critique kills weak ideas and lets the strong ones live.

Unfortunately, this is not what Darwin meant. The "fittest" does not mean the biggest and strongest and toughest. It's not fitness as in pumping iron every day. It's fitness as in conforming to circumstance. Does it fit the situation? Natural selection according to Darwin kills off many big, strong species and lets many small, weak ones survive. *Tyrannosaurus rex* died out. The butterfly did not.

Harsh critique as a form of idea selection favors whoever can argue best, not who has the best idea. The two are not at all the same. It might be true that arguing best to get your idea approved means you will argue best to force it through implementation too—you need a tyrannosaurus for that, not a butterfly. But that just means your company runs by the law of the jungle, where everyone has to fight for everything, all the time. That's a sick culture, not a strong one. It's a sure-fire formula for killing off good ideas.

Worse is when these harsh methods are actually an inquisition. Remember the purpose of the Spanish Inquisition: to root out heretics. Harsh criticism in companies does the same. It makes everyone conform to conventional wisdom—"our way of thinking"—whether you know it or not. You please the boss with tough questions that match what you think the boss thinks. The basis of harsh critique is usually the expert intuition of whoever has the most power in the room. And as we've seen, expert intuition is not a method for innovation.

A Dragon's Den is above all a filter: among many competing ideas, you let a few squeeze through. Of course you should not accept all ideas your staff propose. But you should consider them. And that means you apply creative strategy to new ideas. You ask the proposer to fill in the matrix, formally or informally, with the problem, the pieces of the problem, sources, and precedents. That's not critique—it's guidance. You can then decide which few are ready for a review meeting. For that, instead of a Dragon's Den, call it a Dark Room, as in photography, where you help innovations develop. The idea might never see the light of day, but at least you gave it a chance.

Or, give every unit the ability to innovate to some degree and only bring up to the "dragon" the projects that cost too much for a unit to do alone. Many companies do this, for example, Amazon. Then instead of breathing fire, the dragon helps the unit head figure out how to try out the idea, perhaps as a pilot, either with extra corporate funds or without. In all cases, review meetings should seek to improve ideas, not tear them apart. If you do it right, the flaws of each idea will come clear. You don't need a dragon for that.

Customer Insights

Several innovation methods look to "customer insights" for their creative ideas, at least in part. So this item deserves some attention on its own.

Customer insights are helpful to have. Certainly you should learn as much as possible about what customers do and think. That information helps you understand the situation you face. It rarely leads directly to creative ideas. It is especially hard to get customer insights about an innovation because it does not exist yet. If you asked users about the Apple II, would they tell you to replace the green screen with a graphical user interface and mouse? Of course not. Customers can comment on existing products and services, but that's all.

And if a product or service is something new and very different from what they already know and use, customers tend not to like it at first. Why?

They're used to the old product or service, and they don't want to take the time to learn how to use the new one. That's why innovations that end up succeeding often do poorly in early focus group tests.

If customer insights include reference to an element of another product or service that the customers admire, then that precedent can go on the insight matrix. It might even be a key part of your creative combination. Otherwise, customer insights help you analyze the problem but do not help you find a solution. For that you need creative strategy.

Design Thinking

In the past few years, design thinking has become a common method for innovation in business. It began as product design, but then the designers proposed to use their same methods for all kinds of business problems. One popular version of design thinking comes from a recent handbook, *Business Model Generation*. The book lists Alexander Osterwalder and Yves Pigneur as authors but tells us that the Innovation Hub—"An amazing crowd of 470 practitioners from 45 countries"—cocreated it. So the handbook is a good summary of current thinking on this subject from a wide survey of the field.

In particular, the book gives you "techniques and tools from the world of design that can help you design better and more innovative business models." The two key steps are to list the nine "building blocks" of all business models and then fill in the blocks using six methods from the world of design.

Here are their nine blocks of design thinking: Key Partners, Key Activities, Key Resources, Value Proposition, Customer Relationships, Channels, Customer Segments, Cost Structure, and Revenue Streams. To apply this to creative strategy, we can immediately see that this list could be used as our left column of the matrix: the pieces of the innovation we seek. So far so good.

Here are the six design methods you use to fill in the blocks: Customer Insights, Ideation, Visual Thinking, Prototyping, Storytelling, and Scenarios. Uh oh, now we have a problem. In creative strategy, our next step is to do a treasure hunt for what works. These six design methods tell you something else entirely. Here's a summary of what they offer:

Customer Insights = ideas from customers
Ideation = brainstorm new ideas

Visual Thinking = convert your thoughts into images
Prototyping = build a quick-and-dirty model using your preliminary ideas
Storytelling = what your customers experience as they move through your model
Scenarios = different directions your model could lead

We've already talked about Customer Insights, and Ideation is just another name for brainstorming. As for Visual Thinking, it's good to convert your thoughts into images, but first you must have the thought. Visual Thinking gives you no help on coming up with the thought in the first place. It's the same with Prototyping, Storytelling, and Scenarios; they don't tell you how to get the idea that you then prototype, work through as a story, and imagine taking in different directions.

Above all, design thinking is a pitch for designers themselves to join or lead innovation teams for all kinds of business problems. After all, innovation amounts to the design of a new product, service, or business model, so designers can certainly help. Yet the attempts so far to formalize design methods for business are mistaken.

Ironically, good designers actually use a form of creative strategy in their own design work. They are masters of eclectic combination. If designers can apply that same skill to business problems, in addition to their visual expertise and customer awareness, they can play a key role on any creative strategy team.

Design for Six Sigma

There is a recent twist on design thinking that is making headway in big companies especially: Design for Six Sigma, or DFSS. Six Sigma is a program that promotes quality at every step of production, so DFSS takes that a step earlier, to the design of the product itself. It begins with "Voice of the Customer," a form of "customer insights" from the general design thinking method. You gather customer insights and then select or combine what the customer said to make a short list of the most important ones. For each item on the list, you decide what will best satisfy the customer on that item.

Here's the problem, again: How do you decide what will best satisfy the customer for a particular item on your list? This requires a creative leap to come up with something that solves the problem the customer raised.

Sometimes the answer is obvious from the customer comment: "the handle is too small" gives you the idea to make the handle bigger. For minor design changes to a product, this kind of checklist improvement is fine. But it doesn't work for innovation. If the customer using the Apple II says, "I don't like the green screen," DFSS does not lead you to "graphical user interface and mouse." Only a search—like Jobs's visit to Xerox—will give you the answer.

At best, DFSS gives you a long list of minor changes to your product. But it doesn't stop there. Next, DFSS details the technical specifications to produce each item, and where you might encounter quality problems at each step. And then you propose solutions to those quality problems. Again, we find the same question: How do you propose a solution to a problem? If you don't do the search of creative strategy, you rely on your direct experience. For many problems, that works. But it's not innovation.

The final result of DFSS is a long list of actions to build into the actual production of the product. After that, regular Six Sigma takes over. As we can see, at the key stages where you propose solutions—to the problems the customers raise or the quality problems you foresee in production—DFSS has no method for innovation. At those two points, you can use the insight matrix to innovate beyond the experience of yourself and your customers.

Even with that improvement, the whole DFSS method is flawed from the view of innovation. DFSS starts with your product or a product idea, and then you go get customer insights about it. But DFSS gives you no guidance on how to come up with the product idea in the first place. For that reason, DFSS is fine for altering existing products. It's not good for innovating beyond your existing products, or services, or business model.

Divergent Thinking

Has anyone ever told you to "think outside the box"? That's a form of divergent thinking: don't think what you usually think, think something else. Apple made divergent thinking famous with their advertising slogan, "Think Different." Innovation requires divergent thinking because the result is something different from what you've been doing.

But again we ask: How do you think divergently exactly? What's the method? I know how to think inside the box—that is, my usual routine. But if I'm going to do something different, I face a universe of possibilities and no guidance at all for how to decide which one to choose. In brainstorming they tell you to just list as many ideas as you can think of, no matter how "wild." If that's divergent thinking, it's easy. But does it do any good?

Here's the problem: divergent thinking is backwards. It's not the start of innovation. It's the end. You don't start by thinking outside the box. You proceed through the steps of creative strategy, and the result is something that "diverges" from your current thinking. Divergent thinking as a first step works if you want to generate wild ideas. But it's not the path to innovation.

We can understand the wish to think "different" or "outside the box." It's true that when you're stuck thinking one way, and it doesn't get you anywhere, you need to think something else. The first step is to recognize that your current thinking isn't working and so you need an innovation. That calls for presence of mind. For that, you need to stop thinking what you're thinking. People do this all the time. They "take a step back," which is very different from "take a new direction." After you "step back," you try to state and restate the problem and its pieces, in order to do a search.

The search itself solves the puzzle for how to think outside the box. You look in as many other boxes as you can.

Gut Instinct

When you get what you think is a creative idea, and you can't explain how you got it, you might say: "It's just my gut instinct." Lots of successful executives will tell you that's how they work: they trust their gut. But exactly what does that mean?

The new science of the brain makes a distinction between instinct and intuition. An instinct is something we're born with as humans; they are actually very few, and almost all physical, such as self-preservation, sex, and pleasures of the five senses. An intuition is very different: it's a product of memory. Something about the situation reminds you of something else you experienced. If you can't name the past example, you call it "gut instinct." A more accurate term might be "mysterious memory."

Many of these mysterious memories are well founded. Then we call them "expert intuition," as we saw in Part I. That is, your past experience qualifies you as an expert about a particular situation, and your judgment based on that is sound. That's usually the case when an executive's "gut instinct" is right on the mark. But sometimes gut instinct can lead you astray. You might say, "I have a bad feeling about this," or "I just know this will work," but in reality your experience is not sufficient to make you an expert in this case. Unfortunately, because you seldom know exactly the memory you're drawing on, it's hard to tell the difference between good and bad judgments of this kind.

Many professions rely on expert intuition every day. If you have only mere moments to make a decision, you have to rely on expert intuition. A nurse in an emergency room, a soldier in battle, a firefighter entering a smoking building—they all rely on past experience to tell them quickly what to do. Usually they can't explain why they did what they did, but an eminent scientist, Gary Klein, has interviewed dozens of experts right after their decisions and teased out what went through their minds at the time. In every case, past experience ruled the day.

Creative strategy goes one step beyond expert intuition. That flash of insight in the shower draws on what you've stored in your mind from the past. In that way it's a form of memory too. But it draws on things far beyond your personal experience. In quick decisions, you're pulling from the front shelves—your strongest, most recent, and most personal memories. If you have more time, and your mind is relaxed, you wander into the back shelves, up and down the aisles in a leisurely fashion, pulling something here, something there, from everything that's in your mind. That includes what you've read, what you've heard, and images you've seen, as far back in time as you can remember.

The insight matrix mimics what goes on in your mind when you have a flash of insight. Except that the shelves—the sources of your treasure hunt—cover the world rather than just your personal experience. Gut instinct can work for rapid decisions, but if you can find the time, try creative strategy instead.

IDEO

IDEO is a design firm that pioneered the application of design thinking to business problems. Today it is the best-known business design firm in the world. That's why it deserves its own entry here.

In 2001, one of IDEO's leaders, Tom Kelley, published *The Art of Innovation* to explain its design method. It's classic design thinking, where you conduct research and observe your market, client, customer, and so on. And then you brainstorm. Kelley even titles a chapter "The Perfect Brainstorm," where he tells us that "brainstorming is practically a religion at IDEO." He gives you rules for how to do it. Let's look at the main ones:

Be visual
Defer judgment
Encourage wild ideas
Build on the ideas of others
Go for quantity
One conversation at a time
Stay focused on the topic

Some of these rules are simply good communication practice for all kinds of business situations, not just brainstorming. It's good to be visual, to defer judgment, to build on the ideas of others, and to have one conversation at a time. That's true for meetings of any size or purpose. If your company has bad communication habits, perhaps an IDEO brainstorming session will teach you better manners. That's all to the good. But as for innovation, that's a different story.

IDEO tells you to "encourage wild ideas." This is standard advice in brainstorming. But creative strategy tells you something very different: look for pieces of the puzzle that someone, somewhere, has already solved to some degree. That's an entirely different task from tossing out wild ideas.

IDEO tells you to "go for quantity." Kelley even begins his brainstorming chapter with the previous quote from Linus Pauling about having many ideas as the way to have a good idea, which we saw earlier was not at all how Pauling himself came up with his best ideas. The treasure hunt in creative strategy doesn't go for quantity, it goes for quality.

IDEO tells you to "stay focused on the topic." Creative strategy tells you something very different: as you search, you might change your understanding of the problem. Your topic might change.

We can even revisit the rule to "build on the ideas of others." In principle this is good, but how do I do it? IDEO tells you to build on the ideas of others with "wild ideas" in "quantity." Creative strategy tells you something very different: build on an element your teammate found with an element that you find.

If brainstorming is key to IDEO's method, and their rules of brainstorming do not foster innovation, then why is IDEO so successful?

For that we turn to another book, *How Breakthroughs Happen* by Andrew Hargadon, who worked at IDEO as a designer. He tells us that IDEO forms project teams with members who worked before in a range of very different industries. So for a toothpaste client, the various team members might have experience in shoes, airlines, banking, radio, and so on.

Their job is to take elements that worked from those other industries and adapt them to the toothpaste problem.

Aha! It's a form of creative strategy, or at least a decent hybrid.

So if you must brainstorm, make sure to have people in the room from very diverse backgrounds, and tell them to draw from what they've seen before. Even so, that's not as good as the full creative strategy method, where you don't force people to toss out ideas in a meeting but rather give them time to search both beyond their own experience and, in lone moments, to let their minds wander far back in the shelves of their memories to things they've seen and learned that won't spring to mind in a brainstorming meeting.

In sum, IDEO's brainstorming techniques can teach you how to communicate better in your daily work, but they don't produce innovation. The method they use, of teams drawing elements from their diverse experience to make a new combination, comes close to creative strategy. To come even closer, ask the team members to look beyond their own experiences too for a full what-works scan.

Imagination

Most methods of creativity rely on imagination, the wonderful ability of the human brain to think up something new. It's the essence of brainstorming, for example. The key step is to use your imagination to come up with an idea, and someone then puts it on a list. Artists use their imagination. Inventors use their imagination. Innovators use their imagination. And so on, for all kinds of creativity.

But how does imagination work? Good imagination works as creative strategy: a new combination comes together in your mind from previous elements. Bad imagination works as fantasy: I dream up something impossible. I can imagine a pill that costs only a dollar and cures every disease in the world, but that kind of imagination does not help you come up with a course of action. For example, if we start our planning by imagining our company's "ideal future," the truthful answer is "infinite profits" or some other such goal we can never reach. How do you make a plan for that?

A cousin of imagination is visualization: try to see in your mind the future you want to achieve. That's supposed to help you achieve it. But we're back to the same problem. What if I visualize something impossible? Some people think that's fine. If you go after an impossible goal, you might only reach halfway. Isn't that better than setting and achieving an easy goal? Aim for the stars and reach the moon, versus aim for the anthill and reach it.

Alas, this is not much help for innovation. If I aim for the stars, such as a pill that only costs a dollar and cures every disease in the world, won't I at least reach the moon, in the form of a pill that costs two dollars and cures half the diseases in the world? Of course not. The problem is this: when I imagined that pill, I had no idea how to make it. This kind of visualization only works if you have a good idea already of how to proceed. For example, if you visualize losing fifteen pounds in two weeks, you might only lose five pounds in five weeks. But for either result, you know what to do ahead of time: eat less and exercise more. That's not innovation. It's willpower, to implement a solution you already know. Visualization might help you change your habits to have more willpower, but it does not give you a creative idea.

For innovation, we don't know the solution beforehand. If Jobs imagines "the best small computer in the world," that doesn't help him build it. Only when that imagination has real content, from Wozniak and Xerox, can Jobs imagine the next great computer. And that's creative strategy.

Mind Mapping

A mind map is a diagram of words with lines between them. You start with one word, which makes you think of other words. You write down those new words and draw lines to them from the first word. Now you do the same for the new words. And so on, until you run out of time, paper, or words.

Some advocates of mind maps tell you it's a technique for creative thinking. But once you understand how innovation actually works, you see right away that mind maps are simply a form of personal brainstorming, with all the same obstacles to innovation built in. Freeing your mind to toss out ideas is not how creativity happens. A mind map is not a what-works scan; it does not search your mind for precedents you know or search beyond your mind for precedents to discover.

A mind map can be useful as a simple brain dump: to get down on paper what you think about a topic and to see connections among ideas. This can help organize your thoughts for a paper or presentation. But that's not innovation. If you want to use mind mapping for innovation, search through what you wrote down for useful precedents, or for ideas that spark where to search beyond your own mind. But don't spend too much time mapping your list, that is, drawing lines between the words. Instead, collect the precedents from the list and arrange them in an insight matrix.

Not-Invented-Here

Here we consider a well-known obstacle to creativity: Not-Invented-Here. You find it especially in R&D or marketing departments, where people pride themselves on being creative. People actively refuse to borrow elements from outside, because "we're different." Only we can understand our situation and our company, so only we can come up with ideas that apply to it.

That's partly true. Every company is different, every person is different, every snowflake is different. No two are ever exactly the same. And people in a company and in a situation are best placed to judge what's best for that company in that situation. Creative strategy recognizes that every solution needs to be different; each new creative combination is unique. And it puts in the hands of insiders the judgment of what elements to select and combine.

So the formal method of creative strategy solves Not-Invented-Here, at least on paper. What happens in people's minds is something else. You can force someone to do a what-works scan, but you can't force them to do it well. It takes humility and courage to admit you don't have the answer and you have to search.

Overcoming an ingrained attitude of Not-Invented-Here takes more than introducing creative strategy. It's cultural change, and that takes more time, or more drastic action. You might need a creative strategy for how to do it, that is, find elements that worked for other companies in defeating Not-Invented-Here.

Play

Many companies give their people toys to play with. Google is the most famous example of this: there's a whole room filled with toys and games employees can play with at any time. There are more toys and games in the lobby and scattered around other public spaces. Other companies use toys or games in workshops, where you start off with a round of play before you get to work.

Why?

Because play stimulates the right side of the brain, and that makes you more creative. Right?

Wrong.

We now know that there is no right side of the brain. If you play a game or with a toy, the most important thing that happens is you learn how to play that game or to use that toy. That's learning, not innovation. It might also relax you, which is good for letting your mind wander and make connections. But different people relax in very different ways: listening to music, chatting with friends, exercising, gazing out the window, doing yoga, walking in the park, cooking, and so on. Very few adults actually relax with toys. And they need to relax at different times, when their minds are wandering about some problem their normal work can't solve. Your mind doesn't wander while you're playing a game: it concentrates on the game.

Playing together can break down social barriers and so foster teamwork, and that's good for creativity. But exposure to other ideas and information, not play, stimulates the creative mind. And relaxing activities, more than play, help creativity by calming the mind.

R&D

Many companies give responsibility for innovation to a Research and Development department. For innovations that depend on advanced science, it makes sense to have a group of scientists working together in one unit. But many business innovations happen without advanced science, even in high-tech fields; as we saw before, Apple bundles, improves, and markets what others invent. R&D should not be the only innovators in your company, and R&D should look outward, not just inward, for elements to combine. Creative strategy is itself an R&D method, where the R is search rather than laboratory experiments, and the D is creative combination.

R&D departments should routinely use creative strategy as a means to guide their everyday work. That makes their own original research one of the sources on the insight matrix for every project they do. The world beyond their own lab gives them other sources to search.

Six Thinking Hats

One of the world's leading authorities on creativity is Edward de Bono. His 1985 book *Six Thinking Hats* remains popular today. For any problem, de Bono tells you to think about it in six different ways, wearing six different hats: process, objective, intuitive, negative, positive, and creative. For a group, each person picks a hat and plays that role.

That's all fine—it's good to look at a problem from different angles—but that's not innovation. These six points of view do not result in a creative idea.

But look, one of the six angles is "creative." Does de Bono tell us how to do that? He does. His advice: lateral thinking. He first explained that in a 1973 book *Lateral Thinking*. You use random words or objects and try to apply them to your problem, give an opposite view to accepted truth about the problem, or change the problem to make it backward, impossible, or fantastic. These methods all stir the pot of your mind so creative ideas pop out.

We see right away that lateral thinking is not creative strategy. It does not tell you to look for elements elsewhere that solve pieces of your puzzle. In essence, the techniques of lateral thinking amount to stimulating the right side of the brain. After all, De Bono came up with his creative method in the early 1970s, almost three decades before neuroscience revealed how learning-and-memory produces creative ideas. It should come as no surprise to find that his methods are out of date.

Time Off

Another feature of Google's creative workplace is time off for professional staff. One day a week is all yours, to work on a project of your choice. This technique came from 3M, where you can take off 15 percent of your time. This is an excellent organizational technique to give people the bureaucratic freedom to pursue new ideas at their earliest stage. At both companies, you can then apply for funding and more formal time to make the innovation happen. Wonderful.

But still we ask: For my time off, how do I come up with an idea worth pursuing? Google and 3M give no guidance on that. If you add creative strategy to the mix, that would do the trick.

Trial and Error

Many people believe that there is no method for creativity. It's simply a matter of trial and error. The more things you try, the better your chances that something will work. As Thomas Edison once said, "If I find 10,000 ways something won't work, I haven't failed. I am not discouraged, because every wrong attempt discarded is another step forward."

This seems to be a clear endorsement of trial and error as a creative method. But Edison also said this: "Everyone steals in commerce and industry. I've stolen a lot, myself. But I know how to steal! They don't know how to steal!"

Now we can understand both quotes together. First you "steal" from others, then make a new combination. When that fails, you search again and try another combination. And so on, until you find a combination that works. This is not trial and error. It's hunt-combine-try, hunt-combine-try, hunt-combine-try. . . . The repetition also develops expert intuition, where you recognize faster each time what might or might not work.

Sure enough, historians now think Edison made no truly original inventions himself. His light bulb, for example, came from Joseph Swan's bulb and Lewis Latimer's filament.

Others think that trial and error means "conduct experiments." Experiments are good, but they are not the same as trial and error. Scientists do lots of search before they design an experiment, to increase the chances the experiment will work. There are not "10,000 ways something won't work," as Edison counts: there are millions. You can waste huge amounts of time and money on trial and error. And failed experiments tell you far less than a successful experiment. Successful past experiments are building blocks for the next set of experiments.

Some people advocate trail and error as an attitude more than a method. They want the company to accept failure as a normal part of innovation. If everyone is afraid to make an error, they won't dare any trials. There is merit to this view; many good ideas fail, and the company culture has to allow that. The irony is that companies that won't tolerate any failure are least likely to embrace its complete opposite, an attitude of "try anything." Instead, offer creative strategy as a prudent way to experiment. Companies are more likely to accept failure if you can explain why your experiment is worth a try—a creative combination of past elements that worked.

Last but not least, trial and error can lead you to kill off experiments too soon. Don't accept failure too easily. Remember that even in creative strategy, after you start implementing your idea you need new ideas to add to it. Hunt-combine-try beats trial and error throughout an innovation's life.

TRIZ and SIT

A popular innovation method among engineers comes from Genrich Saulovich Altshuller, a Soviet scientist. In the 1940s and 1950s, he analyzed 40,000 patents to develop his "theory of inventive problem solving"—TIPS, or TRIZ in Russian. Altshuller made a list of forty inventive principles that account for all these inventions. He then devised a grid of thirty-nine problems as both rows and columns. In the cells of the grid, Altshuller filled in which of the forty inventive principles solve the intersection of those two problems.

For example, if your problems are temperature and loss of time, Altshuller fills in that cell with four inventive principles: parameter changes, mechanical substitution, skipping, and mechanical vibration. So you combine those four things to solve your two problems. Each inventive principle applies to many different combinations of problems: for example, parameter changes helps solve 229 different pairs of problems.

Got it?

Poor Altshuller. He worked so hard, but the whole idea was misconceived from the start. He studied the results of 40,000 innovations, not the method the inventors used to create them. For example, we can follow Altshuller and fill in a grid with the fundamental problems that the features of the first Macintosh solved, but that is not even remotely close to the actual method Jobs used to invent it. He combined the small machine that his partner, Steve Wozniak, had already invented, with the graphical user interface and mouse that Adele Goldberg and her Xerox team had improved from Doug Engelbart's earlier design. We can fill in a grid with the fundamental problems that the features of Edison's light bulb solved, but his actual method was combining Swan's bulb and Latimer's filament. And so on through the annals of innovation.

If you want to innovate, do what other innovators did. That's creative strategy.

There is also a modern variant of TRIZ: systematic inventive thinking, or SIT. TRIZ inspired SIT's "five thinking tools," which we find in a 2002 book by Goldenberg and Mazursky, *Creativity in Product Innovation*. The authors boil Altshuller's forty inventive principles down to five creativity templates that cover the majority of new product innovations:

Attribute dependency
Replacement

Displacement
Component control
Division

None of these templates involves the creative combination of elements that worked elsewhere. Instead, you manipulate the current features of the product in five different ways. For example, you take the legs off a chair and replace them with a different element that can perform the same function of keeping the chair off the ground. But how do we find that element? The only guidance we get is to start "in the immediate environment," such as "wall, table, carpet." If you can't think of something that replaces the legs, try a different template.

This method does not preclude creative strategy—your idea for an element to replace the chair legs might indeed come from something else that works. But SIT does not lead you to that. And let's compare the two methods outright. SIT tells you to take your existing product and perform five thinking experiments on all its many features, individually and in combination. Creative strategy starts instead by asking you what's the problem with your product that makes you want to innovate, and then you search for elements to combine that solve it. Of the two, creative strategy comes much closer to how innovations actually happen.

Workplace

Before, we touched on the idea of a creative workplace a bit in "art" and "play." A playful, artistic workplace aims to stimulate the creative right side of the brain, versus the analytical left side. But science has overturned that model of the brain. A creative workplace also helps you relax, which is good but still misconceived. People relax much better out of the office completely, and most use means other than art or play. A third element of the creative workplace is everything else: if the chairs, desks, walls, halls, and decorations are kooky and offbeat, you'll have more innovation. A conventional workplace yields conventional ideas. A creative workplace yields creative ideas.

At least that's the theory. But if you look at where innovation actually happened, you typically find drab walls and offices. For example, Google's current offices are hardly conventional: you can sit in a sling chair with your laptop, in front of a wall of red dots in an op art pattern on a see-through plastic bubble, or lean against a replica taxi. Yet Google's revenue still comes overwhelmingly from its original innovation, Internet search ads. Did the Google founders get that idea in a creative workplace?

We can reconstruct how the original Google guys, Larry Page and Sergey Brin, came up with their great idea thanks to *The Google Story* by David Vise and Mark Malseed. In the late 1990s, Page and Brin were graduate students working under Professor Rajeev Motwani of Stanford's computer science department. Through a series of creative combinations, the Google guys put together four precedents: a conventional data-mining algorithm, the reverse-link ranking of academic citations, Altavista's search engine, and Overture's online ad revenue system. Their workplace was nothing special: the standard cubicles and offices of universities around the world.

The workplace can matter for innovation, but not for stimulating creativity. Much more important is how people in power treat ideas from each other. In this regard, anecdotal reports indicate that Google is indeed a creative workplace. Their executives encourage the exchange of ideas, regardless of hierarchy, and seek out new ideas rather than suppress them. You can have toys and games and colorful décor galore, but how your boss treats you matters far more. You can have drab walls and boring offices, but a culture that loves innovation is far more important.

For example, a recent article by Jonah Lehrer tells the tale of Building 20 at MIT. In 1943, the Radiation Lab needed more space, fast, so MIT threw up a huge, drab three-story building with narrow hallways, thin walls, and poor ventilation. Dozens of scientists crammed into it, and helped win the war with innovations in radar. After the war, until MIT tore it down in 1998, Building 20 was home to a changing mix of scientific teams that made breakthroughs in fields from video games to linguistics. From the very beginning, scientists reported that chance meetings in the long corridors with others working on very different problems led to lots of new ideas.

A workplace that helps people working on different problems run into each other, and a culture that encourages them to talk openly to each other about their work, are the keys to a creative workplace. We know from creative strategy that what they really get from each other is sources to search or precedents to apply to their own problems. The most boring building can be the most creative place, depending what happens inside.

Youth

If you want to innovate, hire younger staff. They retain more of a child's innate creativity than older staff. Right?

Not quite.

Children are more uninhibited—that's true. They will draw a cat flying to the moon, or a purple carrot, or an arrow with curlicue feathers. That's different from any kind of creative solution to a real problem the child might face. For that, you want to draw on as many sources as possible, and that gets easier, not harder, the older you get. It's true that many adults become narrow in their outlook and don't search widely for elements to combine. But they still have the ability to do so, if they just decide to do it.

Younger staff are consumers too, so they do bring views of your younger customers. That's helpful, in the same way your older staff will bring views of your older customers. Younger staff will ask naïve questions that make you think twice about old ideas and routines your company takes for granted. That's helpful too. But that's not innovation; it's questioning conventional wisdom. What you need next is an idea to replace conventional wisdom. For that, younger people might be more uninhibited—or not. Often they are busy learning the ropes and trying to fit in. In that case, older, more secure staff who don't worry about fitting in any more might think with a more open mind.

If younger staff are more willing to take risks for new ideas, that's easy enough to understand. Often they don't have families to help support, or mortgage payments, or other burdens that make you more risk-averse the older you get. Even though your ability to get creative ideas increases with age, your willingness to take risks for those ideas often declines. If the company culture makes innovation difficult or punishes failed experiments, older staff might simply be too burned out to try again.

Many people who argue that young people are more creative cite as evidence the long list of young innovators in history. Einstein and Picasso were only twenty-six when they had their big breakthroughs. Mozart composed at the age of ten. Jobs was only twenty-four when he had the idea for the Macintosh. Well, let's look at each case. Einstein combined the work of five other scientists for his big idea, $E = mc^2$. Picasso combined Matisse's 1906 painting *Happiness of Life* and an African sculpture (that Matisse showed him) to make his breakthrough painting *Les desmoiselles d'Avignon*. And Mozart was less an innovator than a great mimic and combiner of all the styles of music he found while touring Europe as a performer. All three of these youthful innovators used creative strategy—not youthful spirits—to make their innovations. As for Jobs, we already saw that he did the same too. Youth might make you more willing to innovate, but creative strategy helps you do it at any age.

So ends our review of creative methods that compete with creative strategy, either to make you a more creative person or to design an innovation. The crucial point for all of them is how you actually get an idea to solve a problem; these methods either skip that step entirely or rely on the magic of imagination. A few can be quite compatible with creative strategy—like art or collaboration or time off—as long as you keep to the core discipline of searching for elements that worked elsewhere to make a new combination. Understanding, practicing, and mastering that discipline is the key skill for innovation.

12
Strategy

An innovation must be both creative and strategic: something new (creative) that gives you a feasible course of action toward a worthwhile goal (strategic). Some popular methods of strategy make an explicit promise to give you that new direction, and these are direct alternatives to creative strategy. Other popular strategy methods make no special claims to yield innovation but can crowd out creative strategy and thus block innovation.

In most cases both sets of methods are actually forms of analysis and do not yield a creative idea. With some modification, you can adapt these methods to creative strategy: use them for analysis, and then use creative strategy for your strategic idea.

Analysis

This is the most popular and generic method of strategy, the way "imagination" is the most popular and general method of creativity. Many of the following methods are forms of strategic analysis: they help you understand your situation but do not produce an idea for what to do about it. Analysis is a good thing. It's just incomplete as a method of strategy. If you do your analysis first, and then do creative strategy, there need be no conflict between the two.

Blue Ocean Strategy

In 2005, Kim and Mauborgne published the book *Blue Ocean Strategy*. Since then, their method has quickly become very popular in the business world. It offers a way to avoid the "red ocean," where competitors bloody each other, in favor of the "blue ocean," where no one yet competes. Instead of new products for existing customers, or new customers for existing products, you seek new products for new customers. If you get there first, you gain first-mover advantage and plenty of time before competitors arrive to turn the ocean red again.

This is clearly a method for innovation. And it's not a new idea. Hamel and Prahalad proposed it in their 1994 book *Competing for the Future*. They called their virgin market "white space" instead of "blue ocean." Christensen and Raymor reprised the idea in their 2003 book *The Innovator's Solution*. Certainly it's an appealing idea, so no wonder it keeps coming up. The question for us is: How do you do it exactly?

Blue ocean strategy offers these steps. First you paint a "strategy canvas," where you list key "factors" that rule competition in your industry and how different segments of the industry fare in each factor. For example, in the wine industry "aging quality" is a key factor, where premium wines rank high and budget wines rank low. Right away we recognize the strategy canvas as a method to analyze your situation. It does not give you a strategic idea—at least not yet.

Next, you take your factors and decide which ones your company should "reduce," "eliminate," or "raise." And, are there any new factors to "create"? These are fine questions, but blue ocean strategy gives you no guidance on how to answer them. For example, we learn that Yellowtail Wines created "ease of selection" as a new factor by reducing their selection to only two types of wine and simplifying the label. But we don't know how they came up with that innovation. And we get no guidance on how to get this kind of idea ourselves.

This is the classic problem with strategy methods of all kinds. You take an analytical framework that describes your current situation and then make a magical leap to fill in the framework for the future you desire. With blue ocean strategy as your guide, you take your current industry strategy canvas and draw your desired canvas over it. For example, Yellowtail reduced "aging quality" but created that new factor, "ease of selection." You can see how Yellowtail's new strategy canvas differs from industry norms, factor by factor. We get a good picture of the result. But we still don't know how Yellowtail came up with their new strategy in the first place. How did they decide to increase "aging quality" rather than something else, like "ease of selection"? And why didn't they create a new factor like "personalized labels"? Unfortunately, blue ocean strategy does not tell us. It has no method to figure out which items of the strategy canvas to change, and what to change them to.

What you find instead is more and more detail on how to do the analysis. After you draw the industry strategy canvas, you go interview a wide range of managers and customers in your industry, in "alternative industries," and in industries that are related or might be so in the future. An "alternative" to wine is beer, so you look at that too. Restaurants are a related industry. And so on. From the view of creative strategy, this could be a good exercise, if it were clear that you were looking for elements that work elsewhere that you might want to borrow for yourself. Unfortunately, blue ocean strategy tells you to gather "strategic insights," for example, that an accounting department wastes a lot of time making phone calls to confirm foreign exchange payments. There is no obvious way to translate that kind of insight into an element for your own strategy.

Nevertheless, blue ocean strategy tells you to take all the insights you gathered and now draw six new strategy canvases for your company. Six! That's because a blue ocean strategy can take one of six paths: it "looks across alternative industries," "looks across strategic groups within the industry," "redefines the industry buyer group," "looks across to complementary product and service offerings," "rethinks the functional-emotional orientation of its industry," or "participates in shaping external trends over time." Whew! How to translate the strategic insights into a strategy canvas for just one of these paths is mysterious. To do it six times is six times as mysterious.

You spend two weeks drawing and redrawing, and then the teams come together in a "visual strategy fair." Each team posts its six canvases around the room, and then you invite judges to pick their favorites. You end up synthesizing a single canvas that shows what you should "reduce," "eliminate," "raise," and "create." Congratulations, you have your blue ocean strategy!

Alas, it's still the same old problem: you use a framework to analyze your current situation, and then you fill out the framework according to how you want it to be in the future. The only link between the two is "insights" from your analysis. The insight step remains mysterious in blue ocean strategy as in other conventional strategy methods. Only creative strategy solves the mystery of the insight step: you combine precedents from elsewhere in a new combination.

If you want to integrate creative strategy into blue ocean strategy, look for specific "elements that work" rather than "insights" in general. As such, your strategy canvas can point you to new sources to search beyond your own industry or market, to enrich your creative combination.

Case Method

It's seldom explicit, but many executives believe that the best way to come up with a creative strategy is to be a creative strategist. It's the people, not the method. Put the right people on the problem, problem solved.

But how do you find the right people? That's a tough one. Senior executives have a track record, so you can judge their prior work to some degree. But what about hiring junior executives? It's hard to know from a resume and an interview if someone is a good strategist. So some companies give job candidates a strategy case to solve. That shows how well they will solve strategy cases in the job they're applying for. Or at least, that's the idea.

If those candidates went to business school, the case method is familiar to them. They know what to do. A case is a description of what a real business did, plus questions about what they should do next. Harvard pioneered the method in the 1920s, and today most business schools use the case method to teach strategy. So the case method has a major impact on the practice of strategy in companies around the world.

Does the case method foster creative strategy? In one way, it does. Each case a student studies becomes an "example from history," as Clausewitz would call it. That case becomes a potential source for a future insight matrix. Unfortunately, the case method of teaching strategy does not see it that way. On the first page of every Harvard case, there's a disclaimer: "Cases are not intended to serve as endorsements, sources of primary data, or illustrations of effective or ineffective management."

We can understand the part about endorsements and primary data. But the last phrase basically tells us not to use the case as an "example from history." That's partially so as not to offend the subjects of the case if it shows them in a bad light. But it also comes from Harvard's case method theory: all strategic situations are different, so you cannot apply one to the other.

Now we have a problem. The cases themselves foster creative strategy, but the case method contradicts it. So how do students take what they learned in the classroom and apply it later at work? In that interview for a strategy job, and later in their strategy assignments, they have two choices. They can treat each case as unique, as the case method tells them, or they can break from the case method and draw on the cases themselves as examples from history, as Clausewitz counsels.

One time after I gave a talk on the foibles of the case method someone from the audience came up to me and said they use the case method all the time where she works—but a different version. She explained: Copy and Steal Everything—C.A.S.E.

Otherwise known as creative strategy.

Competitive Strategy

In 1980, Michael Porter of the Harvard Business School published the book *Competitive Strategy*, which was based on a course he taught there. Since then, his general method—competitive analysis—has spread beyond Harvard to become nearly universal in strategy courses in business schools and among strategy consultants and practitioners in companies around the world. Even his specific methods, such as the famous "five forces," are still the most popular among the many versions of competitive analysis that have sprung up over the years.

Porter solved a specific problem: much strategic planning in business went straight to setting a mission, vision, goals, and objectives without any systematic analysis beforehand. The subtitle of Porter's book is "Techniques for Analyzing Industries and Competitors." And that's what he gives you. Note that the subtitle is not "How to Come up with a Strategic Idea." So Porter's methods do not compete with creative strategy. Go ahead and do competitive analysis *à la* Porter—or anyone else—as your first step. But don't spend too much time on it. Leave enough time for the search phase that creative strategy demands. And don't make the classic mistake of doing your analysis and then holding a brainstorm meeting to "generate solutions." Instead, use the insight matrix.

All the versions of competitive strategy that have arisen over the three decades since Porter's original feature the same limitation. They are methods of analysis. They don't tell you how to get a creative idea. Some versions admit this, at least to some degree. For example, in 1999, Pankaj Ghemawat wrote a Harvard Business School *Note* on "creating competitive advantage," where he explains the limits of the method he outlines: "This note takes an analytical approach to strategy. In actuality, of course, many of the greatest advantages come not from analysis, but from entrepreneurial creativity and insight. . . . The final step in the analysis . . . is to find favorable options. The generation of options is ultimately a creative act."

Bravo, Professor Ghemawat. He admits that his method shows you how to analyze your situation, not generate creative ideas for strategy. Unfortunately, this kind of self-awareness is rare in the strategy world. More typically you get "analysis" or "diagnosis" or "research" that mysteriously yields a strategic idea.

Sometimes strategists who use competitive analysis actually do practice some version of creative strategy: after the analysis, they search widely for precedents on key elements of the problem to arrive at a creative combination. But you'll seldom know that's what they did. They present their work in the language and format of competitive strategy, not creative strategy. It helps to make explicit the key steps that should follow strategic analysis, rather than fooling yourself into thinking that the analysis itself generates strategy. Making these steps clear removes the mystery of where the ideas actually come from. As with any discipline, a greater awareness of what you're doing helps you study what you did and how to improve it.

Critical Thinking

Some methods cite critical thinking as a key part of strategic thinking. There are many definitions of critical thinking, but most are similar. Here are the most common:

1. Disciplined thinking that is clear, rational, open-minded, and informed by evidence
2. The mental process of actively and skillfully conceptualizing, applying, analyzing, synthesizing, and evaluating information to reach an answer or conclusion

By these definitions, creative strategy is a form of critical thinking. But most models of critical thinking differ in some key way from creative strategy. Usually they involve only analysis, not synthesis. For example, W. G. Sumner defines critical thinking as "the examination and test of propositions of any kind which are offered for acceptance, in order to find out whether they correspond to reality or not." By this definition, critical thinking is not a method to come up with propositions—that is, ideas—but to evaluate them. If these ideas are proposals for future strategy, that evaluation should conform to creative strategy. For that, your critical question asks: Is strategy made up of precedents from real sources that solve elements of the problem at hand?

Execution

Which is more important, strategy or execution?

Here is a common attitude in the business world: there are lots of good ideas, so it's execution that makes the difference. If you execute poorly, any strategy will fail. In a popular 2002 book, *Execution: The Discipline of Getting Things Done*, Bossidy and Charan observe that most top executives spend too much time coming up with a strategy and not enough time making sure the company executes that strategy quickly and well. Top executives should not just come up with a strategy and delegate its execution. They should spend most of their time leading the execution too.

Bossidy and Charan are probably right that top executives don't spend enough time on execution. But that doesn't mean that execution is more important than strategy. They are equally important, the way all links in a chain must be strong or the whole chain is useless. Good execution of a bad strategy is just as bad—and maybe worse—than bad execution of a good strategy. If you observe that your execution is bad, don't just jump to the conclusion that you need better execution. You might first need a better or more complete strategy. Remember the Parker story from Part I? Washkewicz had a good overall strategy, but he needed further strategic ideas on how to make it work. Execution in that case called for further innovation on every element of the strategy. But Washkewicz saw it as only a matter of execution.

Often people don't execute well because they don't have good ideas for how to solve new problems that arise along the way. The answer to this is not "better execution." First you need creative strategy, again, for that particular problem. Then you need good execution, again, until another new problem arises, and so on. Good execution needs creative strategy.

Experts

Call in an expert. That's how you figure out what to do. Many strategy consulting firms bank on this: their staff have lots of experience working at or consulting for many companies in your industry. They've seen everything. They can apply all that to your problem.

Another way companies call in the experts is by promoting them. You did great at a specific technical task—marketing, finance, operations, what have you—and the company promotes you to a job with more responsibility. In your new position, how do you figure out what to do? You rely on the expert: yourself. After all, that's why they promoted you, because you already know what to do.

It's good to be an expert. Experts can solve most of the problems that arise in business. But that doesn't mean experts are best at innovation. For an expert to innovate, the first thing you have to tell yourself is, "I don't know the answer, but I can find it." You have to take off your expert hat and put on your innovator hat. Experts know the answer; innovators find it. This step is an act of humility and courage.

But perhaps you're in a company, or consulting for one, that believes in experts and nothing else. In that case, become an expert in something else: creative strategy. Develop and practice your skill in rapid appraisal, the what-works scan, and creative combination.

Gap Analysis

Many strategy methods include gap analysis: describe (A) where you are, (B) where you want to be, and then (C) determine how to get from A to B. Usually, some kind of recommended framework guides you, for example, Porter's five forces breaks down A and B into five categories. Some creative methods do the same, for example, design thinking might tell you that customers want products of a certain look, size, cost, and ease of use. That makes four categories for A and B. Now you do C, and fill in the gap between.

The problem with gap analysis is C. You need ideas for how to get from A to B. Where do those ideas come from? That depends whether the company seeks to innovate or not. If not, you take benchmark results or rely on your own expert intuition. In other words, you know how to get from A to B, so you fill in what you know. If the company seeks to innovate, that means you don't know how to get from A to B. What do most companies do in that case? As usual, they brainstorm.

If you want to use gap analysis with creative strategy, A and B can be part of your situation analysis that helps you see where you need to innovate most. When we get to C, instead of brainstorming, you can put B at the top of your insight matrix and go from there. And remember that as you search, you might change your view of B.

It is not always clear at the start of gap analysis whether or not you need creative strategy. In many cases, benchmark results and expert intuition can fill part of the gap, but not all. You reach a point where you should stop and admit that you don't know the rest of the answer. Now you need creative strategy. Put the pieces you already know on the insight matrix; for benchmarks, the sources are known, but for expert intuition you should force yourself to remember at least one example of where you saw that piece work well.

In general, though, you should restrict gap analysis to execution. Once you have your idea for innovation, you can use gap analysis to fill out your plan for marketing, operations, finance, and so on. In that case, B is the creative combination from your insight matrix. As a planning tool, gap analysis is fine. As a strategy or innovation tool, it's not. Creative strategy is a much better method for arriving at a creative idea.

Good to Great

Since it came out in 2001, *Good to Great* by Jim Collins has been one of the world's most popular business books. What a title! Who doesn't want to go from "good to great," as a person or a company? And Collins echoes Steven Covey's famous *Seven Habits of Highly Effective People* to give us seven habits of companies that went from good to great. What's not to like?
Here is Collins's list:

1. Level 5 leadership
2. First who, then what
3. Confront the brutal facts
4. Hedgehog concept
5. Culture of discipline
6. Technology accelerators
7. The flywheel

We can skim over 1, 3, 5, 6, and 7 because they don't involve creating your strategic idea. Number 1 describes how five levels of management should lead their staff, in order to explain that top leaders must act differently from the other four levels that they probably rose through in their career. Number 3 is simply good advice, always: no wishful thinking. Number 5 matches well what Bossidy and Charan say about execution. Number 6 reminds you to keep up with the latest technology in all aspects of your business. And number 7 tells you to keep developing new initiatives that fit your strategy and relate to each other, to add momentum like a flywheel.

That leaves numbers 2 and 4. Here we have a problem. Number 2 is similar to Kotter's change management model, which told you to form your "guiding coalition" before you have a strategic idea. Collins tells you to decide "who's on the bus" before you come up with a strategy. In both versions—Kotter and Collins—that's bad advice. If you're a manufacturing firm and you want to move into services, you have to have that idea first before you add an expert in services to your team. "Who" should follow the idea, not precede it.

As for number 4, Collins invokes the old proverb, "The fox knows many things, but the hedgehog knows one great thing." In other words, do one big thing well, rather than try to do lots of little things. But how do you decide what your "one big thing" should be? Here Collins is no more help than other conventional methods of strategy. He compares eleven "good to great companies" with eleven competitors in the same industries, and concludes: "Strategy per se did not distinguish the good-to-great companies from the comparison companies. *Both* sets of companies had strategic plans, and there is absolutely no evidence that the good-to-great companies invested more time and energy in strategy development and long-range planning."

Huh? That can't be right. Collins confuses "time and energy" spent on strategy and the quality of strategy. Okay, good-to-great companies did not spend more time deciding on a strategy, but Collins cannot possibly mean that good-to-great companies did not have strategies of better quality.

As for how to come up with your own hedgehog concept, Collins tells you to answer three questions:

1. What can you be the best in the world at?
2. What drives your economic engine?
3. What are you deeply passionate about?

Clearly, the first of these questions is the heart of the matter. The answer is your strategic idea. Unfortunately, the only guidance Collins gives on this question is bad advice: go with your core competencies. This is a trap.

You might be good at something—your core competencies—but you might not be better at it than others, so you won't succeed if you go for that. So if you shouldn't just pick from you core competencies for your big idea, what should you do? Collins has no answer.

The second question tells you to find an "economic engine" that differs from and is more profitable than the economic engine of your competitors. How do you do that? Collins doesn't say.

The third and final question tells you to do what you're passionate about rather than get passionate about what you do. This sounds nice, but it's next to useless for figuring out what to do. Take any ten top executives at a company and ask them what they're really passionate about, regardless of what they or the company are actually doing now, and you will get a long list of diverse pursuits that might not include what the company does at all. Or, just as likely, someone is passionate about a part of the company that's failing and has no future.

The third question is a form of wishful thinking—that we all can and should do what we're passionate about—and so violates Collins's advice elsewhere to "confront the brutal facts." It's entirely possible, and often likely, that what everyone is passionate about is a terrible business idea. Of course you try to find people who are passionate about your idea, or motivate them to become so, but that's a terrible way to decide on a strategy in the first place. More likely—and this is how things really work—a winning strategic idea motivates people to work on it. People get excited about the chance of success; that's the reality of the business world. First, you need a good idea. For that you need creative strategy.

Innovator's Solution

In his 1997 book *The Innovator's Dilemma*, Clayton Christensen describes how big firms did not adopt new technology because they feared it would compete with the old technology they already sold. This was a clever application of Schumpeter's classic "creative destruction" to a single firm: Schumpeter showed how capitalism advanced through new companies with new ideas "destroying" old companies based on the older ideas. Perhaps the clearest example of Christensen's version was Kodak rejecting digital technology because it competed with film.

Christensen's book made the "dilemma" quite clear. But how do you resolve the dilemma? For that he and Michael Raynor came out with another book in 2003, *The Innovator's Solution*. Most of the book follows the usual formula of conventional strategy methods: it gives questions you need to answer for your strategy. For example, "What products will customers want to buy?" or "Who are the best customers for our product?" or "Getting the scope of the business right." For a method to answer these questions, we have to wait until chapter 8, "Managing the Strategy Development Process."

Here we find a contrast between two kinds of innovation strategy: "deliberate" and "emergent." The authors clearly prefer emergent strategy as a way to create "disruptive innovations" for the unpredictable world we face today. Henry Mintzberg first named and described "emergent strategy" in the 1980s, and the *Innovator's Solution* borrows heavily from his work. Christensen and Raynor tell us that strategic ideas "bubble up from within the organization" as "the cumulative effect of day-to-day prioritization and investment decisions" made by managers throughout the company. These managers respond to "problems or opportunities that were unforeseen in the analysis and planning stages" of deliberate strategy making, and the result is "emergent strategies." When an emergent strategy succeeds, "it is possible to formalize it, improve it, and exploit it, thus transforming an emergent strategy into a deliberate one."

In this formulation of emergent strategy, Christensen and Raynor take us no further than Mintzberg did more than two decades ago. They give no guidance for how to respond to the unplanned "problems or opportunities" you encounter in an emergent strategy. Yet again, on the crucial point of how exactly you get a creative idea for strategy, we find no help at all.

Christensen and Raynor do offer one more step: the "discovery-driven planning" of Rita McGrath and Ian MacMillan. Once you have your "emergent" idea, you do a different kind of planning that builds in learning and rethinking your plan as you make new discoveries from implementing the plan. This is good advice for planning. But McGrath and MacMillan make no claims about how you come up with that "emergent" idea in the first place. *The Innovator's Solution* offers no help there either. Once again, on that crucial question of how you come up with a creative idea to try out, only creative strategy provides an answer.

Issue Tree

The "issue tree" is a popular problem-solving tool that some practitioners apply to strategy, most famously from McKinsey & Company. It's a search for causes: write down your problem, list all the causes of the problem, then list the causes of each cause, and so on until you can't go any further. The result looks like a tree. This is technically analysis, as in chemistry: you break down the problem into its components. McKinsey and some others go further to say your final tree must be "MECE," mutually exclusive and collectively exhaustive. This is actually misleading advice; many items are interrelated in reality and so can never be mutually exclusive, and you are fooling yourself to think you can ever exhaustively foresee all the problems that might arise in a complex strategic situation.

Some practitioners use the issue-tree format for a "decision tree," where you list and break down all the possible answers to a problem and assign values and probabilities to each one. For simple problems with finite, known variables and outcomes, that can work. But don't use it to come up with a creative idea, a strategy, or an innovation. For those, listing all possible answers to a problem is literally impossible, and assigning values and probabilities to future outcomes is naked guesswork that you dress up in numbers to convince yourself that you're being rigorous.

On the other hand, an issue tree can help in rapid appraisal, to pin down a problem and break it into elements. The top line and rows of the insight matrix are essentially a shorthand issue tree that you might abstract from a messier, more detailed one that you build and revise along the way. But do not try to put a detailed issue tree, such as a MECE one, as the rows of your matrix. More than ten rows, and you have made the problem too complex for your brain to see a combination, or to revise with key leaders and key informants. You want just the main branches of the tree on your matrix. And beware spending too much time poring over your tree, breaking it down further and further. More insight into the problem comes from discovery, not analysis, in your rapid appraisal interviews and what-works scan.

In the end, remember that an issue tree, of any kind, does not give you a creative solution. For that you have to search.

List Options

Most problem-solving methods tell you at some point to "list options." They might call them "alternatives" or "solutions" or "actions" or even "strategies." You make a list and then evaluate each item on the list. That evaluation leads you to pick one option over the others. Problem solved.

Or is it?

The real question is what method to use to list an option, even a single one. The usual method is brainstorming—you throw out an idea from the top of your head. Then you or someone else throws out another one. And so on. Then the evaluation step selects one of the options.

Here's the problem: telling someone to "list options" gives them no guidance on how to think up a good option in the first place. No matter how good my method of evaluation, if I have bad options to evaluate, I will end up with a bad idea.

Listing options is popular for two reasons. First, it solves the problem of what to do with five people in a room with five different ideas. The solution is simple: you list five options. That's fair. But is it creative? Not likely. The insight matrix gives a better method for five people in a room to follow. Second, listing options prevents you from just accepting the first idea that pops into your head. Unfortunately, it still relies on ideas just popping into your head, just more of them, or more heads. Remember that creative strategy spends weeks coming up with a single option. Listing options comes up with more than a single option in a matter of minutes. Which method might produce options of higher quality?

Participatory Strategic Planning

Most strategic planning methods within organizations today are participatory in some way—that is, staff beyond the top rank of executives join in at some point. The advice to do so comes from none other than Peter Drucker, perhaps the most influential business expert of all time. In 1954, Drucker's first major book, *The Practice of Management*, argued forcefully that top executives and department managers should both participate in the setting of each other's goals. Those department managers should then do the same with managers one level down, and so on through the organization. This was a key element of one of Drucker's biggest ideas: "management by objectives." Each level must fit their own objectives into the level above them, and the only way to do that is to participate in setting both. Otherwise, the objectives you set will stray from the overall company objectives.

This makes perfect sense. Once again, though, we face the old problem of how you decide on the content of your objective. Alas, Drucker gives no help on that, other than the usual advice to know your customer and the trends of your industry. So you organize a meeting where two levels of executives meet to set objectives for both. That's a good start. Now what do you do, once you're in the room? How exactly do you get an idea for what goal to set? Drucker doesn't say. Ten years later, his *Managing for Results* gives a bit more guidance: you need an "entrepreneurial idea" that overcomes "restraints" that face the business, corrects the "imbalances" of the business—such as the wrong size—and turns "threats" into opportunities. But once again these are problems—restraints, imbalances, threats—with no method to solve them.

Since Drucker's 1954 call for different levels to set goals together, a whole specialized field of practice has grown up where internal and external consultants run participatory strategic planning sessions for companies. Unfortunately, they don't solve the core problem of how you determine the content of an objective. Instead, they concentrate on the participatory method itself. Here's an example, compiled from a small set of firms that specialize in this kind of planning. I don't name them here because I don't want to pick on anyone in particular. Hundreds, perhaps thousands of facilitators make exactly the same mistake.

Here are the steps:

1. *Design*: Agreement on pathway and process for moving forward
2. *Problem*: Agreement of what the problem is and why
3. *Vision*: Agreement on image of the ideal future state
4. *Solution*: Agreement on solution(s) that everyone is willing to support
5. *Implementation*: Agreement on an action plan for implementing the decision

The facilitators propose Step 1, which the participants then discuss, amend, and agree on. Steps 2–4 are pure brainstorming, where everyone throws out ideas that you then rank and vote on. For Step 5, you typically divide into sub-teams by function, with some kind of full-group endorsement of each piece at the end. Notice the only word that repeats in each step: *agreement*. The aim of this method is not to come up with a creative idea for strategy, but for the people in the room to agree on a strategy.

Of course agreement is a good thing. But it's not the same as a creative idea. Unfortunately, "management by objectives" often becomes "management by committee," where instead of a creative idea you get the most popular idea. And innovations, by definition, are unpopular in some or many quarters of a company. Change hurts, more for some than others. Remember again the Parker story: if Washkewicz had used this participatory method, the group would never have come up with a retail strategy that transformed their core business so dramatically.

But most companies that use participatory strategic planning don't aim for innovation in the first place. They set financial targets—like "grow revenue in each division by 15 percent"—and then do a round of participatory strategic planning to push those targets down through the organization in the form of action and financial plans for each unit. Top executives then review each set of plans yearly or quarterly. Everyone spends a lot of time setting and reporting on goals. They all hate it, but they keep doing it, thinking it's the right thing to do. The result is that there is no time, and no method, for coming up with creative ideas for strategy at any level.

Creative strategy, by contrast, aims specifically for creative ideas. It can be as participatory as you want to make it, and it gives a good start to planning as well. But it has one disadvantage: it takes time. Participatory strategic planning typically takes up one or two full days, and that's it. You write up the results and get back to work. To use creative strategy instead, you have to start weeks or even months ahead of the due date, and the search itself takes up more total time than a single workshop. Creative strategy saves lots of time on the front end, when many firms do elaborate analysis before their planning workshops.

But it's not really the amount of clock time that matters so much, it's the mental energy to think about strategy. Most executives don't have "mental time" for creative strategy. They're busy. Participatory strategic planning lets them think about strategy only two days a year, in a way that does not push them to have creative thoughts in any meaningful way. Participatory strategy planning amounts to exactly the kind of "busy work" that most executives find very easy to do. Perhaps that's the true reason it's popular. If so, that makes it a huge obstacle to adopting creative strategy.

Scenario Planning

In 1973, several Arab oil exporters cut supplies to the United States and Western Europe because of their support for Israel in the Yom Kippur War. Thanks to Pierre Wack, head of corporate planning at Shell, the company had already made contingency plans for a dramatic rise in the price of oil. The other oil companies were caught by surprise. In just a few years, Shell went from the eighth largest to the second largest oil company in the world.

Since Wack's 1973 success, "scenario planning" has become a common strategy method in the business world. That's a good thing—if it entails the same kind of contingency planning that Wack did at Shell. You make predictions on several scenarios you think might happen in the future, and then decide whether any of them is likely enough or important enough to warrant current actions or at least contingency plans. Note that scenario planning does not help you create the content of those actions or plans. For that you need creative strategy, as usual.

Unfortunately, some companies make the same mistake with scenario planning as others make with competitive strategy. You do your scenario analysis, and then brainstorm actions and plans. Or, your "analysis" or "scenarios" or "research" mysteriously produces actions and plans without any explicit steps that show where those actions and plans came from.

Again, some scenario planners might do a version of creative strategy: after they lay out their scenarios, they search widely for precedents on key elements of the problem to arrive at a creative combination for actions or plans. The result is one insight matrix for each scenario. The discipline of precedents makes the scenarios more realistic, and the multiple scenarios reflect the uncertain reality you face.

Scientific Method

So many innovations start with breakthroughs in science. The transistor, for example, led to countless innovations in modern electronics. Scientists use the scientific method. So innovators in any field should use the scientific method too. Right?

Right. But you might need to change your idea of how the scientific method works. Many people think that the scientific method begins with a hypothesis. Then you conduct an experiment to confirm or disprove your hypothesis. If the results disprove it, you come up with another hypothesis and test that.

All well and good, but that's not the scientific method. It's the experimental method. The scientific method has many parts, and the experimental method is just one of them. Certainly experiments are vital. But the scientific method begins well before you make a hypothesis that starts your experiment. For example, how do you come up with a hypothesis? What's the method for that?

Let's ask the founder of the scientific method, Roger Bacon, from thirteenth-century England. Here's what he says: "At first one should believe those who have made experiments or who have faithful testimony from others who have done so . . . experience follows second, and reason comes third."

Look where Bacon tells you to look first: in the laboratories of other scientists. In other words, what works? Next comes your own "experience." By this Bacon means your own experiments. Third, you try to fit together what came out of the first two steps. The hypothesis for your own experiment comes from your scan of what other scientists have done before you. That's why science advances, rather than each new scientist reinventing the wheel with a hypothesis you dream up out of thin air.

The scientific method does not tell us exactly how to get from the results of previous scientists to your own hypothesis. For that we look to Thomas Kuhn's *Structure of Scientific Revolutions*, about how scientific breakthroughs actually happen, by "flashes of insight." They are creative combinations of what other scientists found, plus new observations about the natural world that better tools produce. For example, Galileo's innovations came from combining a new Dutch invention, the telescope, with the calculations of Copernicus, which in turn came from combining an old idea of the Greek Aristarchus, new tools of trigonometry from previous decades, and the celestial data of Ptolemy.

From this understanding of how science advances, we can conclude that creative strategy is a form of the scientific method.

SWOT

What's the most widely used method of strategic analysis in the business world? We have no way to know for sure, but my guess is SWOT: strengths, weaknesses, opportunities, threats. Lots of companies realize they should do some kind of analysis before brainstorming "solutions," but competitive strategy, scenario planning, blue ocean strategy and most other forms of analysis are a huge amount of work. Instead, you can do SWOT analysis in a single brainstorming session. Then you follow that with another session to brainstorm solutions. Problem solved!

From the view of creative strategy, of course, this formula is massively misconceived. The fault lies with the second part: brainstorming solutions. SWOT is a valid method of analysis if afterward you do creative strategy. You can even do more formal analysis, like competitive strategy, and then plug that into the four categories of SWOT. Then try to convert a strength into an innovation problem for the top of the insight matrix, then a weakness, then an opportunity, and then a threat. One or more of these problems might give you a good place to start.

Some companies use SWOT not to determine an overall strategy but to help plan for an objective they've already set. That's fine, as long as you remember that SWOT is a method of analysis only. It does not produce a creative idea, an innovation, or even a strategy. For that, do creative strategy next.

Systems Thinking

In economics they warn you about "partial analysis"—that is, you leave an important factor out of your equation. In strategic thinking, the parallel is systems thinking—that is, include all important factors in your strategic analysis. And note how they interact: one part affects another part, which affects a third part, and so on through the whole system.

This is excellent advice. But as with strategic analysis in general, it does not give you an innovation. It helps you understand your situation. That's all.

Peter Senge calls systems thinking the "fifth discipline" in his popular book of the same name. Systems thinking plus four other disciplines are key skills for the "learning organization," which innovates through constant change to your interconnected company system. Everybody is connected to one another and to the outside world, so new problems lead to rapid innovations where the whole company adjusts to the new reality as one smooth system.

This all sounds good, but again we miss a crucial step. How exactly does systems thinking, and everyone communicating well with one another within the system, produce an innovation? The missing link is creative strategy. Systems thinking helps you understand the problem and its elements on the insight matrix. Good communication means you can form teams quickly and easily to do creative strategy formally or informally as problems arise, and you can implement the innovation more easily because everyone understands it.

So ends our review of strategy methods that compete with creative strategy. We saw that most of them are actually methods of strategic analysis; they do not tell you how to get a strategic idea for what to do. As with competing creativity methods, some of these strategy methods can be compatible with creative strategy, like competitive strategy or SWOT. You can use your favorite method of strategic analysis to identify your most important strategic problem, and then use creative strategy to solve it.

Make sure not to carry your analysis forward into the idea itself—that is, don't lay out your analytical framework and then fill it in with strategic actions, even if those actions come from elements that worked elsewhere. Once your analysis gives you a strategic problem, follow the steps of creative strategy: break the problem into parts, search widely for elements that fit each part, revise your list of parts and sources as needed, and end with creative combination.

References

Here you will find a set of miscellaneous materials that give more background to creative strategy. The first section is a brief summary of the method that you might want to use as a reference guide as you proceed through it. The second section is a review of the sources I found in my own what-works scan of strategy and innovation. These sources enabled me to put together the idea of strategic intuition that creative strategy puts into practice. The last section lists books and articles I refer to in the text.

Creative Strategy at a Glance

Purpose

Creative strategy is method for innovation of all kinds, in three parts: Phase 1 breaks down a problem into elements, Phase 2 scans sources to find precedents that fit each element, and Phase 3 combines a subset of those precedents to solve the problem.

In contrast, conventional innovation methods typically have two steps: first, in-depth research and analysis about the problem; and second, brainstorming a solution. This yields strong analysis and weak solutions.

Creative strategy reverses the emphasis; it quickly mines your own understanding of the problem and then spends more time searching widely for solutions. That's how most innovation actually happens: creative combination from new sources.

Participants

Creative Strategy Team

These are the people who will carry though all three steps of the method. Sometimes the team has senior members who do more of Phase 1 and junior members who do more of Phase 2. The whole team joins in Phase 3. Diversity of work and life experience is a big plus for team composition.

Innovation Leaders

These are the people who will decide on and head the innovation initiative that results from the method. Sometimes the decision makers are different from the innovation heads, and sometimes it takes time to identify them all. Innovation leaders are most important in Phase 1.

Key Informants

These are people inside and outside the company who have special insight into the problem, or good leads for sources to scan, or insight into the precedents you discover. Innovation leaders are all key informants too. Key informants are most important in Phases 1 and 2.

Innovation Staff

These are the people within the company who will implement the innovation idea that results from the method. Some or all of the innovation leaders, and some key informants, are part of this group. As a group the innovation staff participate only in Phase 3.

> *Note:* In small companies, it is possible for the creative strategy team, innovation leaders, and innovation staff to be all the same people.

Activities

Phase 1	Phase 2	Phase 3
Rapid appraisal	What-works scan	Creative combination

Creative Strategy Phases

Phase 1: Rapid Appraisal

In brief interviews with innovation leaders and key informants, and quick study of documents and data they cite, you pin down the problem: Where do you most need to innovate? Then together you break down the problem into smaller parts, including the key obstacles to overcome. These parts are the elements of the puzzle you need to solve.

Phase 2: What-Works Scan

You search the world for sources, which are companies and organizations that have solved any elements of the puzzle in different situations. You find out exactly what worked for which elements, why, and how you might adapt these precedents to your own problem. This phase takes up most of your time.

Phase 3: Creative Combination

You condense the best elements you found in the scan and lead a workshop for whoever will implement the innovation. In the workshop, participants select and combine a subset of precedents to arrive at the innovation, and start a plan for how to implement the new idea. The selected precedents give you the basic outline of the plan.

Insight Matrix

This is the main organizing tool for all three phases of creative strategy.

Phase 1: The problem goes at the top and the elements of the problem are the rows.

Phase 2: The sources for the search are the columns, and precedents you find are the cells.

Phase 3: Selected cells make your creative combination.

The following model matrix shows only seven sources (S) and five elements (E), but in reality the chart continues with as many columns and rows as you need. Here we see twenty-two precedents (X) found. The seven circled precedents are the creative combination. Planning begins with whatever data and activities come with those seven precedents.

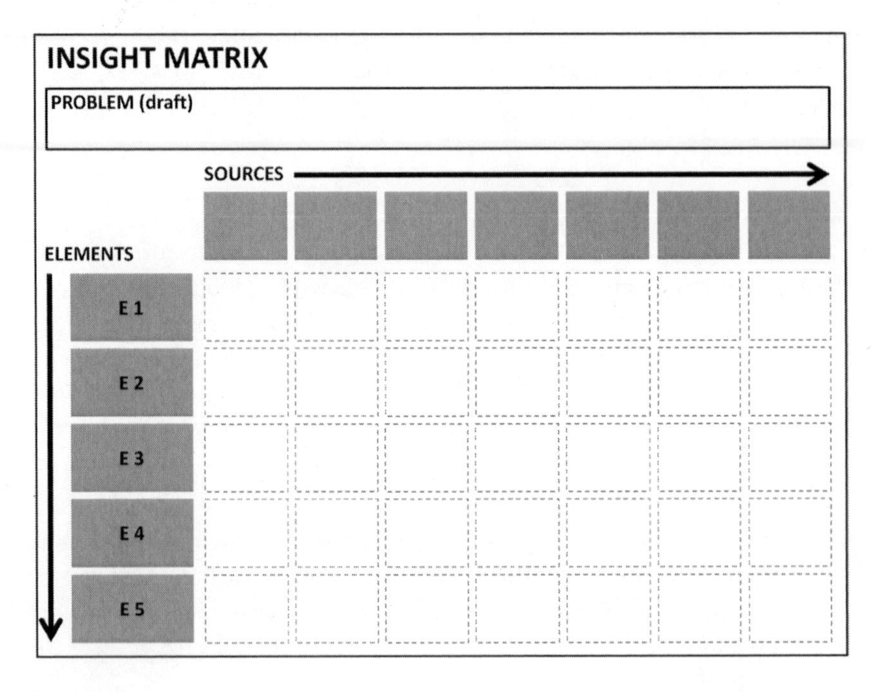

Figure A.1
Phase 1: rapid appraisal.

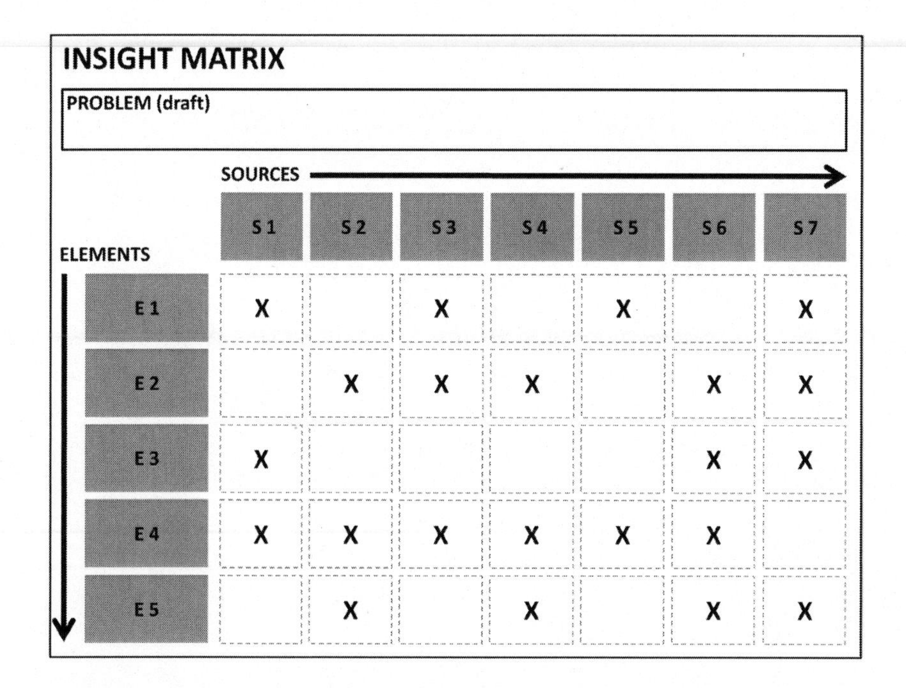

Figure A.2
Phase 2: what-works scan.

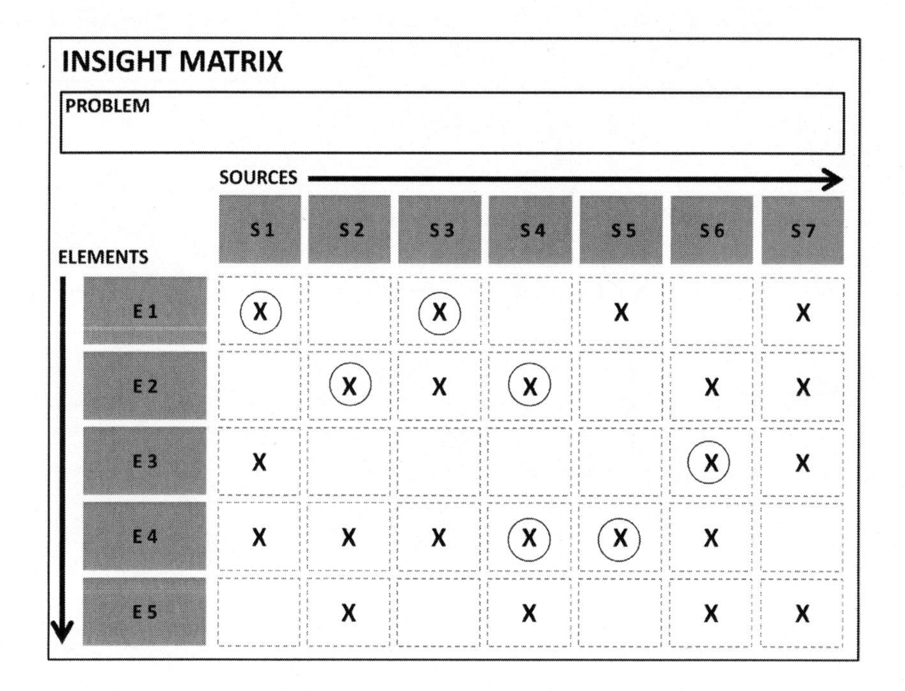

Figure A.3
Phase 3: creative combination.

Phase 1: Rapid Appraisal

Purpose and Participants

This phase identifies what problem your innovation needs to solve and breaks the problem down into elements. It includes interviews with key leaders and informants and the study of documents and data about the problem. The creative strategy team interviews innovation leaders and other key informants, to state the problem and break it down into its elements, and to elicit from them leads for other key informants and sources to scan. The interviews point to documents and data that the team consults for more insight into the problem and leads for the scan.

Actions

Identification

Identify innovation leaders who will decide on or lead the implementation of the innovation. This is often an executive team for the division or other unit of the company that has the problem. Sometimes the problem spans divisions, for example, marketing and finance, so include key leaders from all relevant units.

Interviews

Ask the innovation leaders what they think the problem is and what the obstacles are to solving it. Get a history of the problem within the company, including any previous attempts to solve it. Show them your matrix with draft statements of the problem and its elements. Convert obstacles they mention into problem elements. Ask if they have ideas for sources and key informants. The interviews can be in person, by phone or e-mail, or via videoconference.

Documents and Data

Ask interviewees for reports, memos, studies, customer research, websites, or other materials that might help describe and explain the problem and its elements or might point you to sources and other informants. The team does not create new documents or collect new data.

Introductions

For each person you interview, you need an introduction from a key leader who has already agreed to and approved the creative strategy project. The introduction can be in person at a meeting, by phone, or most typically by e-mail. The introduction should include the interview purpose: to understand the problem and its elements in order to guide a what-works scan.

Iteration

After a few interviews, the problem and its elements are often different from when you began. You also identify internal experts on the problem not on your first list. That means another round or two of interviews. You may have to revise the problem and its elements.

Insight Matrix

You show your draft insight matrix at each interview and alter it as you proceed. When you get approval of your final draft of the problem and elements at this stage, make sure key leaders know that these can change depending on what you find in the what-works scan.

Evidence

At each interview, ask for evidence to help you understand both the problem and how the informants see it.

Phase 2: What-Works Scan

Purpose and Participants

In this phase, the creative strategy team interviews key informants and researches sources inside and outside the industry in search of elements that solve the different elements of the problem. The team spends most if its time on this phase.

Actions

Teamwork

The creative strategy team divides up the search, by elements or sources or both, and agrees how and when to update one another as they proceed. One person keeps a master matrix to record all the updates.

Start

The best place to start the scan is with the evidence, key informants, and sources that key leaders named in the rapid appraisal. One clue leads to another.

Documents and Data

Scan reports, memos, and studies for examples of successful elements, and for mention of other evidence, key informants, and sources to investigate next. Some evidence helps you evaluate elements in order to judge whether and how they actually work. Make sure to review the business press and academic literature at least five years back for precedent leads.

Key Informants

Ask key informants for examples of successful elements and for ideas about other key informants, sources, and evidence to investigate. Some key informants help you evaluate elements in order to judge whether and how they actually work.

Sources

Information on sources comes from key informants and from all the documents and other material you encounter in your search. For each source, you want to pinpoint precedents that produced an effect for that source similar to the effect you want it to have for your relevant problem element.

Write-Up

For each promising precedent you find, write up a one-page sheet: description, why you think it works for the source, and how it might apply to your own innovation problem.

Iteration

As you scan, your understanding of the problem and its elements might change. Revise the insight matrix accordingly. For major changes to the problem statement, check back with innovation leaders.

Note: In some cases, the creative strategy team might do creative combination during the scan:

- If the team includes innovation leaders and innovation staff
- If the innovation leaders want a report with recommendations rather than a workshop

Phase 3: Creative Combination

Purpose and Participants

In this phase, the creative strategy team helps innovation staff complete two steps: select and combine a subset of precedents from the what-works scan that solves the innovation problem, and begin planning how to implement the new idea.

Actions

Workshop Preparation

Send participants these preworkshop materials ahead of time:

- The insight matrix with the problem, elements, and sources filled in and X's for matrix cells where you found at least one element
- A write-up of the problem and elements
- A one-page sheet on each element: a description of its source, why you think it works for the source, and how you might adapt it to your own problem

Workshop Agenda

Day 1: Morning

- Full-group introduction and review of preworkshop materials
  Remind the group that this is not a brainstorming session; the group should propose an idea that is not on the element list and write up a one-page sheet in the same format.
- First breakout session
  Each small group takes the first two elements and selects elements most feasible and worthwhile to adopt, writes briefly why, and articulates any preliminary ideas on implementation.

Day 1: Afternoon

- Second breakout session
  Each small group takes the next two elements and selects elements most feasible and worthwhile to adopt, writes briefly why, and articulates any preliminary ideas on implementation.
- Full-group reports and discussion

Day 1: Overnight

- Insight matrix summary
  Facilitators put selected elements into a summary insight matrix and revise and compile the one-page sheets for each element.

Day 2: Morning

- Full-group reviews and discusses overnight materials
- Third breakout session
  Each small group reviews and discusses overnight materials and proposes edits (add, delete, change).
- Full-group reports and discussion

Day 2: Afternoon

- Fourth breakout session
  Small groups divide by function and expertise to start a preliminary action plan on the elements most relevant to them: who does what next, when, for each element.
- Full-group reports and workshop conclusion

Sources

Here I present the sources I found in my own what-works scan for how to get creative ideas for strategy, plus some more recent sources. Some of these references appear in the main body of the book as well. They are gathered here and sorted by field.

History of Science

The great work here is Thomas Kuhn's *Structure of Scientific Revolutions.* Kuhn shows how scientific breakthroughs actually happen, as a form of creative combination from what others have done before.

We noted in the section on "Scientific Method" that the method's founder, Roger Bacon, gives similar advice.

Isaac Newton named his sources and told us: "If I have seen farther, it is by standing on the shoulders of giants."

Sir Peter Medawar, winner of the 1960 Nobel Prize in Physiology or Medicine, agrees: "Everything that a scientist does is a function of what others have done before him: the past is embodied in every new conception and even in the possibility of its being conceived at all."

Einstein is a good example. His theory of special relativity—famously $E = mc^2$—combined the achievements of these five scientists:

Hendrik Lorentz, the Netherlands—transformation equations for light speed
Ernst Mach, Austria—relativity of mass to speed
James Clerk Maxwell, Scotland—light as energy and mass
Hermann Minkowski, Germany—space-time equations
Henri Poincaré, France—relativity of time

Neuroscience

The turning point for the new theory of learning-and-memory was a 1998 paper by Brenda Milner, Larry Squire, and Eric Kandel, "Cognitive Neuroscience and the Study of Memory." Squire and Kandel followed up the next year with a book, *Memory: From Mind to Molecules.* And the year after that, 2000, Kandel won the Nobel Prize. Other neuroscientists have since written books on the subject for a general audience: Barry Gordon and Lisa Berger, *Intelligent Memory*, and Gerald Edelman, *Wider than the Sky.*

For the neuroscience of presence of mind, see Sharon Begley's 2007 book, *Train Your Mind, Change your Brain.* For a review of more recent research, see William Duggan and Malia Mason, "Strategic Intuition," in *Handbook of Intuition Research* by Marta Sinclair.

Further back, Seiji Ogawa presented his first MRI breakthroughs in a 1990 paper to the National Academy of Sciences, "Brain Magnetic Resonance Imaging with Contrast Depending on Blood Oxygenation."

Psychology

Despite the advances of learning-and-memory in neuroscience, the left-right brain continues to dominate cognitive psychology, which is the behavioral study of how people think. In this tradition, Daniel Kahneman won the 2001 Nobel Prize in Economics for his laboratory studies on the two classic modes of thought, reasoning and intuition. He wrote up his work in a popular book, *Thinking: Fast and Slow.* Kahneman runs clever classroom experiments where he gives subjects mathematical puzzles to solve, and the subjects consistently make the same mistakes. To Kahneman, this shows that their intuition was faulty: if they had thought more about the puzzle, using reason, they would have gotten the right answer.

Unfortunately, Kahneman's research doesn't apply to strategy, creativity, or innovation—or indeed any real-world situation where the right answer is not subject to mathematical proof. In the real world, you have to make a series of educated guesses that depend on your own learning-and-memory. The "guess" part uses your intuition. Learning-and-memory lets us recast Kahneman's model to "Intuition: Fast and Slow." Expert intuition is fast, and strategic intuition is slow. You cannot solve a real-world problem without one or the other, or sometimes both.

Herbert Simon's early studies of expert thinking helped win him the Nobel Prize in Economic Sciences in 1978. A more recent pioneer of expert intuition is Gary Klein. His 1998 book, *Sources of Power*, reports on his studies of experts in action: firefighters, emergency room nurses, and soldiers in battle. For the first time, a research psychologist explained how intuition works in terms that fit the advances in learning-and-memory, although Klein did not know that at the time. It's fitting that his book came out in the same year, 1998, as the breakthrough paper on learning-and-memory by Milner, Squire, and Kandel.

Klein's work on expert intuition has drawn a substantial following in the past decade among other cognitive psychologists. My own work on strategic intuition is solidly in Klein's footsteps, and in his debt.

Military Strategy

The great work here is *On War* by Carl von Clausewitz. It first appeared in 1932 and has remained in print ever since. Military academies around the world still use it, and so do many university courses in political science.

Clausewitz has his fans in business strategy too. Three of them from Boston Consulting Group's Strategy Institute published a book in 2001 that selected excerpts from *On War* that are most useful for a business audience: *Clausewitz on Strategy*. The first set of excerpts is on *coup d'oeil*—that is, flashes of insight. We also see a clear emphasis on *coup d'oeil* by Ulrike Kleemeier in her chapter, "Moral Forces in War," in a 2007 book, *Clausewitz in the Twentieth Century*, edited by Hew Strachan and Andreas Herberg-Rothe.

But these cases are rare. Most scholars of Clausewitz concentrate on his views of strategic analysis rather than of strategic thinking, as in the *coup d'oeil*. For a recent application of Clausewitz to military thinking, see a 2005 monograph I wrote for the U.S. Army War College, "Coup d'Oeil: Strategic Intuition in Army Planning."

Asian Philosophy

Four Asian traditions describe aspects of creative strategy: Hindu, Buddhist, Dao, and Zen. Over the centuries and across vast regions, each of these philosophies has developed its own rich and diverse tradition. Here we single out just a few works that relate most closely to the key step of presence of mind.

The *Bhagavad Gita* from ancient India is a sacred text of Hinduism that gives the philosophy of yoga. The Gita is a war story: in the middle of the battle, the god Krishna lectures the warrior Arjuna. One of the early uses of yoga was training for soldiers: if you've done yoga, you know the warrior pose. One of the key disciplines of yoga is presence of mind, which meditation promotes.

In northern India, the Hindu Siddhartha founded Buddhism, which spread a few centuries later to China. There it met the Dao. Two great works of philosophical Dao, the *Dao De Jing* of Lao Zi and *The Art of War* by Sun Zi, both discourse on presence of mind. A blend of Buddhism and Dao became known as Zen in Japan. There, Miyamoto Musashi's *Book of Five Rings* gives another lesson in presence of mind.

We come full circle to Sharon Begley's book, *Train Your Mind, Change Your Brain*, cited above under "Neuroscience." She reports on brain scans of Buddhist monks, to pinpoint the mental mechanism of presence of mind. See also my article in the *Peking University Business Review*, January 2008, "Strategic Intuition: East Meets West in the Executive Mind." And these are the principal sources for personal strategy: presence of mind gives you better ideas, but it also makes you happier and healthier. For this angle, see also *The Art of Happiness*, a book by the Dalai Lama and an American psychiatrist, Howard Cutler.

Business Innovation

In the middle of the twentieth century, the great economist Joseph Schumpeter portrayed innovation as the key force of economic growth. We can see elements of creative strategy in his essays, "The Creative Response in Economic History," "Change and the Entrepreneur," "The Instability of Capitalism," and "The Process of Creative Destruction." For Schumpeter, the entrepreneur is an innovator who operates at any level of an organization, from start-up to maturity, and on any aspect of the business. New combinations from previous achievements, which defy prediction by previous analysis, are the heart of Schumpeter's view of how innovation really happens.

We can find other glimpses of creative strategy in the business literature, back as far as James Webb Young's 1940 marketing handbook *A Technique for Producing Ideas*. Webb's technique is very much creative combination. Henry Mintzberg's 1994 book, *The Rise and Fall of Strategic Planning*, criticized all methods of strategic analysis, most famously Porter's competitive strategy. But to see how business innovation really happens, we must dive into the sources that chronicle the innovations themselves.

For Google, we have *The Google Guys* by David Vise and Mark Malseed. For Louis Gerstner's transformation of IBM, see his own *Who Says Elephants Can't Dance?* For early Microsoft, there's *Hard Drive* by James Wallace and Jim Erickson. Howard Schultz tells his own Starbucks story in *Pour Your Heart Into It*. Ray Kroc does the same for McDonald's in *Grinding It Out*. And so on through successful innovations across the business world. Each of these books gives us enough of the story to see where the innovators got their ideas.

For other innovations, we can piece the story together from various sources, for example, a series of short articles on Rose Marie Bravo tells us how she got her idea to turn around Burberry's. For most innovations, we have no record. The innovators do not tell us how they came up with their ideas. But wherever we are able to find out, the answer is the same: creative combination. Sometimes we just get the pieces the innovator put together, but sometimes we get the flash of insight too, for example, Schultz in a Milan coffee bar or Kroc when he first saw the McDonald brothers' hamburger stand in San Bernardino, California.

The inspiration for the insight matrix came from Steve Kerr, GE's first chief learning officer in the 1990s. He took the Trotter Matrix, which Lloyd Trotter used for tracking what worked in his factory division, and used it to help with the what-works scan at GE's Crotonville campus. Robert Slater cites the Trotter Matrix in *Jack Welch and the GE Way*. Details of Kerr's version come from interviews in 2002, after Kerr left GE for Goldman Sachs.

Social Enterprise

The sources for innovation in social enterprise are similar to business examples: you find creative combination, and sometimes the flash of insight too, in various sources that tell the story. So for Muhammad Yunus and the founding of microfinance, we have his own book, *Banker to the Poor*. For the strategy of nonviolent disobedience that ended legal segregation in the United States, we have *Parting the Waters* by Taylor Branch. *Uphill with Banners Flying* by Inez Irwin tells how Alice Paul led the campaign that won American women the vote.

Again, most innovations in social enterprise remain mysterious: we have no record of how the innovators got their ideas. But wherever we can piece together the story, it's creative strategy again and again.

The techniques of rapid appraisal came mostly from social enterprise, especially in the field of international economic development. The key pioneer was Robert Chambers, who first described the method in a 1992 paper for the Institute of Development Studies in Sussex, England. The method is now widespread in that field.

Art

Many people see art as the most creative human activity. In one way, finding creative strategy in art is very simple: study exactly the sequence of a single artist's work to see what resembles at each stage the subject or style or medium of previous works. Art historians do this all the time. For example, Stephen Greenblatt's *Will in the World* cites key sources for many of Shakespeare's major plays. And Daniel Wakin tells us about Mozart and the Czech composer Josef Mysliveček:

> "Mozart was indeed a master imitator, capable of working in a wide variety of styles," Maynard Solomon writes in his biography, *Mozart: A Life*. It was a skill Mozart was proud of. In Mysliveček, Mozart found a model of the Italianate style and its graceful melodies and elegant rhythms. He borrowed ideas from Mysliveček's works for his first opera seria, "Mitridate," and themes for early symphonies of his own. He arranged a Mysliveček aria, which became the popular "Ridente la calma," and was for a time considered the composer of Mysliveček's oratoria "Abramo ed Isacco."

But to find artists themselves citing their own sources, that's much harder. Either they don't leave any record of where their ideas came from, or they claim what they did came purely from their own imaginations. As with business innovation, in those cases where we are able to track down the details, we typically find creative combination.

Some artists admit it. T. S. Eliot, the British-American poet, won the Nobel Prize in Literature in 1948. He said, "Immature poets imitate. Mature poets steal." Jim Jarmusch, a modern filmmaker known as an innovator, said this:

> Nothing is original. Steal from anywhere . . . Devour old films, new films, music, books, paintings, photographs, poems, bridges, street signs, trees, clouds, bodies of water, light and shadows. . . . And don't bother concealing your thievery—celebrate it if you feel like it. In any case, always remember what Jean-Luc Godard said: "It's not where you take things from—it's where you take them to."

Yet this honesty—and humility—are rare. Harold Bloom became one of the world's best-known literary critics thanks to his book *The Anxiety of Influence*, about how past achievements are both a blessing and a curse: they give you plenty to steal, but if you steal too much, you are a copy-cat, not an artist. Most artists solve the problem by taking from more than one source, as Jarmusch counsels. As a child prodigy, Mozart performed throughout Europe and learned all its various styles of music. Mysliveček was only one of many composers and musicians Mozart borrowed from in his works.

Education

John Dewey pioneered "creative" education more than a century ago. He led a shift from traditional to progressive methods that you find today, especially in the United States, from nursery school through graduate school. Instead of lecturing students on theories and facts, the teacher guides them in self-directed discovery. There are many variations on this theme. The Harvard case method is perhaps the most famous example.

Unfortunately, Dewey renounced most of these methods later in his career. His 1916 book *Democracy and Education* launched the progressive education movement, and his 1938 book *Experience and Education* criticized it. But it was too late. The movement had already spread through schools of education especially, that to this day continue to graduate legions of teachers eager to put Dewey's methods into practice.

Dewey's 1938 critique was simple. He intended his methods for kindergarten and the early grades, when you had to introduce new material "progressively" to children, following their own interests. That was the only way to hold their attention. At each higher grade, you progressively introduced more traditional forms of instruction that covered the "basic material" that all children need to learn.

And where does that basic material come from? Here is Dewey's answer: "[T]he achievements of the past provide the only means at command for understanding the present."

Contrast this with the first guide to the Harvard case method, *The Case Method of Instruction*, of 1931:

> Education . . . deals with the oncoming new in human experience rather than with the departing old. . . . The . . . accumulation of human experience is inevitably the taking of what is given rather than the creation of what is new. If we teach people to deal with the new in experience, we teach them to think. . . . In any event, all a teacher can hope to do is to develop, first, an appreciation of the almost infinite complexity of modern business problems, second, the hopelessness of reaching a definitive and unequivocal solution, and third . . . the solution of this dilemma by some carefully reasoned but, in the end, common-sense line of action.

Now we can understand why Harvard cases warn the reader not to take the case as an "example from history." In progressive education, the past is no guide to the future. That's why Dewey eventually rebelled against his own followers.

For creative education in science, we turn to Thomas Kuhn. At the end of his study of creative leaps in science, *The Structure of Scientific Revolutions*, Kuhn offers advice on training future scientists. Coincidentally—or not?—Kuhn went to a progressive school as a child, and his parents were shocked to find that the school never taught him to read. He was already in second grade. So they did it themselves.

Kuhn criticizes traditional science education for teaching only the results of successful experiments—for example, how radium atoms decay—plus the experimental method of designing experiments to confirm hypotheses. This leaves out the most important piece: how Marie and Pierre Curie came up with their hypothesis that radium atoms decay. Kuhn wants science students to study in detail the "examples from history" that led to creative leaps. That's the best way for them to learn how to make such leaps themselves.

So too in all fields, not just science. And that takes us full circle. If your field is innovation, you learn how to do it by studying examples from history, which are the details of how past innovators got their ideas. And that leads us to creative strategy.

ACKNOWLEDGMENTS

I would like to thank the following companies and organizations for helping me to pilot the ideas and methods found in this book:

Abdul Latif Jameel (Saudi Arabia), Amazon, Army Research Institute, Association for Strategic Planning, Aviva (UK), BearingPoint, Becton Dickinson, Bibby Financial Services, Booz + Co., Capitaland (Singapore), Cheung Kong GSB (China), Clariden (Singapore), CNAM (France), Crain Communications, Deloitte, Deutsche Bank (Germany), Eckerd Family Foundation, The Economist (UK), Eisai (Japan), Ericsson (Sweden), Exetor, Federal Home Loan of Seattle, Finance Development Training Institute, GIBS (South Africa), Grant Thornton, HEC (France), Hewlett-Packard, IIPM (India), IMAX, Interdisciplinary Center (Israel), Investment Industry Association (Canada), KAIST (Korea), LendLease (Australia), Marketing Executives Networking Group, Microsoft, MILE (Saudi Arabia), NADAV Fund (Israel), NASA, National Black MBA Association, Navigant Consulting, National Black MBA Association, New York City Department of Education, Nokia (Finland), Novartis (Switzerland), Novozymes (Denmark), OCBC Bank (Singapore), Ogilvy & Mather, Ohio Banker's League, L'Oréal, Pension Real Estate Association, Research Affiliates, Siam Cement (Thailand), Siemens (Germany), Skadden, Sony Music, Special Libraries

Association, Statoil (Norway), TEDxEast, Truliant, TUM (Germany), UN Federal Credit Union, US Army War College, Vestas (Denmark), Virgin Mobile (UK), WHU (Germany), World Economic Forum (Switzerland), Young Presidents' Organization, Ziff Brothers Investments.

I would also like to thank the following individuals for their ideas and help in developing and piloting creative strategy: Amy D'Onofrio, Lynn Ellsworth, Ken Favaro, Jasmin Franz, Shirley Grill, Paul Ingram, Kevin Kelly, Steve Kerr, Maurice Lam, Jim Schrager, and Nadim Yacteen.

Last but not least, I owe a great debt to Myles Thompson for his editorial guidance and to Bridget Flannery-McCoy for her intellectual and technical contributions to the book as a whole.

BIBLIOGRAPHY

Aeppel, Timothy, "Changing the Formula: Seeking Perfect Prices, CEO Tears Up the Rules," *Wall Street Journal*, March 27, 2007.

Andrew, James, Manget, Joe, Michael, David, Taylor, Andrew, and Zablit, Hadi, *Innovation 2010*, Boston Consulting Group, April 2010.

Beatty, Sally, "Boss Talk: Plotting Plaid's Future," *Wall Street Journal*, September 9, 2004.

Begley, Sharon, *Train Your Mind, Change Your Brain*, New York: Ballantine, 2007.

Bossidy, Larry, and Charan, Ram, *Execution: The Discipline of Getting Things Done*, New York: Crown Business, 2002.

Branch, Taylor, *Parting the Waters*, New York: Simon and Schuster, 1988.

Businessweek Online, "Rose Marie Bravo, Burberry," January 12, 2004.

Chambers, Robert, "Rural Appraisal," Discussion Paper, Institute of Development Studies, University of Sussex, December 1992.

Chesbrough, Henry, *Open Innovation*, Oxford: Oxford University Press, 2006.

Christensen, Clayton, *The Innovator's Dilemma*, Boston: Harvard Business School Press, 1997.

Christensen, Clayton, and Raynor, Michael, *The Innovator's Solution*, Boston: Harvard Business School Press, 2003.

Chua, Roy, Morris, Michael, and Ingram, Paul, "Embeddedness and New Idea Discussion in Professional Networks," *Journal of Creative Behavior*, 44, 2, 2010.

Collins, Jim, *Good to Great*, New York: HarperBusiness, 2001.

Covey, Steven, *Seven Habits of Highly Effective People*, Free Press, 1989.

Dalai Lama, and Cutler, Howard, *The Art of Happiness*, New York: Riverhead, 1998.

deBono, Edward, *Lateral Thinking*, New York: Harper Colophon, 1973.

——. *Six Thinking Hats*, New York: Little Brown and Co., 1985.

Drucker, Peter, *Managing for Results*, New York: Harper & Row, 1964.

——. *The Practice of Management*, New York: Harper & Row, 1954.

Duggan, William, *The Art of What Works*, New York: McGraw-Hill, 2003.

——. "Coup d'Oeil: Strategic Intuition in Army Planning," Strategic Studies Institute, U.S. Army War College, 2005.

——. *Napoleon's Glance*, New York: Nation, 2002.

——. *Strategic Intuition*, New York: Columbia Business School Publishing, 2007.

——. "Strategic Intuition: East Meets West in the Executive Mind," *Peking University Business Review*, January 2008.

Duggan, William, and Mason, Malia, "Strategic Intuition," in Marta Sinclair, editor, *Handbook of Intuition Research*, Cheltenham, UK: Edward Elgar, 2011.

Easwaran, Eknath, *The Bhagavad Gita*, New York: Vintage, 2000.

Edelman, Gerald, *Wider than the Sky*, New Haven, Conn.: Yale University Press, 2004.

Gerstner, Louis, *Who Says Elephants Can't Dance?* New York: HarperCollins, 2002.

Gillmore, Inez, *The Story of Alice Paul and the National Woman's Party*, Fairfax, Va.: Denlinger's, 1977.

Gladwell, Malcolm, *Blink*, New York: Little, Brown, 2005.

Goldenberg, Jacob, and Mazursky, David, *Creativity in Product Innovation*, New York: Cambridge University Press, 2002.

Gordon, Barry, and Berger, Lisa, *Intelligent Memory*, New York: Viking, 2003.

Greenblatt, Stephen, *Will in the World*, New York: Norton, 2004.

Hamel, Gary, and Prahalad, C. K., *Competing for the Future*, Boston: Harvard Business School Press, 1994.

Hammer, Michael, and Champy, James, *Reengineering the Corporation*, New York: HarperBusiness, 1994.

Hargadon, Andrew, *How Breakthroughs Happen*, Boston: Harvard Business School Press, 2003.

Herold, J. C., *The Mind of Napoleon*, New York: Columbia University Press, 1955.

Ichniowski, Casey, and Shaw, Kathryn, "Insider Econometrics: Empirical Studies of How Management Matters," National Bureau of Economic Research, Working Paper 15618, December 2009.

Johnson, Steven, *Where Good Ideas Come From*, New York: Riverhead, 2001.

Kahneman, Daniel, *Thinking: Fast and Slow*, New York: Farrar, Straus & Giroux, 2011.

Kandel, Eric, "Nobel Lecture," Karolinska Institutet, Stockholm, December 8, 2000.

Kelley, Tom, *The Art of Innovation*, New York: Crown Business, 2001.

Kesmodel, David, "Boeing Teams Speed Up 737 Output," *Wall Street Journal*, February 7, 2012.

Kim, W. C., and Mauborgne, Renée, *Blue Ocean Strategy*, Boston: Harvard Business School Press, 2005.

Kleemeier, Ulrike, "Moral Forces in War," in Hew Strachan and Andreas Herberg-Rothe, *Clausewitz in the Twentieth Century*, Oxford: Oxford University Press, 2007.

Klein, Gary, *Sources of Power*, Cambridge, Mass.: MIT Press, 1998.

Kotter, John, *Leading Change*, Boston: Harvard Business School Publishing, 1996.

Kroc, Ray, *Grinding It Out*, Chicago: Regnery, 1977.

Kuhn, Thomas, *The Structure of Scientific Revolutions*, Chicago: University of Chicago Press, 1962.

Lao Zi, *Dao De Jing*, New York: HarperCollins, 1988.

Lehrer, Jonah, "Groupthink," *New Yorker*, January 30, 2012.

McGrath, Rita, and MacMillan, Ian, "Discovery-Driven Planning," *Harvard Business Review*, July-August, 1995.

Milner, Brenda, Squire, Larry, and Kandel, Eric, "Cognitive Neuroscience and the Study of Memory," *Neuron*, 20, 1998.

Mintzberg, Henry, *The Rise and Fall of Strategic Planning*, New York: Free Press, 1994.

Mintzberg, Henry, and Waters, James, "Of Strategies, Deliberate and Emergent," *Strategic Management Journal*, 6, 1985.

Mintzberg, Henry et al., *Strategy Safari*, New York: Free Press, 1998.

Musashi, Miyamoto, *Book of Five Rings*, New York: Overlook, 1974.

Ogawa, S., Lee, T. M., Kay, A. R., and Tank, D. W., "Brain Magnetic Resonance Imaging with Contrast Depending on Blood Oxygenation," *Proceedings of the National Academy of Sciences*, 87, 1990.

Osterwalder, Alexander, and Pigneur, Yves, *Business Model Generation*, Hoboken, N.J.: Wiley, 2010.

Porter, Michael, *Competitive Strategy*, New York: Free Press, 1980.

Rasiel, Ethan, *The McKinsey Way*, New York: McGraw-Hill, 1999.

Robinson, Ken, *The Element*, New York: Viking, 2009.

Schorn, Daniel, "The Brain Behind Netflix," CBS News, February 11, 2006 (interview December 3, 2006).

Schultz, Howard, *Pour Your Heart Into It*, New York: Hyperion, 1997.

Schumpeter, Joseph, "Change and the Entrepreneur," in Harvard University Research Center in Entrepreneurial History, *Change and the Entrepreneur*, Cambridge, Mass.: Harvard University Press, 1949.

——. "The Creative Response in Economic History," *Journal of Economic History*, 7, 2, November 1947.

——. "The Instability of Capitalism," *Economic Journal*, September 1928.

——. "The Process of Creative Destruction," in *Capitalism, Socialism and Democracy*, New York: Harper & Brothers, 1942.

Senge, Peter, *The Fifth Discipline*, New York: Currency Doubleday, 1990.

Simon, Herbert, *Models of Thought: Volume 2*, New Haven, Conn.: Yale University Press, 1989.

Slater, Robert, *Jack Welch and the GE Way*, New York: McGraw-Hill, 1999.

Sperry, Roger, "Nobel Lecture," Stockholm Concert Hall, Stockholm, December 8, 1981.

Squire, Larry, and Kandel, Eric, *Memory: From Mind to Molecules*, Scientific American, 1999.

Sumner, W. G., *Folkways: A Study of the Sociological Importance of Usages, Manners, Customs, Mores, and Morals*, Ginn and Co., 1940.

Sun Zi, *The Art of War*, New York: Oxford University Press, 1975.

Surowiecki, James, *The Wisdom of Crowds*, New York: Doubleday, 2004.
Time, "Women in Fashion: Rose Marie Bravo," Online Edition, February 9, 2004.
Vise, David, and Malseed, Mark, *The Google Guys*, New York: Delacorte, 2005.
Von Clausewitz, Carl, *On War*, New York: Penguin, 1982 (1832).
Von Ghyczy, Tiha, Bassford, Christopher, and vonOetinger, Bolko, *Clausewitz on Strategy*, Hoboken, N.J.: Wiley, 2001.
Wakin, Daniel, "A Composer Forgotten by All but Mozart," *New York Times*, March 4, 2007.
Wallace, James, and Erickson, Jim, *Hard Drive*, Hoboken, N.J.: Wiley, 1992.
Young, James, *A Technique for Producing Ideas*, Lincolnwood, Ill.: National Textbook Co., 1988 (1940).
Yunus, Muhammad, *Banker to the Poor*, New York: PublicAffairs, 1999.

INDEX

THE HUNTING ANIMAL

Also by Franklin Russell

WATCHERS AT THE POND

THE SECRET ISLANDS

Franklin Russell

1817

HARPER & ROW, PUBLISHERS, New York

Cambridge, Philadelphia, San Francisco, London, Mexico City, São Paulo, Sydney

 For information address Harper & Row, Publishers, Inc., 10 East 53rd Street, New York, N.Y. 10022.

FIRST EDITION

Designed by Ruth Bornschlegel

Library of Congress Cataloging in Publication Data

Russell, Franklin, date
The hunting animal.

1. Predation (Biology) 2. Hunting. I. Title.
QL758.R87 1983 599'.053 82-48131
ISBN 0-06-015106-4

83 84 85 86 10 9 8 7 6 5 4 3 2 1

CONTENTS

THE HUNTING ANIMAL

PROLOGUE ○ The Cougar

"The hunt . . . a deep and permanent yearning in the human condition."

ORTEGA Y GASSET
Meditations on Hunting

The cat moved along the ravine in daylight, it was said, and could appear in the open fields, or in the woods, without a hint of warning. Its victims were the domestic animals of Jacob Michael Cain, who had owned the farm two hundred years before me. The barn he had built there, of solid slabs of hemlock, still stood. I had started my life close to nature, and had remained a naturalist, despite twenty years of city dwelling. Now, I had come to this farm from other countries, unprepared for its reminders of a past that I had largely forgotten.

I had been a professional conservationist, a planter of trees, an expert in the control of erosion, but I had also been a professional hunter. I was a writer but I had started as a farmer. In rebuilding the barn, I found a roll of paper, thrust into an auger hole in one of the heavy beams, which contained an inscription. The paper fell apart when I withdrew it, but one line remained legible. "We Killed the Great Cat Inside the Run."

An old neighbor told me that at one time the creek running down the ravine had been called Cougar's Run. It was certainly an ideal place for a hunting ambush. A large cat could remain clandestine in sumac shade there, and I could imagine how it might be a frightening spirit in the narrow valley that was my territory.

The valley was wild, secluded, and precipitous, and the rocks of the run—or stream—were a kind of twisted and stepped highway leading down to the Delaware River. In times of drought, the deer walked to the banks of the ravine to reach their only source of water. Hidden in the ravine, I could look upwards and see them silently passing, high above me. I had given up hunting, but here I resumed it. The energy of the cat drew close. It flowed up the rocks, passed invisibly through the undergrowth, and the jugulars of the deers hissed in the shade.

I found a cave which overlooked the ravine, perfect shelter in any season. There I could wait as the cat had waited—but with a rifle, so that I might have venison whenever the mood took me. This meat became as significant to my family as the vegetables and fruits that I grew in a two-acre garden.

In the long hours of hiding there, though, I occupied a separate world of introspection where reverie could mature into reality. The stimulus was Nature in its impartial offerings of song and fruit, death and birth, and a sense of imminence: Something important is about to happen. It did not matter that I was surrounded by oaks and maples, ash and hemlock; the trees might well have been ghostly gums of the Australian Murrumbidgee, or kahikatea in New Zealand, or the dwarf palms and bamboos of Indian sal forests.

The aloneness of the hunter, and his thoughts of his hunting past, are the very genesis of primitive energy. He is always a young man, then, and making his most daring journeys. He will not think of middle age, and even the responsibility of his family will be dim as he pauses, every sense alert for the sound of what he plans to kill. This is really the only time that he is fully alive. All the rest is the dreaming time.

I paused among the pollens of early summer. An American ovenbird bobbed at the edge of a quiet pool, but it was Kilimanjaro that I saw reflected in the water. Wood thrushes uttered their fluting cries, but I was hearing again the unforgettable harmonics of Mackenzie wolves in the Saint Elias Mountains of the Yukon. In the background, the cougar stalked Jacob Michael Cain's cows. Almost visible, the cat slipped through the undergrowth before me, trod on the ferns that I had transplanted to decorate my expansive garden near the colonial house.

The ghostly snarl of the cougar joined the cries of other cats from the nights when I had lived in Africa and India. I was taken back, brutally, to the time when a leopard had broken into a barn on the Transvaal farm where I lived, killing all the poultry, and even my pet cats, which slept in the same barn. One of them hung, partially eviscerated, from a nail above the harness racks.

Throughout my life, I had used animals as metaphors to describe human events and express personal feelings. There is great risk in this if the human events that sponsor the fables are not understood. Now it seemed to me that the cougar was using me to describe primitive and frightening situations which I had previously avoided. Event by event, lost connections reenacted themselves. Nothing occurred willingly. The bloodied pet fell from its nail and sprawled at my feet. Antarctic winds blew. The brain-fever bird cried out that it was January on the Ganges. The cat became a serial nightmare. I grew to dread its liquid growl within the cougar's run.

1 ○ The Buffalo

The ritual never changed; the buffalo always came north. It was described as the grandest spectacle in all of nature, the juggernaut advance of millions of great creatures across one quarter of a continental wilderness. There the animal was triumphant over its environment, so successful that a beast became the architect of the grasslands, with weather and soil its servants.

In the 1860s, Jonah William Campbell, the son of an Ohio farmer, liked to station himself on the north bank of the Arkansas River, between the Oklahoma border and Dodge City. If he got the right spot, and the hunting camps were not too thick around him, he might command a three-mile view of a curve in the river, in a kind of rude ambuscade for the millions that were heading toward him.

By that time, there were only ten to fifteen million buffalo surviving, as compared with perhaps sixty million in the seventeenth century. But even a small herd of two or three hundred thousand animals was a formidable mass of potential momentum. Such herds tended to be victims of their own size, or success perhaps, impossible to divert, insensitive to massive gunfire, yet capable of hysterical stampede, when a million tons of charging meat would not be stopped by anything.

Campbell would be in his place by the middle of March, blizzards still possible, even likely. The river might be frozen from bank to bank along much of its length, from the Rocky Mountains in Colorado to its conjunction with the Mississippi near Arkansas City.

"I liked to get set up early," Campbell would say, "because by the 1860s, there was a lot of us shooting buffalo and you had to get to the best places real early." His wagon, hauled by mules, carried more than a ton of powder and lead. His heavy brass cartridges were hand loaded and used over and over.

From his commanding position, he could predict that the buffalo would appear some morning between March 17 and March 21. The men on the bluff would remember each arrival with great clarity, to judge from the tales told to their descendants or to history itself. Sometimes, a muffled rumbling sound, vast, inchoate, enveloping, would come stealing across the river in the predawn gloom. The men would stir, sling buckles clinking, ammunition clattering in tin cans. Many had fought in the Civil War. The sight of the prone waiting men invoked redoubts at Appomattox, Bunker Hill, Leesburg, and images of the still and untidy supine dead after such battles.

I came to know Campbell on the Santa Fe Limited, from Chicago to Los Angeles, in the summer of 1932. A young boy, I was on a world tour with my parents, who were Scottish-born New Zealanders. They used the Depression to see the world. In America, we were heading for China, and would reach Chungking.

Campbell was a typical hunting man, extroverted and easygoing. He saw me as a fellow hunter, albeit dressed like a Western gunfighter, six-guns at the hip, imitation leather chaps fastened at the waist, and a villainous scowl set under a wide-brimmed hat from Marshall Field's department store.

"Hi, pardner," he said. "You aimin' to ride the range in that outfit?" He pretended to light my chocolate cigarette.

He told me that he had retired from farming in 1924, a couple of years before I was born, and he was spending his leisure years traveling, visiting some of the places of his youth, and reminiscing about those great and unforgettable days when, between 1869 and 1881, he had been one of the most successful buffalo hunters of the American West. In those twelve years—about the maximum length of time a man could stand the killing without lasting physical damage—he must have shot well over one hundred thousand animals if he did indeed earn, from their hides, meat, tongues, and tallow, the two hundred thousand dollars that he claimed.

"When you're eighty-five years of age," he said, as the train slipped across the Missouri River, "you remember the good things clearer and clearer, like they was really yesterday."

The buffalo appeared as a spreading black stain, at first as a series of fingers reaching for the frozen surface of the Arkansas, and then coalescing into a solid rumbling mass. Despite the frozen ground, the often-deep snow, the herd lifted both dust and steam from its mass, the exhalation of so many lungs, the stamping of up to one million feet in a single herd. Veteran hunters laughed all of one summer after a tenderfoot from New York saw the herd, dropped his rifle and fled, and was never seen again.

There was plenty of reason for apprehension. Campbell himself confessed to a catch in the throat, a surge in the heart, when he contemplated how easily these outwardly stolid marchers could be whipped into stampede. It took little. The slash and boom of rifles might be ignored. But the sound of a distant tornado, the flicker of a lightning bolt, or even the chatter of a disturbed rattlesnake might send them mad. Then, like a tidal wave, the mass rolled into movement.

It appeared to waiting hunters that the animals must come from some inexhaustible fount of abundance. They mashed the landscape flat and moved onward, ever onward. Campbell said a feeling of helplessness was common among buffalo hunters. They felt overwhelmed. Guns boomed incessantly. Animals fell. Wagons clattered. The relentless movement of buffalo on the horizon emphasized that the slaughter had no effect. Thousands died, thousands replaced them. The mind became exhausted.

When large herds arrived at water holes, no scheme had been devised in the evolution of the animal to share the drinking among the masses. It was as if the success of the buffalo had been a rather recent thing, and there had been no time for adjustment. The mob advanced, thickened to a sea of muscular backs, growling like thunder, and then was gone, the water hole a shapeless quagmire into which was punched all vegetation. Nestling birds called feebly from the mush of reeds and mud.

The buffalo so filled their landscape that the hunters of antiquity, wolves, were pinpricks in the walls of their numbers. What could stop an animal which had become irresistibly strong? Control, when hunters, diseases, and natural disasters were not enough, might develop in the personality. Perhaps panic was the functioning epidemic disease, acting like the jaws of several million wolves, and touching the tiny brains. Indian encampments were stamped into pink dust. The mob flowed to ravines, and filled them, and charged on. Then the leaders stumbled, and fell, and were overwhelmed by those behind, who also fell, so that the rush forward became a deadly interior collision.

"They were mad," said Campbell.

One time, the herd was spread out over the ice of the Arkansas River and the waiting buffalo hunters tensed for the right moment to begin firing. Ideally, this was just as the leaders came up out of the water, and enough animals were ashore to encourage those on the ice to continue pressing forward into the guns. But this herd seemed to be in no hurry to cross, and the thickening stain of animals gathered in a wall halfway across the ice. Then some itchy tenderfoot let off a shot. An animal fell. Those around it reared backward.

But those behind, out of sight and not hearing the killing, kept coming forward. At once, there were one hundred thousand animals together, or a quarter of a million tons of dead weight, compressed on ice a few inches thick. From his position at the highest part of the bluff, Campbell saw the center beginning to fall, the motion radiating outward in rings of energy to the sounds of crashing ice and bellowing animals. Flight was impossible because the ice broke faster than hooves could scramble. The herd went down in majestic finality, some of its members later to plague towns along the Mississippi as far south as New Orleans, where they were jammed between wharf pilings, and collected, bloated, among moored paddle steamers.

Campbell fell back as the buffalo came on. Soon, when late spring brought the prairies to verdant life, the growth of grasses would slow the animals down, and definitive hunting could begin. But early in this season, it was opportunistic, chancy, dangerous. A hunter had to have emplaced a finely strung organization of other men—skinners, tanners, transporters—to make profit from the barrage of bullets that he would lay upon the earth.

He had seen most of the hunting methods at work, and felt his was the most efficient. A few years previously, he had hunted with some of the last of the métis of the Red River region—half-breed Indian-Scottish hunters whose lives were dominated by buffalo. They were dispirited by the decline of buffalo numbers, which had revealed their hunting methods as being too wasteful to be sustained. They had neither the patience nor the desire to wipe out entire herds on the move, as Campbell attempted. Instead, they went to the hunt in caravans of several hundred carts, carrying provisions, ammunition, guns, camp gear, and hangers-on in an atmosphere that was more exuberant than precise in its aim to kill.

They drove until they reached a buffalo herd, usually around the first week in June. Indiscriminate slaughter followed, although little effort was made to prevent the herds fom scattering. In 1860, Campbell went to the hunt with a hundred carts. Twenty years before, more than one thousand carts returned from the hunt with a million pounds of dried meat, grease, pemmican, and tallow. Alexander Ross, a traveler with the hunt, said that seven thousand buffalo were destroyed, yielding about two thousand tons of dressed fresh meat, of which a thousand tons was wasted in the field processing.

"They didn't deserve to get rich, the way they worked," said Campbell.

He operated in loose communion with free-lance skinners and meat handlers. They gravitated to him because he was willing to shoot from sunup to sundown, and he could have charged them a fee for the privilege of processing his animals. He knew the herds better than any man on the prairies, it was said, and he had a knack of being exactly where the animals were thickest.

He would never reveal which of the four major herds might yield the greatest kill in any year. Unlike most other hunters, he worked during the winter, as well, which gave him his prescience about the spring movements west, and north. The northern, or Yellowstone, herd wintered along the Yellowstone River in Montana, but plunged far north in summer, all through the territory of the upper Mississippi and the Milk River, into Canada.

The Republican herd came from the south to summer in some of the territories vacated by the Yellowstone herd, mainly between the Bighorn and the Black Hills. The Arkansas herd, from Arkansas, reached into Republican territory in its summer movement northward, entering Nebraska in July and moving back into Arkansas in the winter. The last herd, the great Texas conglomerate, wintered toward the Concho and the Pecos and moved north in spring through the Panhandle to the Arkansas, and so into Colorado, with the others.

The Indians had built cultures upon such mass. One tribe, the Blackfeet, started coming out of a seminomadic, bare-subsistence way of life in northern Saskatchewan about fifteen hundred years before Campbell hunted. Their poverty made them hungry for change, and eager for invention, which is within the core of all the best hunters. But without game, they could be nothing much. They themselves needed to be invented, by an animal they had not yet met.

They encountered buffalo in the valley of the North Saskatchewan River and devised a method of adapting their manpower to overcoming the irresistible force of the herd. They attacked in winter blizzards, when the buffalo sought shelter in timber. The Blackfeet, massed in bands, drove them out into snowdrifts.

It was a strategy of killing, but dangerous and uncertain. Big herds would not be driven and might wheel on the hunters. Genius was needed to make buffalo driving an all-season event, with a more certain result. But the Blackfeet had achieved that first requirement of good hunting: intimacy with the game. They became killers disguised as shepherds.

Their success brought them south, and they found a steady thickening of buffalo as they got among Yellowstone animals. Blackfoot myths are not dated, but perhaps between five hundred and a thousand years ago, a Blackfoot hunter learned how to "call" the buffalo. He was being assailed by insects, as are the buffalo throughout the summer, and stood up in full view of the small herd he was watching. He started flapping his robes. Some of the buffalo cows walked toward him. He ran to a ridge, and flapped again. The cows broke into a trot. The rest of the herd followed.

This became a gallop, a charge. The hunter barely saved his life by flinging himself down behind a boulder.

This was magic. The victim's own power had been used to bring it within range of the lance. The Blackfeet might not know that a robe-flapping hunter resembled a light-coated buffalo calf. But they had seized upon the maternal anxiety of the buffalo cow as a means of killing the bulls as well.

Each of the herds had been appropriated by Indians, long before the eastern Americans arrived on the scene. They had fought for hunting rights among themselves from the moment they got horses from the Spaniards. The Comanche, for instance, which had not been a buffalo-hunting tribe before the horse, or particularly fierce, were transformed, and took near-control over the Arkansas herd, along with the Cheyenne and the Kiowas, who also had property rights to the Texas herd.

This hunt was no creeping of men through the grass, no sudden drives from snow-clogged woods. Instead, it was an equestrian theater, brave men with eagle feathers streaming from their harnesses. These were possibly the most colorful, proud, able, and technically proficient hunters who ever set out in pursuit of game.

"My father was on the Chisholm," said Campbell, "and he never got over them Indians."

In 1855, a member of the Walla Walla Council, Lieutenant Lawrence Kip, was waiting for an Indian delegation to arrive at an outdoor meeting.

"We saw them approaching on horseback in one long line," wrote Kip. "They were almost entirely naked, gaudily painted and decorated with their wild trappings. Their plumes fluttered about them, while below, skins and trinkets and all kinds of fantastic embellishments flaunted in the sunshine."

Kip said that the Indian was trained from early childhood to almost live on horseback. "They sat upon their fine animals as if they were centaurs. Their horses, too, were arrayed in the most glaring finery. They were painted with such colors as formed the greatest contrast, the white being smeared with crimson in fantastic figures, and the dark colors streaked with white clay. Beads and fringes of gaudy colors were hanging from the bridles, while the plumes of eagle feathers, interwoven with the mane and tail, fluttered as the breeze swept over them, and completed their wild, fantastic appearance."

It was impossible to live near the buffalo without adapting to the insistence of their numbers, the pressure of their arrival. Their advances created rituals within rituals, natural history extending itself into cultural schemes of perception. When a year's supply of food could be gathered in hours, there was then time for indulgence, decoration, and the development of style. The eagle-feathered Indian, omnipotent on a horse, killed white men as sport.

Campbell was no horseman and so was uncomprehending of how a horseman without a saddle could slip behind the body of his mount, and fire a rifle over the animal's back, or from under its belly, at full gallop. He simply did not believe that the Indians of the early part of the nineteenth century had been able to reload flintlocks, and fire, all at the full speed of the horse. Like most frontier-type men, he looked more to the deficiencies of the Indian.

"There was the booze," he said.

He had very strict rules about drinking during the hunt. "Some men drank all the time," he said, "but it never made sense to me. You have to put a tighter hold on yourself when you are hunting. There, you are really free, and it was a temptation to many to drink as much as the body could take."

The answer was not to drink at all. It was mainly because he was a teetotaler that Campbell got to know the Indians better than most other buffalo hunters. In the early seventies, he was invited to at least one performance of the legendary sun dance, which was the Indian way of invoking spirits to make the hunting good, through dancing and fasting. The Indians equated the ecstasy of dancing with the pains of hunger, the elevation of the mind through the punishment, or suffering, of the body. Campbell was astounded by some examples of warriors' resistance to pain.

"I saw this fellow drive sticks through his chest, attached by thongs to a big pole, and then leap around like he was crazy, and the sticks ripped right out of his chest, and you could see the flesh just hanging there, all ripped," said Campbell. "It was the most awful thing I ever did see."

The sun dance was the hunters' obeisance to that great spiritual presence, the mystic dark hordes that came over the horizon each year, all-providing, all-encompassing. It was an elaborate marriage of animal and man, in ceremonies that might last days. Buffalo skulls, buffalo thongs, buffalo hides, were symbols of the bounty the Indians invoked, while the eagle feathers were the representation of themselves as fierce and successful hunters. The Mandan, in the northern plains, developed a special dance, the most complicated, probably because they were almost last on the receiving line of the buffalo bounty, and needed extra inducements to bring this mountain of meat over the horizon to them.

This dance caught the imagination of George Catlin, in the 1830s, who saw each hunter actually disguised as a buffalo, wearing a mask tanned from an entire buffalo head, horn and hair complete. The identification of the hunter with his victim was made symbolically complete by the young bucks, as buffalo, dancing around the old men, the experienced hunters, sitting in a circle.

"When one becomes fatigued of the exercise," wrote Catlin, in his *Indian Tribes of North America,* 1847, "he signifies it by bending quite forward, and sinking his body towards the ground; when another draws a bow upon him and hits him with a blunt arrow, and he falls like a buffalo—is seized by the bystanders, who drag him out of the ring by the heels, brandishing their knives about him; and having gone through the motions of skinning and cutting him up, they let him off, and his place is at once occupied by another, who dances into the ring with his mask on; and by this taking of places, the scene is easily kept up night and day, until the desired effect has been produced, that of 'making the buffalo come.'"

"Of course," said Campbell, "them northern Injuns weren't nothing to do with the ones I was dealing with, the Sioux, and the Comanches, whom you couldn't trust a score of feet from your horse, or gun, or any grub you had."

In the hunt, all inventiveness leads to technology, as intimacy with the animal sharpens the capability to kill more quickly and easily. Hunter and prey fuse into this ecstasy of effort. The Blackfeet were decorating their killing lances with symbols of the hunt, invoking rituals which made them more ready to hunt, more eager to improve the invention that had brought them out of the snows to this prairie prosperity. They were ready to invent the piskin.

I remembered the word for years before I learned what it meant. Campbell wove a fabric of event, a teeming, Brueghel painting of words. I, enchanted, understood little, but was changed forever. The Indians appear in serried silhouette, against a bulking of Montana clouds, overlooking their herd of grazing animals. It does not matter whether they have received the horse by now, or not, because the piskin works for both men on foot and men mounted. At first, piskins were stockades, with angled fences directing the herd to its place of entrapment and slaughter. But later, the piskin might be simply a cliff to which the buffalo were driven.

Campbell had heard of, but had not seen, the most famous of these cliffs, the Sun River Jump, located west of modern Great Falls. Both the operation of these jumps, and his technique of shooting, depended upon regulating the movement of the animals for the most efficient killing.

"It was a real tricky thing," Campbell said, "to shoot in such a way that they don't bolt, or move out of range, or disperse too much. The best shooters caused the buffalo to move together, so they could be shot together."

A Blackfoot buffalo caller fasted for days. He prayed incessantly for the divinity of guidance, which is also the power that all great hunters possess, a psychic connection with the victim. The Blackfoot caller became gifted and possessed when the right visions came down to him from a sky marching with columns of migrating spirits. The Indians in silhouette move forward. The buffalo, shortsighted but hearing screams, move correctly. Their hooves cut a grassy plain which stretches from the Front Range of the Rockies, its undulating surface broken infrequently by rimrock cliffs where streams have cut ravines.

A broad valley is visible beyond the turning buffalo, many thousands of acres of grazing. The buffalo cannot see far, but they can smell the distance, its contents. As their pace increases under pressure, they go into a wide and shallow draw that points toward the valley. The screams become piercing. The trot becomes a compressing charge.

The women, the children, and the old are waiting at the base of the cliffs of the Sun River Jump. They are attending a myth. It is a slow-motion fall of gods from the skies. Around them is the debris of ancient drives: bones, ossified skins, skulls, twenty-five thousand tons of bits and pieces scattered over five acres.

The first animals seem to glide, feet outstretched, and driving into soft soil. The front legs break, and the flying animals somersault and roll, bellowing. The followers also fly, but crash onto their brothers. The rimrock cliffs throw back astounded gasps, whistles of crushed lungs exploding air, the snap and rattle of bones failing as the horde cannot stop itself from flying at the edge of the Sun River Jump.

Campbell prided himself on the thoroughness of his hunting, and by the fact that he never tired of shooting. Hunting is obviously an art, as the Indians demonstrated, but the white man turned it into a business. If Campbell's secret thoughts could be known, it would be revealed that he believed he had turned a bloodthirsty business into something that was artistic.

"It was the locomotive, though, that actually conquered

the West," said my father, an amateur historian, and an expert in trains.

"It was the rifle that opened it up," said Campbell.

He was accustomed to the heft and power of the .50 caliber Sharps, which had replaced the light and mass-produced Springfields of the early buffalo-hunting days. The Sharps had devastating hitting power and did grievous damage to anything it hit. The Indians said of it that "it shoots today and kills tomorrow." The Sharps, which was made in Hartford, Connecticut, had to be lodged on a stand, because of its sixteen-pound weight, too heavy for saddle use. But pretty much any buffalo would go down under its blow at six hundred yards or more.

At around six o'clock in the morning, Campbell would leave his camp and ride until ten o'clock. This was deliberate timing. The buffalo would be bellyful with morning grazing by then, and not inclined to panic. He, on the other hand, would have ridden far enough to get a notion of the strategic placement and thickenings of the buffalo for miles around him. Given luck, and the right kind of planning, he might be able to shoot for several days in this place. He staked out his horse, tied on knee pads, swung two heavy rifles off the saddle, along with a hundred shells, put on gloves, and began crawling toward his victims.

If he had chosen well, he would be within gunshot—about a hundred yards from the dim-sighted creatures. The trick was then to pick the leader in each of the scattered groups within range, usually an old cow, swinging her head and twitching her tail while she kept glancing around her as a sign of authority.

He knew it was no use aiming for the heart or the head. A heart-shot buffalo could gallop for five hundred yards before going down, and that was too far to walk for the skin. A head-shot animal, on the other hand, was capable of almost anything. It might even charge the rifleman and trample him to death. Campbell fired for the lungs. This was both a crippling and a mortal wound, which caused hemorrhage and intense shock. It stopped the animal from bolting while it struggled, vainly, to regain its breath.

When the bullet struck home, the victim snorted and a shower of blood sprayed from her nostrils. At the sound of the explosion, a score of animals would look toward the stricken animal. Receiving no instructions except the signs of her distress, which might also be her impatience with flies, the other animals resume grazing. Still suspicious, a large bull is struck by the second bullet before he gives a snort of warning. A third animal starts into a trot and is stopped short, gasping. Campbell has developed a rhythm of killing, in which he always knows which animal must die next. He tries to drop them in compact groups so that the skinners, who will arrive in the afternoon, need only to turn from one animal to begin skinning the next.

By eleven o'clock, his first rifle, smoking hot, lies cooling beside him. The concussion of the firing has deafened him temporarily, as usual. His right shoulder and arm, even his hand, are all sore. He is worried that such prolonged firing might permanently damage his hearing, as it has done to many others. He probably saves it only because he will work no more than a dozen years on the prairies. Other riflemen kill for twenty years, or longer, and most are deaf at fifteen years.

The skinners come close behind the rifleman, usually four or five of them working together behind a good gun. They whet their knives on small field grindstones, prop up the slain animals on their backs and slit their skins from jaw to tail, with a long cut down the inside of each leg and around the neck. They drop the buffalo on its side and then rip off the skin with a horse. Working fast, they spread the skins out on the prairie, hair side down, sprinkling the flesh side with arsenic to repel insects. In five days, they will have to race back to this place and arrange the shipment of the dried and stiff hides to the East.

In early March, the buffalo turned north. Sometimes,

their spring coats were so dense and lustrous they seemed to glow in evening suns. The calves, yellow-robed and frisky, trotted over a flush of grasses. Half a million square miles of prairie could never be eaten out. The cows, pregnant from the midsummer rut of the previous year, gorged in readiness for late-spring births.

In the search for uncorrupted pasturing, in which the later hordes would not have to graze in the footprints and the dung of those who had preceded them, there was a visible discontent. Too much was not enough. The water holes became focus points in the march, at first briefly detaining, but then, as the animals kept coming out of the wintering territories, turned into arenas of disaster. Old bulls were mired in the mud, and died. Calves played in the mud, got stuck, drowned, or choked. "You could smell the stink of the wallows from miles away," said Campbell.

He killed with pleasure in the spring, when the hunting country was fluid. Water birds were clamorous in their departures from wetlands to northern breeding places, and grass and flowers transformed every view of the prairie country. Campbell, although an Ohioan, had a fierce love of the prairies. "Free country," he called it. As he lay on his back, in the summer nights, watching the canopy of stars revolving, he heard the mutter of invisible hordes, distant thundering when panic struck, the occasional clash of heavy collisions, the melodic fluting of wolves.

Each glorious prairie morning, he raised his head cautiously from his sleeping pallet to inspect the ebb and flow of the rutting season, which would continue until the fall. No animal on earth, it was said, could stand against a buffalo bull fighting for his share of cows. The fighting began with first light. Campbell never shot fighting bulls. Rather, it was better to shoot all around them. The monotonous boom of the Sharps cut left and right around a bull making short stabbing runs that sent an adversary staggering to his knees. The collision was so severe that the attacking bull went down too, bloody red eyes gleaming. He rose, whirled, and flicked froth from his mouth, to charge again, as the cows for which he was fighting stood, gasping blood in their ruined lungs, all around him.

It was not a hunt in any sense that might be divined from the Stone Age people, but a massacre that satisfied another lust from the ancient past: the need for blood beyond real need. Wolves trailed the buffalo columns, some of which stretched out fifty miles long in the route of march. The attempts of the wolves to kill were foiled as much by the mass of victims as by the energy of their flight. But once calving started, the wolves closed in. The calves were taken. Now those bulls which had been wounded in mating fights and thereby separated from the herd were hemmed by wolves. They backed up to the walls of canyons, their eyes bitten out, their noses ripped off. They reared, hearing the soft scuff of feet approaching. Blind heads came up and they wheezed through mangled mouths after the wolves had bitten out their tongues. Death came hard to such powerful creatures. They were hamstrung, disemboweled, but survived for days.

"It was a fever," said Campbell.

In the East, the tales of the buffalo hunt inflamed all ambitions for freedom, opportunity, and wealth. The West was an inexhaustible hunting territory. The Kansas Pacific, and the Atchison, Topeka and Santa Fe, ran competing lines in the tracks of the moving buffalo. The first train that tried to reach Dodge City was stalled for hours in the middle of a dense mob, ten miles long and three miles wide, probably dammed up in its march by the crack and boom of rifles, pistols, and muzzle loaders coming out of Dodge itself where the locals blasted away, firing from roofs, the windows of their shacks, from piles of crates, baggage, and dark mounds of buffalo skins.

The train itself bristled with guns and rocked with continuous broadsides into the stolidly marching animals. Everybody killed—prospectors, farmers, gamblers, tourists, whores, firemen, salesmen, and the optimistic hundreds who hoped to become buffalo hunters. For years, the Eastern newspapers had carried stories of how wealthy people mounted expensive expeditions to kill buffalo.

British noblemen shot thousands of buffalo. Grand Duke Alexis, son of Czar Alexander II, hunted with George Custer and General Philip Sheridan. Washington Irving, Horace Greeley, John James Audubon, and scores of others passed through the buffalo herds with gun, notebook, and engraving equipment. But in the 1870s, it was the time of common people, the ordinary hunters who shot for livelihood.

Campbell, though sensitive to the natural charm and beauty of the prairie world, was not at first troubled by the grossness of his killing. Instead, he was dismayed that so much meat must go to waste. There was simply too much of it to process. The markets were too distant. Refrigeration was still in the future. The skins, or robes, brought good prices, worldwide, and so did the tongues, which became a restaurant delicacy. But the sheer bulk of felled meat was mostly left to rot where it had fallen. The real hunter, always economical, and thinking about next season, must be concerned.

Campbell sought to remedy the waste by fully exploiting his killing for himself. He had observed the Indian drying the meat into pemmican, enriching it with nuts, dried berries and fruits, slicing it, and dipping it into wild honey. Campbell hung up the hams of the fattest bulls in mesquite trees, and left them there for the winter; it was an unspoken code of the frontier that one man did not cut down another man's meat. The hams would be ready at any time during the following summer.

Buffalo humps never reached the Eastern markets, but they were esteemed in the West, hung in trees for months, crusty, going green, while Campbell shot his way a score of miles distant, but with the flesh left behind him perfectly preserved and seasoned, waiting to be sliced and salted and fried in deep tallow. Buffalo meat, hung over the winter, was sliced in the warm May sun, red and juicy, and pleading for hot skillets, loads of gravy, and groups of hungry prairie wanderers.

Campbell often lived on buffalo hump and tongues for months at a time. He boiled the tongues until they were tender and then fried them in the marrow of hipbones. He cured his buffalo meat by digging large square holes and lining them with fresh green hides pegged at the edges. Into a hole went half a ton of salted meat, which was left there for eight days. Then it was smoked, resalted, and cured.

"There was too much of it to be fully appreciated."

It was sometime in the middle 1870s that Campbell began noticing that something was going wrong with his hunting idyll, which was incidentally making him rich. Accustomed to large-scale death, a machine-age processing of nature, he slowly found himself touched by the plight of the buffalo. Its success had always been too outrageous for there to be any real security to it. Nature itself, he understood, punished all excess. Fire, flood, drought, blizzard: these were the real catastrophes of the buffalo. But Campbell began to see himself enmeshed in a disaster of another kind, of which he must become the final victim if he remained a hunting man.

How this came to him was probably through the insistence of spectacle, the degradation of his hunting range, the squalor of the frontier. Near Dodge, thousands of acres of prairie were staked with drying skins. The railroad station was buried, concealed, by mile-long dark barrows of baled skins, awaiting shipment East.

But perhaps it was the cumulative effect of mindless death. As a professional hunter, many years later, I would note the phenomenon of elation at repeated killing, followed eventually by a lethal exhaustion of the senses, guilt, then tears. Instead of becoming hardened to the travail of innocent animals, the hunter finds himself drawn down among them, putting his own feelings into a growing identification with their suffering.

For Campbell, this probably began with his shock at seeing buffalo on fire. The sound of a prairie fire, he would say, was like that of a train crossing a distant wooden trestle bridge, a thrum, a rumble, a roar. The buffalo were too shortsighted to ever see the approach of flames until it was too late. But the sound roused them. Sometimes they ran toward the flames, then panicked when they realized their mistake. The flight became an internal explosion of bodies, the vanguard charging the rear guard.

Terrified of fire himself, Campbell could survive such entrapment by digging a shallow hole in the soft earth, and pulling as much earth in on himself as possible. In a brisk wind, the flames traveled at forty miles an hour, and in gusts, at sixty. They ran down the buffalo, which disappeared in the pall of smoke. Campbell shuddered when he heard the voices. The flames did not drive evenly, or burn long in one place. After they had passed, it was the buffalo themselves which were burning, the shaggy manes of bulls brilliantly alight in a black smoking landscape. Calves and cows got to their knees and bellowed. They ran in haphazard circles, or stood rooted in the smoldering earth, eyes seared white in scorched faces. Dungheaps burned as beacons after the last of the animals had collapsed of burns and shock.

The buffalo were hunted by the natural rage of earth. More than one hundred thousand animals drowned in failed crossings of the Arkansas River. Charles Goodnight, a Southwestern rancher, once rode for five days through drought-stricken territory where "dead buffalo lay on the ground, for as far as I could see in every direction, so thickly fallen that an agile man could have travelled a hundred miles, jumping from carcass to carcass, without ever touching the ground."

In life, the buffalo overwhelmed the landscapes of plenty; in death, they filled the memory with an appalling squalor. Felled in drought, decimated in tornadoes, scorched by fire, or shot only for the hide and the tongue, or some choice steak, they lay naked in the prairie sun until they collapsed in rot. A secondary industry arose, feeding hogs on the carcasses. But the hogs went wild and eventually they had to be hunted down too.

The dead buffalo strewing the plains reminded many human observers of a battlefield, although the Civil War had produced nothing as horrifying as this. Men were buried after battles, but the buffalo were not. In these poisoned landscapes, flies became a surreal form of life. Great green blowflies rose in clouds from carcasses. Campbell had to stop eating meals in daylight because he could not get the food into his mouth ahead of the ravening flies.

He could never forget the stench. In calm and dusty weather, the people of Dodge City claimed, the air turned green. Everyone wore bandannas over nose and throat. Excursion trains left Kansas City, and even Chicago, filled with riflemen who blasted away day and night at the masses of buffalo amid the stink of animals killed from previous trains. Civil War veterans who thought they had experienced the worst, gagged on the smell of the Western frontier.

Campbell had been ahead of his time when he began hunting the year around. But by the 1870s more and more hunters were following his example, tagging along behind the moving buffalo twelve months in the year. They worked in pairs, in threes, in family groups, and were ready to devote all their lives to this single hunt. Even at that date, three men could kill and skin five hundred animals a week, and gross $1,750. Only the goldfields offered any comparable chance for such swift wealth.

By the beginning of 1870, Campbell realized that the main Central Western buffalo hunt was played out for his kind of hunting, not so much by a shortage of animals as by a superabundance of hunters. "It was getting downright dangerous to shoot in some regions." What he did not know was that a revolution in tanning was at hand, developed in Germany and Pennsylvania, by which the "soft" leather of buffalo robes, formerly not durable, became tough, resilient, and very valuable.

Campbell was leaving Kansas for the Far Western hunt, abandoning the Arkansas hordes in favor of the much more dubious rewards of the Texas herd, which was contained within Comanche territory. The Comanches had already indicated they would fight to preserve their hunting control of the Texas animals, and they had killed many hunters seeking to intrude, in some instances wiping out entire parties.

For a brief time, as the orders for hides flooded in from New York, and Europe, a dressed hide was worth a week's wage to a workingman. A buffalo stampede began, not of animals but of Eastern hunters-to-be, of railroad workers laid off for the winter, of residents caught up in the swirl of the hunting fever. Within twenty months, it was estimated, twenty thousand hunters, and their crews, were in the field, for the beginning of perhaps the greatest massacre of animals ever performed by one species upon another.

Campbell joined a hunting party that planned to penetrate Comanche country in the Texas Panhandle, and defend itself against massed Indian attacks. In this period—1872–1873—between six and seven million buffalo were felled in the western Kansas hunt, a quantum jump in the killing which obliterated, rather than decimated, the herds. Campbell reached a place called Adobe Walls, on the Canadian River, at the end of the Kansas slaughter, at the same time that the Comanches assembled a war party of seven hundred to wipe out his group.

At dawn, June 27, 1874, Campbell was wakened by the screams of attacking Indians. He slept with a Winchester at his side and a Colt under his saddlebag, and so, unlike the other residents and visitors to the station, who were racing about in their long johns trying to find guns and shells, he was ready to fight instantly. He raced out of the saloon, and saw that the attacking braves had become hung up in the killing of some horses and two men who had been sleeping in their wagons by the corral.

Campbell had always been fussy about his firearms, and his Winchester, never intended as a buffalo gun, was one of the first of the so-called double repeaters, bolt-action weapons which could fire twelve shells as fast as the rifleman could aim, fire, and work the bolt. As the Indians came out of the corral in a dense screaming mass, Campbell probably killed twenty of them immediately with his pistol and rifle. Almost at the same instant, the booming of Sharps began as the heavy guns of other hunters came into action, the .50 caliber bullets killing three or four men each at near-point-blank range. The charge was stopped, Campbell remembers, with dead braves at his feet.

Meanwhile, of course, the price of hides steadily tumbled. The Texas herd did not last long. The Comanches, in retreat, often massacred their own animals to prevent hunters like Campbell from profiting from them. Soon Campbell himself withdrew from direct hunting, and became a hide and meat dealer. Before the end of that decade, a noose of hunters' camps was strung through Nebraska, Wyoming, Colorado, and the Canadian West. The hunters pressed the remnant of the herds against the mountains and other natural barriers. No matter where the animals attempted to travel, the rifles were there. They could not come north with the spring, or go south in the fall. They could not move.

For the Indians, it was not merely the loss of lands, the mortalities of braves uselessly defending ancient hunting territories. It was the destruction of an entire culture which had been systematically built upon the permanence and bounty of unlimited numbers of buffalo. The flash, the spring, the vigor of the Indians was lost to something they could not fight: grasslands empty of the sacred game.

Their fury was felt deepest, perhaps, by Red Cloud, in his futile exhortation to the Great Father not to build any roads through the Black Hills of the red people. But it was

Chief Sitting Bull—who had made the celebrated remark about the white man keeping only one promise: "They said they would take our land, and they did"—who brought the era to a close. He could not stem the white man's invasion but he could make good the Comanche trick of massacring the herd before the white man could hunt it. He found the last twelve hundred buffalo grazing in the United States, in western Dakota, in 1883, and with a force of one thousand braves, he surrounded the herd and completed the final buffalo hunt.

The effect of Campbell's dense history on a very young mind was strong. He was to leave the train in Utah, at an engine-change point. The thunder of guns could still be imagined in this expansive landscape, and the fall of majestic animals under such a wide and open sky.

The slaughtered buffalo left behind a cemetery of bones. In fact, the Kansas plains could not be plowed until most of them had been picked up. Skulls, rib cages, the massive leg bones of the last seven million, were so thick that they blocked the coulters and moldboards of the steam plows that began twanging the tough roots of prairie grasses before Sitting Bull performed his massacre.

But there was money in bones, which made combs and the handles of knives, which could be ground up into fertilizer, or used in the refining of sugar. At twelve dollars a ton, and with the ability to pick up about three thousand pounds of bones a day, a smart man might extend his hunting fortune. Campbell owned wagons, and teams, and he sent his people out at once. They brought back five thousand tons of bones.

"There sure were a lot of bones," said Campbell, a number of times.

The men picked up only the heaviest bones, of course, and so their harvest was but a part of the total tonnage strewing the prairies. Records were kept. The bone hunt provided a final measurement of the scope of the earlier hunting. In all, the bone pickers brought in two million tons.

"What did you do after the bones were gone?" my father asked Campbell.

"Oh, a little of this, a little of that," Campbell said.

He was gone from the buffalo hunt, including the bone hunt, by 1882, and we took our train ride together in 1932. In those fifty years, there was a long silence. What had become of Jonah Campbell? What did he do? My father elicited no anecdote, no memory, no information. All identity stopped in 1882.

After that, a caparisoned Indian might be seen sitting on his horse, like a sentinel, looking into the wide empty silences of the eastern prairies in spring, apparently awaiting herds which could no longer come. Without the herds, a sun dance had no meaning, and the ability to withstand pain was just another old habit that no longer served the myth of the hunting animal.

2 ○ The Tiger

"The object of this hunt is imperial. We are the rulers here."

RALPH STANLEY-ROBINSON
Jubbulpore, 1935

In the modulated gloom of the gun room, the steel of heavy polished rifles caught the glow of the sun in the garden outside. I had learned to identify most of the weapons. There were light and cheap Winchesters, for guests. Sometimes, Mannlichers would be left there for a while, although German weapons were more admired for their workmanship than for their suitability in a worldwide empire.

The favorite weapon was undoubtedly the double-barreled Express, by all accounts the most accurate, which, with its relatively enormous .470 caliber bullet, could hit nearly as hard as a Schneider, or the American Sharps, but without the cumbersome weight of those two foreign weapons. There was also the Paradox, a short, heavy, deliberately clumsy weapon, possessed of staggering hitting power, really a hand-held cannon that fired a one-inch ball.

"It is really a weapon of great brutality," Ralph Stanley-Robinson was fond of saying. A light Kashmir blanket lay over his wasted legs. "It can only be used sensibly when the tiger is cornered, and will not submit to its wounds, and it is necessary for the hunter to go into the thicket."

Stanley-Robinson, an old friend of my parents', had been crippled in a tiger incident a few years before, but he was still referred to as "Sir Tiger," because of his legendary knowledge of hunting the animal in the forty years between 1897 and the present, 1937. He had been, like my parents, a tea planter, but he had also been an unofficial tiger-control officer, available at any time to travel hundreds of miles to rid districts of troublesome animals. He had also been a shikari of note, a solitary hunter, who always brought back noteworthy trophies from fifty-to-seventy-day hunts in many parts of India.

I was allowed to keep my bird-collecting shotgun in the gun room; it looked like a toy against the massive weapons all around it, with its tiny gauge, firing pellets too small to damage the plumage or skins of small birds. Stanley-Robinson was in the billiard room, next to the gun room, anxiously peering through the lace curtains silently billowing in a warm morning wind richly scented by the flowers of the four-acre garden. He looked up as I came in. "Oh, there you are," he said. "I was wondering where you were."

"I just got back," I said.

"You've been in the park?"

"Yes. I have a new specimen."

Stanley-Robinson was intensely interested in my bird collecting. "You go into the park alone," he would observe approvingly, "and spend hours out there, trying to get your specimens."

Sometimes, it took me a month to get the exact bird I wanted. It was not sufficient to shoot just any bird of a desired species. Some would mount well, others would not.

"It's why we rule India," he said. "Have you not observed that the Indian cannot do anything alone? Look at your chum Gupta. He follows you round like a puppy dog. The Indian does everything in groups."

"Oh." I was discomfited about Gupta. I never thought of him as a puppy dog.

"He cannot function alone, and he cannot work at midday, and so his kind will never govern this vast place."

I was not English, as Stanley-Robinson was, but it was true that the Indians did not have a sense of personal discipline that I could understand. Gupta was fat, and I was lean. His parents were slothful, and mine were industrious. He laughed at my jokes, but had none of his own. He revered my gun, but was frightened to touch it. Though he was in awe of my stuffed bird collection, he had no hobby that was his alone. His father fell down the veranda steps of our house trying to bow and depart at the same time. When Indians were alone, they were clowns, like the storytellers who used to come to our place with tales of tiger hunts, displaying horrendous scars and missing fingers or limbs.

But even when they were in groups, and I was alone among them, they still revealed themselves as a people eager for subjection to the steel-willed British youngster looking for birds in the canopies of their trees. The idea of empire could not be challenged because it was organization, and it replaced the chaos of some thousands of years of their history. It did not matter that they were intelligent, and ingenious, and humorous, and likable. I bullied Gupta, and was secretly contemptuous of him. Yet I loved him dearly.

The crunch of gravel outside announced the arrival of motorcars.

"Ah," said Stanley-Robinson, rubbing his twisted, livid hands together. "They're back." He wheeled his chair swiftly across the Turkestan rug on the tiled floor, and out into the cool, dim corridor that led to the lobby of the house. I waited for a while, polishing my gun even brighter.

The gun room was the locus of power, as well as the stimulus to much exciting memory. It spoke to the eleven-year-old boy, but was also evocative for any hunter, in a country where hunting was synonymous with trade, commerce, government, and survival. The influence of the tiger over the affairs of India was about as significant as the impact of wolves, or saber-toothed cats, over bands of human hunters equipped only with stone weapons.

The approach of the tiger, no matter how silently and stealthily the big cat moves, sends alarm tremors running through jungle and forest, meadow and thicket. The harsh cries of jungle babblers and the screams of red-wattled lapwings warn of approaching death. I traveled to the open woodlands of central India, the Madhya Pradesh, to the ringing barks of sambar deer, which sent the tiger warning onward for half a mile. The splendid swamp deer, or barasingha, lift their voices in a thrilling, communal baying. It is like being connected to a network of expectation: the tiger is coming.

On the scrub plains of Rajasthan, black bucks leap vertically, four legs held stiffly together, as their hooves strum the ground in a signal to all who have an interest in the approach of the cat. The gaurs—India's massive, high-shouldered cattle—growl like dogs and trumpet "tiger-tiger" to the forested hill country. I look for birds, but listen to the changes in the cries of monkeys, their chattering turning to screams, their alarms picked up by the birds I seek and sent rushing onward and outward, diminuendo, away from the tread of the invisible cat.

Because I was preoccupied with birds, it was the peacock that I listened for most expectantly. That this gaudy fop should be such a perfect sentinel sent shivers down my spine. He burst out of a mimosa with his weirdly childlike wail, hollow in the dim, early morning light when I liked to hunt. His voice said, "Tiger!"

As the son of a plantation owner who was also an adviser for the fifty-million-acre irrigation complex built by the British, I traveled widely on the Indian continent, and no journey could be made without reference to, and respect for, the tiger. The animal haunted the mind as much as the countryside colored and caressed the eyes. I thought India was the most beautiful place I had ever seen, and I had been all over the world. I could be taken across the Punjab, in what is now Pakistan, and travel into the uplands of Kashmir, where the Himalayan foothills seal off India from the rest of Asia, and could be sure that almost every step of the journey would yield a tiger story.

We gathered around a footprint in the ruins of a fort at Chitor, in Rajasthan, looking at a column of ants filing through it. Our car stopped one night, to allow a bunched herd of barasingha to cross the road, when suddenly, almost as though somebody inside the car had uttered it, a human-like voice said, "Tok!"

"Close the windows," cried the syce, or chief groom, at the wheel of the car. "That's a tiger!"

One cool evening, in Srinagar, that beautiful high city of Kashmir, conversation on an outdoor terrace dining place was silenced by strange cries coming from nearby hills. The Kashmiris laughed. They liked hearing the "pooking noise," as they called it, of tigers. Actually, it had rather an odd resemblance to the warning cry of the sambar, then one of the common deer of India. We wondered whether the tiger could call in its victims. Almost anything was believable about an animal of which there was so much myth, so little fact.

It was, however, the reaction of the Indian himself to the tiger that left me with a haunting sense of imminence that I could observe but not suffer. The Indian was terrified of the tiger. My ayah, that all-purpose Indian woman who might be nursemaid, governess, servant, friend, became almost speechless at the sound of certain bird cries which suggested the presence of tiger. Lahkshman Gupta, my friend, who helped me collect moths and stuff the birds, became tremulous at the mention of tiger.

Once, as guests of a plantation owner who had hacked a property out of the jungles of the Sundarbans, in the deltas of the Ganges and the Brahmaputra, we had just finished collecting some moths from a pergola in the gardens of the house, when we heard a tiger grunting. Gupta froze. When I tried to take a fresh-caught moth from his fingers, I found he had mashed it. The grunting had a contemplative quality to it, as though the tiger were preoccupied with some task. Then he woofed like a big dog. Gupta was running down the gravel path for the house. In a long silence that followed, as I picked up the scattered moth-collecting equipment, moans of exquisite feeling came out of the darkness. Despite myself, goose bumps ran across my skin.

Gupta and I were invited by a rajah to play golf on his private links, or course, and we were wakened one night by a pair of tigers apparently passing on either side of the palace. We were sleeping on a porch, and could hear the animals communicating with each other. Their cries were softly penetrating *ahoo*s that came through the lowered lattice blinds, and lingered in our ears. They sounded like ships in a fog, trying to pinpoint each other's positions, but the sounds were faintly mournful in suggesting that they must fail.

We were on the third floor, but Gupta became very agitated. "We must get up," he said, swinging his pudgy legs to the floor. I did not understand why. "Listen!" I said sharply, because the cries were continuing.

"We must stand in the corridor," he said, his voice rising. I refused to get out of bed. "Custard," I said, an English term for coward. But in a moment, one of the servants came pattering down the corridor to the porch, and asked us if we wanted to stand in the corridor until the tigers had gone.

In Stanley-Robinson's view of the tiger, any hunter of the animal had to be not only dedicated but also British. "Europeans never make good hunters." The true tiger hunter was steely, like an explorer in a journey of discovery, willing to feel the bite of the country, to go among its malarias, and to master its many diseases of bowel and liver. Many shikari died, which gave high drama to the hunting ritual.

For me, the ritual was centered in the hallway of our house, where it spilled out onto the wide veranda that kept the interior well shaded from the direct sun. A sixteen-cylinder Cadillac belonging to my father brought the first of the men to the door. They were rather uniform, mostly lean, tall, perhaps with small and careful mustaches, but certainly all economical in their gestures, reserved in their enthusiasms. Most of them had blue eyes. They greeted Stanley-Robinson in monosyllables.

How many people had been killed? Would the rajah provide enough beaters? "We will need about a thousand men," said Stanley-Robinson. It might take several sweeps to locate the tiger. What were its possibilities of refuge? It was essential to avoid a stalemate, if the animal was wounded and could hole up somewhere. "I don't want anybody killed," said Stanley-Robinson.

Everybody in the house knew the stories. Tigers were presumed to be totally fearless. They came into houses. A month before, wakened by a night bird at midnight, I had looked out my bedroom window, and there was a tiger on the front driveway, a vermilion-clad horror that made me involuntarily start back from the mosquito netting. It had one paw lifted, and was sniffing the house. I was sure that the front door was open, as usual. They were probably still making bread in the big kitchen at the back of the building.

One night in 1906, Colonel Reginald Satterwaite headed for the bathroom of his house at Shillong, in Assam, only to find a tiger in his bathtub.

"I really could not decide," he wrote to a friend later, "whether to run for it, or bluff it out."

Bluff seemed to be the best policy, because it was well known that tigers became quite excited at the sight of running people. Satterwaite held his ground. The tiger slid past him, down the corridor, and into the kitchen. A terrible scream there told Satterwaite that the bluff had worked for him, but that the cook had chosen to run.

After a long moment, the smells from our house must have convinced the tiger that it was too risky to enter. The gun room lay off the main corridor, and the animal could almost certainly smell the guns, which many tigers had come to regard as dangerous. With a shake of its head, the tiger disappeared.

But although the average tiger would never willingly seek engagement with man, the jungles and woods concealed many animals which were always ready to abandon traditional modes of behavior. Age, or lack of it, injuries, or sickness, or provocation, often drove tigers into heavily populated settlements, where, for a time at least, it was absurdly easy to eat well.

John Masters, the novelist of Indian life, was taking an evening walk through the buildings of a bustling military cantonment on the northwestern frontier of the 1920s when an Indian walking behind him was ripped to shreds by a tiger dropping out of a tree. Masters organized a tiger hunt, but was nearly killed by the animal, which had not fled, and in fact ambushed *him* while he was trying to stalk it.

Once the wildlife was known a little, then its language became an extension of the tiger's unseen presence. It was said that a good tiger hunter could tell where he was located in India with his eyes shut, merely by listening to the warning cries of the jungle and forest dwellers. I remember particularly the "phnew" cry of the jackal, which was often a warning of tiger, a bloodcurdling scream that was frightening enough by itself, much less as a warning of a man-killer approaching.

Once, on a picnic, I watched my ayah's face as she listened to an uproar amongst the forest birds, which included the child's cry of a peacock. She was intent, frightened perhaps, but there also seemed to be a kind of gleeful dread in her listening, which told of her conviction that disaster must come, and she was facing it. Then came the peacock's official tiger cry, a vaguely human scream, hollow against the oppressive overcast of the day, an unearthly invocation that was both a warning and a suggestion that a creature was already doomed. The peacock does not fly like other birds; it hurtles. The sight of its untidy body streaming across a clearing proclaimed a hysteria that was also in the ayah's face. After all, the peacock was not even remotely a victim. It was very disquieting, made sinister when nothing happened; no hunting animal appeared.

"Very well," Stanley-Robinson was saying. "It will be necessary to organize the first drive from that old temple near the springs, through the oak woods to the top of the rise, and then down to, and encompassing, all of the valley near the river. Fanshawe, I expect you will find it convenient to split the beaters into three groups."

"Four," said Fanshawe.

"Very well. It is difficult country, and the ravines are attractive escape routes—for the tiger, that is; dangerous to you."

"The supposition is that we will lose a beater or two," said one of the blue-eyed men.

"In that country, it is probably inevitable," said Stanley-Robinson. "In fact, the beaters are basically the bait in such a situation, and if they get into difficulties, then that will be your opportunity. I warn you not to be impetuous with this animal. Keep well back from the beaters and do not risk any close work. When he comes into view, he will be moving very quickly, and because of his experiences, he will know something of your tactics."

In the year 1932, Ralph Stanley-Robinson was sitting in the living room of his Jubbulpore bungalow, a small mahogany table before him, on which he had placed his gin and tonic, his pipe, his sambar leather tobacco pouch, and his copy of Hardy's *Far from the Madding Crowd*. The big windows, really French doors, leading out to the verandah were shielded by latticelike roll blinds. These were let down to the floor and they moved slightly in the wash of air from the punkah moving in the ceiling over Stanley-Robinson's head.

A tiger was known to be in the region of his estate. But it was thought to be a tigress, and a young animal, and so not dangerous. There had been no reports of stock losses, no

Indians menaced. Stanley-Robinson was confident that the animal would find sufficient hunting in some forests of an aristocratic Hindu friend who preserved his deer herds from hunting by locals as a means of attracting tigers to his estate. He was, like Stanley-Robinson, a tiger hunter himself, but that rarity among Indians, a sportsman of the British school, more interested in the quality of the hunting than in the procurement of the trophy.

The tiger came through the French doors at nine o'clock. It brought down the blinds, and broke the doors out of their frames in a shower of glass. It was the blinds that saved Stanley-Robinson's life. Although the cat smashed the table, and Stanley-Robinson's pelvis, it could not extricate itself from the wicker blind immediately, and cartwheeled through the room, destroying furniture, bringing down chandeliers, and filling the house with roars of frustration.

The servants fled out the back of the house, and Stanley-Robinson dragged himself into the hallway, where an old Lee-Enfield sporting rifle was held in the walking-stick rack. But before he could get back to the living room door, the tiger was gone through another set of French doors in a cascade of glass and wood.

"Does anybody have any questions?"

The question that I had, perhaps like everybody else, concerned how it was possible to act sensibly, in crisis, against an animal of such unpredictability. Already, it was ingrained in me that it was impossible to move, think, plan, or even dream, without reference to the animal. I had traveled with my family to many remote places, which gave me a consistency of information about tigers, but no confidence that I was learning new things.

On a typical trip we would be driven from the railway station to the estate of a rajah, who in one memorable instance had achieved respect among the British for his success in preventing all uncontrolled hunting on his vast holdings. When the car slid to a silent stop at the estate gates, a peacock flew overhead, an untidy bustle of plumage, screaming, as my eyes turned immediately toward my ayah's face. Beggars raised the stumps of their arms. The rajah had discovered that not only were handless men incapable of poaching deer, but they were an excellent warning to others contemplating it. Also, they could not pick the forests clean of firewood.

We were quartered in a guesthouse overlooking a man-made green lake of about fifty acres, surrounded by open woodlands. The close-cropped grass, set out in meadows neatly flanked by quiet, shadowed groves of trees, looked to me more like the parkland of ducal estates I had seen in England. Small groups of chital, the dainty Indian deer, grazed along the banks of the lake, and near it were the more robust sambar and barasingha. I expected a gaitered gamekeeper to come striding into view, as he had done on the grounds of my boarding school in England, or to see fox hunters bursting out of the trees. But the memories I had of England were dispelled in a howl of monkeys.

"Perhaps the young man would like to go to the library, or the conservatorium."

I padded down long, darkened corridors, toward predestined appointments with tigers. While the adults drank tea, I took books from the natural history sections of the library, and followed the tiger back to its evolution from the saber-toothed cat.

That ancestral animal had dominated Asia during the early Pleistocene, and it surely must have had a decisive effect on the hunting men of the age. While Paleolithic men and women were barricading themselves inside caves to get through the nights, the forebears of the modern tiger and lion were dividing the Old World between them. The tiger took Asia, and spread southeastward into the islands of the Pacific, southwestward into India. The lion moved to Europe from the Middle East, and then to Africa, some outriders reaching northern India before they were halted, presumably by tigers coming from the other direction.

In this hunting division of the world, the tiger showed the more ingenious adaptation, in its solitary domination of many places. The lion, communal, secure in prides, settled into savanna countries and spent most of its evolution asleep. Or so it seemed to me, after my experiences with that animal in Africa. Meanwhile, the tiger was prowling the slopes of Mount Ararat in eastern Turkey, and the forests of China, before that country was wrecked by human population increases and unsatisfiable demands for wood.

Up until at least five thousand years ago, the tiger was still padding through the forests of poplar and oak that led down the peninsula toward modern Hong Kong. The cat also dominated the scrub oak, walnut, and birch woods of Manchuria. It climbed mountain slopes forested with cedar, hunted above the tree line, in six feet of snow if necessary, and in Siberia at temperatures of thirty and forty degrees below zero.

This was also the animal that moved easily through the stifling humidity of Malaya, through Indian grass jungles where the ground temperatures might reach one hundred and fifty degrees, over mountain passes, at thirteen thousand feet, between Sikkim and Nepal. That was why Stanley-Robinson said it was an imperial animal.

The flexibility of animal was in contrast to the rigidities of the schemes of animal and human life through which it moved. In Nepal, a remote and uncomfortable place which we visited only once in those days, I was told that the tiger was a family creature, often seen in the company of its mate and cubs. But in Maharashtra, a district administrator said the animal was totally solitary.

Traveling India, and absorbing tiger lore, at the window of the car, in the dusky libraries, made the continent exciting, mysterious with its suggestions of sudden death, yet also filled with the colors of its peoples, the luxuries of its rulers, set against the growl of an animal which could not be subjugated by either. Kipling captured this sense of imminency, or invented it, in creating an atmosphere of hunting which was "beyond the frontier" of description, according to T. S. Eliot.

The youngster, propelled through a gaudy, entrancing landscape of possibly ecstatic danger, might be heard singing Mowgli's song:

> *I am two Mowglis, but the hide of Shere Khan is under my feet*
> *All the jungle knows that I have killed Shere Khan. Look, look well, O wolves.*
> *Ahae! My heart is heavy with the things I do not understand.*

The blue-eyed men, whom Gupta, with one of his delicate shudders, called "cruel, like eagles," were getting ready to leave. More motorcars arrived. I loved these moments. The rifles were in their sheaths. Boxes of ammunition were temporary seats. Khidmatgars, or water carriers, bustled around with their containers, uttering high-pitched cries. The beaters sounded like birds as they argued about their positions in the cars. The British brought a unity to India which was hated, but which would be a nostalgic thing after they left.

The British had come to India in the seventeenth century. It was then a peninsula of chaos, a fact which Stanley-Robinson impressed upon me and which most British historians emphasized. There was no central government or even a common idea of Indian identity. Prince fought prince, and rajah battled rajah. It could be said that the only time the Indians came together was when invaders bound them in conquest. The Moguls controlled much of the northern part of the peninsula. Alexander and his Greeks, perceiving the disunity, might have conquered the whole country.

The British found it easy to do so. In fact, they had more trouble with tigers than with Indians. In 1600, when the British East India Company got its charter from Elizabeth I, many thousands of square miles—some said half a million—of India were depopulated by tigers. Farmers, after establishing crops, grazing animals, residences, and roads, were driven from their lands by tigers, the stock destroyed, their workers taken in the fields, and then their families plucked from out of their residences. Travel on roads, in such tiger-dominated country, was impossible without either firearms or great numbers of travelers banded together.

"Very well, good luck to you all," said Stanley-Robinson, shaking hands with some of the men from his chair. "God speed, and good fortune—all those things, don't you know. Keep me in touch, however you can." The cars were loaded and purred away.

"Perhaps you would permit me to assist you in mounting your most recent birds," said Stanley-Robinson.

His interest in the taxidermy came in part, I thought, from my handling of the expensive Belgian bird-collecting gun which my mother had brought back from Europe recently. "My young tiger hunter," he called me, even though I told him that shooting any kind of cat was probably beyond me.

The mosquito season was past, and I had the servants wheel the taxidermy table out of my room and onto the veranda. This was a place of government. From it, India was observed. To it, India came for favors, permissions, indulgences. My father, on the rather rare occasions when he was in the house, sat on the veranda, white leggings covering the tops of his sambar walking shoes, in a high-backed wicker chair. The veranda was a place, a theater, really, for Indian storytellers. They could find employment here, or favors, by the use of mettle and imagination, often displaying their facial scars, their missing fingers or hands, or their exaggerated limps, as examples of their loyalty to some brave shikari master for whom they had suffered the tiger so that he might kill it, and rid their district of its scourge.

A smart Indian—and there were a great number of them—could dine out on his tiger stories, and if he was really good, retire on them to the security of being the headman of the compound, or the syce, who was no longer husbanding horses in those days, but in charge of the governor's long motorcars.

Lying on the veranda so that my eyes were at floor level, I could watch the Indian faces coming up the broad white stairs, heads ascending into view in upward jerks, revealing shoulders, torsos, robes, smiles of supplication, and graceful gestures of the hands. They were a very theatrical and beautiful people. My friend Gupta, ever smiling, came up the stairs. He bowed. I saw him as a fellow bird hunter.

His people had once owned land here, perhaps this land. Some of his people's records were in my father's library. But now all records were vastly improved. They were accurate, rather than imaginative. A great British service to Indians had been to make them aware of who they were by sorting out the records. Two thousand years of chaos, and much of the country depopulated by tigers, had not encouraged national identity.

The Indian records of crop yields, invoices of market deliveries, of debts incurred and paid, rupee by rupee, were all there. But added to them now was the authority of empire, the joining of it all to the web of the outside world. Correspondence from Rangoon, Sydney, Allahabad, and the Seychelles said that the world was circular, not flat, that there was no need to be driven from home by animals or barbarians, that everything could be made comprehensible and unified by using the English language, clipped, efficient, accurate.

"I have four skins ready for mounting," I said. "Could you begin stretching the brain-fever bird, while I start stuffing this jungle babbler? The barbet and the bush quail we can do tomorrow, perhaps."

"I am not very confident that they will secure this tiger," said Stanley-Robinson, as he worked away.

Part of his success as a hunter had come from the closeness with which he worked with local populations, a talent not enjoyed by many other hunters. Despite his disparaging view of Indians in general, he had a deep respect for them as individuals, and as masters of their district lores. It was the mass of Indians that aroused his contempt, helpless as barasingha under the approach of the great enemy.

"They will not listen to the beaters." He shook his head, as if that were his mistake.

In Rajasthan, merely to maintain equilibrium (before the British arrived), villagers had to be united in sweeps through thornbush thickets, slaughtering all the tiger cubs they could find, and praying to their gods that they might avoid the adult tigers. They did not dare attack the full-grown animals, which, once they were aroused to the danger to their cubs, often turned the drives of the villagers into extremely costly operations. Yet it was worth some deaths to keep the population of tigers under any control at all.

The Rajasthanians were not a fierce people. The Naga, occupying the hot tropical evergreen jungles of Assam, Manipur, and Nagaland, were extremely ferocious and aggressive. But the tiger terrified them too, because it was so much harder to control in the entangling growths of jungles. They mobilized up to five thousand people in their tiger hunts, and drove the cats, by the massed clanging of cymbals, the beating of drums, and the screams of the beaters, into labyrinthine traps.

The tiger, guided by high wooden palisades, either fell into a spike-filled pit or found itself at the threshold of a deep ravine, or was confronted by an antique armory of muzzle loaders, ancient cannons, and spearmen. One tiger killed by the Naga was impaled by three hundred and six spears.

It became extraordinary how many Indians had run afoul of the tiger. Eventually, I had to concede that the terror of my ayah was based on fact, not upon her imagination. Her mother had been eaten by a tiger. Her oldest brother lost his right arm to a tiger. Two of our servants had tiger scars, and were proud of them, if also apprehensive that there might be others in store.

Even after the British brought the repeating rifle to

India around 1850, the tiger did not retreat quickly. If anything, its depredations on domestic animals increased. The rifle helped make the villagers safe, by quickly cutting out the worst of the man-eaters. But British methods of animal husbandry increased the numbers of donkeys, sheep, cattle, goats, and domestic pigs through the latter half of the century. This was tiger food.

No record of animal losses was kept, but the British started keeping track of human mortalities from the year 1800 onward. About three hundred thousand people were taken by tigers in the nineteenth century alone, or about eight people every day. If our own experiences in the twentieth century were any guide, the nineteenth-century tigers also took between six and ten million farm animals in the century.

The strength of the tiger, and the great difference in the maximum size of a male and the minimum size of a female, made it highly unpredictable. One tiger of Stanley-Robinson's experience jumped a vertical fifteen-foot bank with a two-hundred-fifty-pound deer clamped in its mouth. The timid villager, hearing the softest sound on the blackest night, might not know, until it was too late, whether the darkness concealed a two-hundred-pound tigress stalking a chicken or a seven-hundred-pound male about to demolish the house with a blow of its paw in search of a cow, a donkey, an Indian.

From the beginning of their conquest of India in the seventeenth century, the British, like the Romans in their own country, understood the importance of fast continental travel. Almost before they shot a single tiger, they erected a national network of rest houses. These were among my favorite places in India, because so many of them told tiger stories, through pictures of personalities affixed to the walls by travelers, or by framed newspaper accounts of how districts had been cleared of man-eaters by brave shikaris.

The rest houses enabled the hunter, the soldier, the

administrator, the visitor, to go from one end of India to the other and always be sure of fresh horses, fresh food, cool drinks, and impeccable attention by highly trained staff. To Stanley-Robinson's hunting stories I could add my own experiences, which included staying in scores of these rest houses, many of which still stand, and are in use today.

The rest houses, like Stanley-Robinson's inexhaustible patience to get his fragile bird skin stretched exactly to the right tension, were monuments to British determination. I could look up from my bed in almost any of them, straight into the fierce eyes of sahibs who had regulated, controlled, and hunted the country, faded sepia photographs of Fotheringhams, Lytton-Smythes, Willoughbys, Stanley-Robinsons, generations of men responding to a country, and the tiger in it: the colonels, the generals, the Fusiliers, the Bengal Lancers, the Royal Marines.

It was impossible to sleep in these places without feeling the breath of the tiger, hearing the boom of the Express, and feeling connected with heroic events. I sipped lemonade where they had eaten and slept. I kept some record of them. There was Lieutenant General Sir Montagu Gilbert Gerard, A.C.S.I., C.B., who specialized in tigers, but also took leopards and bears. General A. A. A. Kinlock, C.B., took only rhinoceros and Captain A. G. Arbutnot, R.F.A., confined himself to bison. The Indian hunt was a study in freedom of choice, because there was plenty of everything.

Lieutenant Colonel Bairnsfather, late 14th Bengal Lancers, looked as fierce as a leopard, but he was a small-game hunter only, which might mean marbled cats, golden cats, leopard cats, jungle cats, fishing cats, desert cats, caracals, lynxes, Pallas's cats, civets, linsangs, jackals, foxes, dholes, otters, pandas, martens, ferret badgers, hog badgers, hares, porcupines, to say nothing of an almost illimitable choice of birds as game.

F. O. Gadsen, late Royal Indian Marines, was a fisherman only, but in a country where fish survived in numbers incomprehensible to an African or a Chinese hunter. Major

Nevile Taylor, another 14th Bengal Lancer, admitted to being more frivolous than his stern-pictured colleagues, a "general hunting" man who also played polo and practiced pig sticking.

Stanley-Robinson went tiger hunting (as a sport, that is, rather than as an assignment to rid a district of a stock or man eater) in the worst of the pre-monsoon heat (roughly March through June), when the vegetation was driest, the woodlands open, and the long grass fallen or burned. "A tiger can conceal itself effectively in grass only five inches high." In temperatures consistently above one hundred degrees, he slogged his way up hills, across scorching plains, marching three to five hundred miles in a typical sixty-day shoot.

Like almost all Indian big-game hunters, he carried the ten-pound Express, the bullet of which looks like a small cannon shell. The weapon was flush-sighted, the two hundred grains of black powder in its massive shells firing a hollow bullet which disintegrated or mushroomed on impact. The blow was so powerful that if it hit sufficient flesh to mushroom at all, the tiger invariably dropped, stunned for a moment.

The Paradox, despite its much greater hitting power, only weighed seven pounds, and Stanley-Robinson carried it mainly for the benefit of any other hunter who might have to join him in a crisis. "Brutal," he would murmur, at the mention of the gun.

He bought almost all his equipment in India ("A ninety percent savings in costs, laddy"), much of his clothing from the army and navy stores at Bombay, and his weaponry from English gun-makers in Calcutta. From England, he brought a good pattern of Norfolk jacket and walking breeches, and had a local durzi, or tailor, copy them. He chose his cloth meticulously, preferring material from the British mills at Cawnpore, or fabric from the Basel Mission at Cannanore.

The ritual of preparation was almost lovingly performed, and it would not take me long to understand that the shooting of the tiger was very much of a secondary event to such superb organization of detail and refinement of choice preceding it. The Indian was superseded in his country by somebody who had learned to know it better. His gaiters were chosen for their resistance to thorns and snakes, and his ankle boots, manufactured of extremely pliant sambar leather, were designed, with their thick, plaited cotton soles without heels, to give him thirty miles of walking a day, for seventy days, without disintegration caused by scuff or sweat. He carried Indian-manufactured knives of inferior quality because British steel, although more durable, was too hard to resharpen in remote places.

His tent was substantial, a one-hundred-pound burden for his bearers, and came from Muir Mills, at Cawnpore. He traveled to Allahabad to get his beds, tables, chairs, wash stands, canvas tubs. His chaguls, porous leather or canvas bags for water (evaporation kept the water chilled daylong), were of the highest procurable quality.

To hunt "fairly comfortably," he needed five camels, which could be hired for about ten rupees a month in northern and central India. He took a khidmatgar, or valet, a water carrier, a dhobi, or washerman, a sweeper, or gun bearer, and at least two grooms. Each man was paid twenty to eighty rupees a month, and fed himself. Stanley-Robinson carried the best guns available, which brought his cost of getting into the field to about one thousand dollars. The actual hunting, or shikar, expenses ran about five dollars a day.

The Indians never understood the strict code of behavior that accompanied the precision of choosing the equipment. They were baffled by men who voluntarily imposed great hardships and dangers upon themselves, more often than not without visible reward. The British shikari got up at sunrise, walked to his next camp, and then went out to beat and shoot until just before sunset. Then he came back to his camp, took his bath, and "arrayed himself in light flannels, and dined," in the words of the Anglo-Indian historian V. S. Merpel. Stanley-Robinson never drank water in the field, unless desperate, and he never drank liquor before sundown. "At dinner," observed a meticulously prepared hunter, General Gerard, "one can take wine or whiskey and soda, as usual."

King George V of England made his last visit to India in 1932. In his honor, a local maharajah organized a royal hunt befitting the emperor of all the Indians. Five hundred elephants were assembled. The elephants formed a line and advanced against a pincer movement of countless thousands of human beaters, slogging their way through brush, grass, and thicket.

It was, by all the accounts, a unique hunt. The royal party fired generally at any movement in the grass. King George and his guests bagged a total of thirty-nine tigers, an extraordinary feat against an animal that is so largely solitary, and which demands, and secures, an individual territory of up to ten square miles. Later, it was murmured discreetly in the gentlemen's clubs where the real shikari gathered that a number of beaters had also been bagged.

The hunt as practiced by aristocratic Indians was not only a most luxurious form of entertainment, it was "an Oriental rather than British form of sport." This meant it was more truly an expression of a national character, because it lacked the mask of self-discipline. In contrast to the sweating shikari slogging alone through the Sundarbans, the thorn country, the deserts, the Indian hunter wore white drill and tennis shoes, and carried an umbrella against the sun. Baskets of iced drinks jingled under the seat of the howdah. There was, in the theory of it, at least, no danger. The ladies came along. The fact of it was that enraged tigers quite often attacked the elephants and clawed mahouts and riflemen off their perches.

Elephants sailed along like battleships, spitting broadsides of fire from their shooting platforms at landscapes staged-managed to be teeming with driven animals. Everything was shot: deer, buffalo, hyena, tiger, leopard, cheetah, cats of any kind, antelope, wild boar. Hundreds of animals died in a good drive.

Records of this hunt were patchy, and no count was kept of any animal killed except the tiger. In seven years before World War I, the Maharajah of Nepal and his guests disposed of nearly four hundred and fifty tigers. The Maharajah of Udaipur dropped at least one thousand tigers during a lifetime of hunting. The greatest Indian hunter was probably the Maharajah of Surguja, who shot his way through colonialism, war, independence, and democracy, until, by April 1965, he reported that he had personally shot one thousand, one hundred and fifty tigers.

In his whole life, Ralph Stanley-Robinson shot nineteen tigers.

After tidying up his work, Stanley-Robinson gave me his clipped good night, and turned his wheelchair away from my table. Then he paused for a moment, in reflection.

"You have such interest in the hunting that I should tell you something. This rajah is a splendid chap, but like so many Indians, does not understand the way we do things. The reason this tiger will be so difficult to kill is because the rajah has already interfered. He has created an animal which, through ignorant persecution, has become vengeful. The rajah himself is in danger. Good night."

A telegram arrived three days after the blue-eyed men left, to say that the tiger had been located, after killing two beaters, but had broken through the Indian lines and had doubled back into thick jungle. Stanley-Robinson wheeled himself up and down the veranda for a couple of hours, before speaking.

"The secret of this kind of hunting is in knowing the animal intimately, its territories and prejudices, its variations in behavior, and above all, its idiosyncracies. Every tiger has a weak spot. It all turns on patience to know. To wait. To exploit the energy and drive of the animal itself.

These are very finely structured cats and they should not be bullied."

Yet, he would admit, sometimes the strength and endurance of the tiger made brutality necessary. He admired a famous nineteenth-century tiger hunter, G. P. Sanderson, who was at his prime around the time Stanley-Robinson was born, in 1870. Sanderson was called to deal with man-eaters in Mysore in that year. Some villagers had managed to trap a pair of tigers in a thicket and kept them there with hundreds of yards of heavy netting. Sanderson entered the thicket with a short-barreled heavy gun when it became impossible to drive them out.

"These were mouse-and-cat tactics, you understand," said Stanley-Robinson, with a chuckle.

It took him five days to place bullets in both the tigers. The weather was steaming hot. There was no water in the thicket area. Despite this, Sanderson still had to enter the thicket, at high risk, to drive the wounded animals into a region clear enough to get straight shots at them. When he killed them, they were still as active and as dangerous as when first trapped.

Sanderson designed a giant spring trap to catch tigers, so powerful that it took six men to prize open its jaws. It never caught a tiger, but it did throw an Indian fifty feet into a tree. Other entrapment techniques were developed by the Mysoreans, who possessed some of the richest land on the continent and were determined to farm. They designed a host of ingenious ploys—traps, ambushes, machines, and other devices to cripple and kill. A favorite was the deadfall type, in which a triggering device held up a huge slab of stone, weighing many tons. When the tiger plucked at a goat tethered under the stone, goat and tiger were crushed flat by the falling stone. One maharajah had mouse-type cage traps built, big enough for tigers and baited with goats, dozens of them trundled into the parklands to tempt the hunting animals.

Late in the nineteenth century, the technique was perfected of laying just enough poison, strychnine, into a goat or sheep carcass so that the tiger would not involuntarily vomit the poisoned flesh up immediately upon eating it. While the strychnine would not kill, it caused the big cat agony, and he roared his pain and rage almost constantly. Meanwhile, a call would go out for somebody like Stanley-Robinson or Sanderson. When the stricken tiger leaped from one thicket to another, the Englishman with the cradled Express was waiting. The .470 caliber bullet was on its way.

On the fifth day of the hunting party's departure, Stanley-Robinson received the news, delivered by a boy who had come from a telephone call received a dozen miles away, that the tiger had been cornered in an abandoned Hindu temple on a golf course thirty miles from the rajah's palace. It had been shot twice, but having no possible escape except through the front entrance of the temple, it charged with such unexpected speed that it ran down two beaters, crippling one. A Paradox had been discharged accidentally in the confusion, killing an elephant being used in the hunt.

"This is really a most lamentable business," said Stanley-Robinson. "Let us first of all have a cup of tea, and then, second, you can tell me again that marvelous story about the playful tiger of the Western Ghats."

It is in my memory today that the incident occurred at Cochin, on the Malabar shore flanking the Laccadive Sea, where Vasco da Gama built a factory in 1502. But there were so many trips, so many courtly Indians. Certainly, we were the guests of a tall and serious rajah who had been educated at Oxford. We became instant friends when he discovered my bird-collecting and taxidermy hobby, and arranged to personally show me his collection of captive birds. It was said that he had the largest private collection of birds in the world. As I put citronella on my forearms that evening, on one of the balconies of his pink palace overlooking a man-made lake, I counted two hundred West Australian black swans on the water in front of me.

"You are fond of wildlife, then," he said softly. "And so you are in for a treat that I have arranged for you, and your family."

The following day, we were all loaded onto the chairs of richly decorated elephants and set out in a convoy on a long journey to an unnamed place. My mahout kept driving his spiked pick into the skull of the elephant with such force that sometimes he had difficulty in withdrawing it from the wounds he had made.

The rajah provided a hunting motif for the trip: he had arranged an "ambush." The elephants climbed for an hour, through dense jungle, and we emerged at the top of cliffs, royal blue carpeting rolling away toward a balcony fenced and furnished with wickerwork, its floor tiled with mosaic marble and carnelian, set at the edge of a precipice that fell into a valley. A stream wandered, twinkling. Cane brakes bulked. Masses of ferns, palms, and the solid, dark red stems of huge teak trees made dense enclosures around our eyes. Brilliantly colored parrots slipped through the tops of the trees, like multicolored blossoms, screeching and caroling their presence in this place.

The servants brought us fruits and sweets, yogurt desserts and rich Indian pastries loaded with cream, wines and sodas and cordials. We spread ourselves out along the balcony just as, timed to a second, the first large Worcester china teapots appeared, and the clink of cups and the rattle of silverware sounded in front of a stammering brain-fever bird.

In this storybook atmosphere, all of us expected there would be a tiger, and the cat showed itself with the same precision as that being demonstrated in the pouring of the tea, head and shoulders appearing out of a cluster of bamboo almost directly opposite the wicker balcony. The face of the animal appeared to be smiling, a big and goofy smile, truly Alice's cat materialized from thin air. The cups were stilled. The servants stopped like statues, poised in attitudes of service, but faces turned toward the giant tiger in the valley.

"It is a totally unbelievable and delicious story," chortled Stanley-Robinson.

This was the scourge of the Sundarbans? This was that frightening roar in Himalaya foothills? This pussycat, gliding into the sun, swishing his tail like a dog? He looked up at us, as if waiting applause. We were held in hypnotic conjunction, thralled to a theatrical moment. Was he trained for this? We will never know.

Moments passed before we could perceive his size, very large indeed, immense, in fact, the largest tiger anybody there had ever seen. He put up his tail, bushed like a house cat's, and danced. He minced, he turned a gavotte, then raced through the long grass with the recklessness of a kitten. All at once, a flock of quail burst out of the grass and the tiger quickly dropped to a crouch, his elbows working like pistons. He appeared to be stalking the flying birds. But it was a parody. He was only pretending to stalk them.

When he came to the banks of the stream, he paused, then ran through its waters in a rush of spray. At once, he twisted to a stop in deeper water, stopped with an exaggerated Hollywood double take, and looked down. Then, with a great swipe of his paw, he raised a column of disturbed water. It splashed all over him. He shook his head, and sneezed three times, very fast.

Then he raced out of the water, tail held low, and disappeared abruptly into the shade of teaks. Polite applause came spontaneously from the balcony, and the clink of well-bred china resumed as the servants went back to work.

I was never to learn the final outcome of the rajah's tiger hunt. One night, about eight days after the cars had left our house, I was wakened at about one o'clock by somebody tugging my arm in the darkness. I could smell the strong medication that Stanley-Robinson took when the pain became very severe.

"Your parents have come home unexpectedly," he said, "and they are taking me to the hospital." He shook my hand clumsily, and with a hiss and squeal of rubber on the tiled floors, disappeared through the bedroom door. Two days later, I was sent to Calcutta. The house was closed. We were gone from India within a month. My birds were given to a museum in Singapore. Stanley-Robinson died in hospital after a year.

Ten years passed before I could finish the Indian journey. This was soon after the independence of 1947. The country looked as though it had been swept by panzers. The dark pall of visible and distant fires lay on the horizons everywhere. It was dangerous to drive in the car, even suicidal in some areas. A European automobile accident could bring a summary lynching. Two English women were torn to pieces, it was said, when they ran out of petrol. Transport was broken. Administration had fled. A hundred clutching hands reached for me as I ducked into a limousine.

There was no sign of the house, or its grounds, or of the trees, or any part of the plantation that had once surrounded it. The villagers turned away when I questioned them. I passed thousands of people in a field in Bengal, overhung by the smoke of a background fire, and heard the shrill ululation of a mob keening for blood. The people had surrounded a small herd of deer, barasingha, I thought, and were clubbing them, hacking them, stabbing them, pulling them to pieces. Haunches were waved high and a bloody head was carried away.

I knew, from my studies of the French Revolution, that many of those who were not allowed to be hunters under the ancien régime became murderers and destroyers in the new republic. I understood that India was being destroyed, as the French forests were leveled and the salmon rivers silted to extinction after 1792. But the actual details of India's destruction could not be pieced together by anybody who had not known the herds of animals before independence, the influence of the tiger before its forests were fired.

I bumped along unkempt roads littered with debris, passed burned railway stations and the ruins of imperial public works, the wreckage of rest houses, the collapse of bridges. The traveler knew this was the insanity of suppressed anger that had no object. The animal marked for death had gone. It refused to be a victim.

I would not get the figures right away; that would take another twenty years. But the Indian lion, in its northwestern enclave of Gujarat, and once only the sport of royalty, was decimated by vengeful Indians who had borne its raids too long without the sahib's guns. The great Indian rhinoceros, also a royal victim, was reduced from thousands of animals to a handful of survivors living in accidental sanctuaries.

The Kashmir stag, which had been such a favorite of Stanley-Robinson, was slaughtered in its many scores of thousands, brought to a crumpled remnant of two hundred animals. The buffalo, which was once only the delectation of a few colonels who liked that kind of shooting, and some ardent naturalists who specialized in photographing them at close range, despite the dangers, dropped from tens of thousands of animals to three thousand.

Stanley-Robinson used to rhapsodize about the hundreds of thousands of barasingha in the middle 1930s, and these herds were trimmed to four thousand animals. The black buck, that delicious antelope, came close to extinction. The gaur, a surly wild ox with its barking call, became only a tiny fraction of its once great numbers. The delicate chital all but disappeared.

I would return to India a dozen times, and wander widely, following rumors of survival. The Brahmaputra valley, which had once hosted so many barasingha, would be found empty. There were animals remaining in Assam, and also Bhutan, and on large estates which had been successfully defended during independence. But the major condition was one of a great desolation.

Then, in the late forties, and the fifties, the extent of this final, ravaging hunt would become somewhat measurable in counting the cat skins that began appearing everywhere. The demise of the tiger could not be chronicled because there were no records, no writers. The skins were always a good currency, and millions now had guns. The tiger had always been a desperate enemy. Everybody hated him. His menace lay equally over all religions, sects, and persuasions.

If it was true that twenty thousand tigers faced independence, and the end of Stanley-Robinson's kind of hunting, then it was probably also true that only about two thousand of them survived liberation from the sway of the cruel and blue-eyed men.

3 ○ The Rifleman

The chiming sound that wakened me was distant but still very clear in the dove gray light before dawn. I looked over to where Horace lay sprawled on his back, one blanket carelessly swathed over his lean and muscular body, still asleep. I sat watching the light grow and listening to the spreading sounds of the forest. A last *chong* of the bellbird hung in the pallid air. Then the sun leaped from range to range of mountains, turning the waiting distance beyond my view into a blaze of colors.

My rifle gleamed beside me. I took the protective bindings from the telescopic sight and began polishing. This was my most valuable possession, a Swiss-made instrument with interchangeable eyepieces which I had not yet had a chance to use. The rifle was a Browning, American designed and Belgian manufactured, semiautomatic in action, and a bit too heavy for hunting in the mountains.

"It's a toy," Horace had said scornfully, referring to the optical sighting device, as he unpacked our gear from the car two days before. We had driven into the foothills of the mountains as far as the torturous gravel road would allow. We were now up at about five thousand feet. The previous day, we had walked perhaps forty miles, hard, grinding travel through foothills of scrub, up through gullies so densely ferned and shaded that our boots were soaked with very ancient dew. We had passed through a landscape that was at war with itself, the scattered clumps of stately pinelike rimu rising from a mongrel crowd of imported trees from Europe, America, and Australia.

Horace wakened with a retching cough.

"Shitabrick!" he growled, and reached for a battered tin of Grey's Fine Cut Tobacco, from which he extracted a fingering of damp stuff and rolled it into a lean, drooping cigarette, known as a racehorse, with which he began each day. He turned over and lit a pile of twigs under a blackened aluminum billy of water which he had set up the previous night. Apart from oaths, he was quite unable to talk until he had drunk at least two enamel mugs of overbrewed, almost black tea.

Horace Henry Sebastian Rangiatikaweko was half pakeha, or white man, and half Maori, or Polynesian: a hybrid dynamo. He was thirty-two, and by profession a fencer, although he also owned a bit of land and did some spare-time farming. He would be dead within four or five years because of the deadly incidence of tuberculosis among young Maoris and because he drank heavily and hence was more vulnerable than was the pakeha.

He earned his living by digging thousands of neat, circular holes in the earth, then ramming into them hand-split birch posts, packing the soil around each with a tamper, and then fixing to the posts eight strands of wire. The staples he used were three-quarters driven so as not to impede the horizontal movement of the wires. The wires were then cranked tight with a wire puller. To these wires were nailed droppers, the staples driven home tight in these smaller posts, which did not touch the ground and which prevented stock from pushing through the wires when they slackened with age. These fences were the best I had ever seen, anywhere in the world. When struck by a hammer, they made a deep-throated strumming that rolled into the hills and might be heard faintly at the other end of the fence, perhaps twenty miles away.

Fencing was one of the hardest jobs a man could do, particularly if he worked in the high country, where two-hundred-pound loads of posts and wire had to be hefted on the fencer's back to the place where he must do his work. The aloneness of fencing tended to make the worker taciturn, hunch-shouldered, a chain smoker, and alcoholic. Or perhaps it was such men who became fencers. All fencers were men of immense pride, in their work first, but also in some ancillary passion. It might be women, or the conviction that all the beer in a pub could be drunk if a man could just stay on his feet for a few days. One fencer came down from the hills and drank ten gallons of beer and ate forty dozen oysters before he needed a nap.

Horace had more than his share of passions, because to his lonely work, his heavy drinking, and a great skill in hunting he had added a final compulsion: a fierce, possessive affection for this isolated, remote country, Aotearoa—Land of the Long White Cloud.

Some of the pakeha said he was born to hunt, which was a high compliment, because hunting in such a mountainous country demanded muscles as well as brains. Others, who did not know Rangi, as Horace was called, felt nervous that he might be wandering the high country, fully armed and perhaps drunk.

"You never know when those fellows are going to go off the tracks," was a common comment about men like Horace.

But it was also recalled that the army had found him good enough to use as a sniper, most particularly during the Sicilian and Italian campaigns, and then, later, as a behind-the-lines scout who, having devised a silencer for his rifle from bulldozer parts, killed seventy-six Germans without ever being heard, much less seen.

He burned himself on the billy, and swore, and then swore again when his limp cigarette fell into the tea. The chiming calls of the bellbird had meanwhile given way to the melodic cadences of the tui, a later-rising bird, and more gaudy, a bold exhibitionist which never skulked to sing. The sun caught his shimmer in a nearby rimu so that he appeared to burst into sight, shaking himself, with a filigreed patterning of fine feathers around his neck and shoulders, like a mantilla of very fine lace.

When Captain James Cook reached New Zealand, in October 1769, he anchored about a mile off a beautiful bay he called Tolaga. Sir Joseph Banks, the explorer-naturalist who would transform the Royal Botanic Gardens at Kew, accompanied Cook, and described the experience of coming to shore. The Englishmen heard a "most extraordinary sweetness of music emanating from the land, of such loudness, moreover, that we were determined that there must be an indescribable abundance of birds."

He understated what awaited the explorers. This was a country of birds, a paradise of birds, a place that birds had reached but which, apparently, their enemies had not. "Mammals were not present on earth in sufficient numbers to have reached New Zealand," wrote W. R. B. Oliver, a museum director, in 1930. No rodents, no snakes, no disease-carrying mosquitoes; it was a sanctuary of birds. One species of quite unaggressive owl, the morepork, flew the night forests, and seemed to prefer hawking for insects to hunting the myriad sleeping birds. The laughing owl avoided the forest altogether and hunted beetles in downs country, uttering dismal shrieks.

It was its own world. Many of the birds had stopped using their wings altogether, preferring to walk, or glide, or climb, rather than fly. In the New Zealand laboratory of evolution, flight seemed to be less an evolutionary advantage than a tiresome consumption of energy that might be better spent singing. One bird, the kiwi, had been so long isolated in flightlessness that it had dropped even the stumps of its wings and so was the only earth creature with two legs and no sign of other limbs.

When Cook and Banks ventured into these chiming forests, they had to brush birds off the barrels of their collecting guns so they could aim at the ones they wished to shoot. Later arrivals to New Zealand shot for food, and their favorite target was the kereru, a native pigeon with sparkling blue and gold plumage, about the size of a small goose. They fired, and the kereru fell, and exploded. Its plump, soft body burst out of its skin. The flesh tasted of wild fruits. The forest, or bush, as it was called, towered into cathedral enclosures where the music carried a purity of innocence because there was so little visible stress of the hunt and death.

Some of this bird music was described only with difficulty, as by the ornithologist J. C. M'Lean, writing about the blue-wattled crow, or kokako. "Few sounds are so enchanting as when a party of these birds is practising a number of rich flute and organ-like notes, many as if in chord, and some ventriloquil. It is only at early morning, when the sun first tips the trees, that such a combination may be heard, for then the clicking and tapping sounds of other tunes are not indulged in."

The mix of song held early travelers transfixed. The warm liquid runs of thrushes blended with the sweet singing of bush canaries, the warbling of stitchbirds, the steeple chimes of the bellbirds and tuis.

Whatever the purpose of bird song, there must have been some profound reason for such symphonic variety in this far land, not faintly matched in Asia, Africa, or South America. There must have been an extraordinary purpose in giving every individual tui a different song, as if the wealth of melody created the need for infinite improvisation, in the manner of Handel at the harpsichord or Charlie Parker on the saxophone.

The bird on the branch looked down at me, arched his neck, the lace shimmering, and began imitating a bellbird. He stretched his neck and uttered a series of rapid, deep-chested *chong*s, doing it better than the bellbird. Then, looking at me sidelong, he uttered a series of *coo*s, like a pigeon. Next came his theme of the morning, his personal song, one that no other tui possessed: a delicate series of descending notes, all in a minor key. Almost immediately, another tui, hidden in the foliage, broke into a soaring run of *whid-loo*s, interjected by the hammer of a bell, and ending in a strong *too*-ee.

The singing forests swarmed with parrots unlike those found elsewhere. The smallest, the orange-fronted parakeet, is little bigger than a canary, while the largest, the kakapo, stands nearly two feet high, is flightless, nocturnal, ground-burrowing, and its booming voice can be heard for two miles. In the high mountains, usually just above the tree line, another parrot, the kea, flourishes as a jokester and a sheep killer. Its extremely long upper mandible proves ideal for cutting through the skin of a sheep to reach fatty deposits around the animal's liver. Yet the kea was evolved in a land that had no sheep. It remains a mystery that it should be so perfectly developed for a kind of hunting which could not have been foreseen in the evolution.

Both Horace and I understood that the birds of New Zealand were "statements" of biology—that is, natural history defined and particularized through living in an environment not found anywhere else. Horace would not put it in my college-taught jargon, but would feel it through his experience, in which his life was an extension of the creatures and plants and the atmospheres of a land that he knew was unique before they sent him away to kill Europeans.

His grandfather, for instance, had possession of a feathered robe made entirely of kaka plumagery, in which red and yellow feathers were artfully combined to make a garment that looked painted by Cézanne, in silken oils. But such robes could be any color at all, because the random mutant feathers of the birds spanned the color spectrum.

"We'll start seeing some kakariki up in this kind of country," said Horace, referring to a small parrot which, before it was trapped and shot out, had developed an appetite for field potatoes.

The Maoris were inveterate bird hunters, and possessed a detailed natural history of almost every species. If they did not hunt for a single brilliant feather, they killed for food, and ate almost anything, from parrots to saddlebacks, yellowheads to red wattlebirds. They managed to equal the beauty of bird song with the onomatopoeic words they affixed to their birds—toutouwai, piwakawaka, mohua, popokatea, korimako, hihi.

We trudged on through light that spilled down the mountains like yellow wine with flecks of gold in it, and the singing of the tuis mingled with the silken rustle of their wings. I had a hundred rounds of nickel-capped bullets in brass cases clinking in an old sugar bag strapped to my waist.

"If we hit the main herd without lots of plurry ammo," Horace had said, "we'll be up shit creek."

We went on up among the hanging fruits of mira and tawa, of wineberries and koninis, through supplejack and karamu. The native fruits and flowers of New Zealand are all unique. By nine o'clock, we had reached a saddle at the six-thousand-foot range and passed into more open country, drier and rockier, where we could catch glimpses through the trees of white mountain peaks, steep rocky slopes, and the occasional glint of water. Downhill now, the fifty-pound pack pushing me forward and the long muscles of the legs protesting. Fantails darted ahead of us, flirting sprays of black-and-white tails.

"Hold it!" Horace drew up short, peering. I bumped into his pack.

Ahead, white figures moved as though in midair, animals sunning themselves against the far side of the gully, visible through a narrow opening in the trees. Horace's rifle was off his back and gripped in a grimy sunburned fist, as he moved swiftly now through the bush. We stayed in cover, with a flanking movement, until the brush thinned, and we crouched, still in deep shade, to peer at the animals. They were perhaps three hundred feet away.

"These are the worst buggers of all," whispered Horace. "They eat every fuggen thing. They're even worse than the deer."

The wild goat, which had come to New Zealand as a farm animal, had become a feral scourge of grazing and bush lands everywhere. Tough, smart, surefooted, and organized, the goats might be driven from the close-tended farms; but in the high country they roamed unmolested most of the time, eating out all the shrubs and young trees that were essential to the long and complicated process of renewing the native forest. They would, if given their freedom, reduce New Zealand to the status of Greece, with its shorn hills, or North Africa, with its desiccated expanses of nothing.

"Let's blast them!"

"I don't know," he said.

My heart pounded.

"Bloody strange to get so close to the buggers," said Horace. "We should let them have it."

We each found a place, and lay down, and began the lineup. I changed the eyepiece in my telescopic sight so that each goat half-filled the field of vision. Horace flipped up his aperture sight arm to expose open sights. We agreed to take the animals from each side of the compacted flock, about a hundred goats altogether. Killing at each edge would drive the goats into the center, where, in the confusion, we would be able to kill more of them.

My viewfinder, with its crossed hairs, reached for its victims. This billy, face content, eyes half-closed, furiously chewing cud, flipping his ears against insects—he would die first. This pregnant nanny, dozing, would be second. I laid out ten magazines, sixty shells, beside me, and levered a bullet into the breech. The billy quivered on the glass, and chewed cud.

We had eliminated goats as major destroyers of the hill flora in our own hill country only with great difficulty, using beaters working through the scrub, horsemen prowling the saddles and ridges, and a spotter airplane circling overhead.

When Horace's hand closed on my left elbow, I almost fired. His intent brown eyes and broken, flattened nose were right at my shoulder. I could see his misshapen, discolored teeth. "No go," he said. "No go, mate. Not worth the ammo. And anyway, we might put the wind up the fellers we're after, and that would never do, eh?"

Shortly after midday, we broke out of the bush into a desolate landscape. As far as we could see, the blackened, twisted trunks of long-killed trees sprang up from grass and tortured arms of scrub. Fire had passed through here a quarter of a century before, but such was the length of forest succession that it would be another hundred years before any of the original trees began reappearing. In that time, of course, the burn would be eaten over, again and again, by the goats and deer that had colonized the mountains.

The paradise of Aotearoa must have its biblical spoiler, and it was not, as may be suspected, the arrival of a hunting cat, the release of the European diseases, or the slaughter of Maori by pakeha. It was, instead, fire. A German traveler of the 1890s wrote a book, *Death of a Land,* in which he painted a flaming picture of events under the long white cloud.

"Scarce anything escapes the fingers of the raging flames," he wrote, "as they ascend high into the greatest mountains and pursue the gentle birds, the nodding shrubs, the delicate blossoms, and drive all to fiery deaths that strike shame and loathing into the hearts of all men who travel this once beautiful land."

As farmers, we used fire to burn out unwanted scrub. Sheep thrived in the rush of grass that followed fire. But we understood that fire was beneficial only in the short run. If used for years, it weakened all vegetative roots and caused "slips" on hillsides, where surface soil slid over its clay base and left open wounds as big as European farms.

The German wrote that everything had been destroyed. But it had not. Some of the forest survived, particularly on slopes of southern exposure, and in damp valleys, of which there were many, and in clusters along the banks of rivers where the flames were diverted for a moment by the proximity of the water, the twists of shingle banks.

In some places, particularly in the Rimutaka Range (where I had procured my first kakariki from a tree-hole nest while fighting a forest fire), large areas of so-called virgin bush still survived. These unburned, uncut regions hosted remnants of the paradise that was destroyed before it could be described. As a result, every New Zealander of sensitivity carried a mental wound caused by burning forests, not so much by the flames as by the thought of there being so many forest dwellers that had forgotten how to fly.

When odd pairs, or individuals, of survivors were sighted in patches of remnant bush, there was a fierce quickening of primeval imagination, as if an American had sighted an army of buffalo advancing or the dodo had been found flourishing on a remote island. Some birds lingered into the twentieth century, and revealed that it was something more than color, and song, that had made this place exceptional.

The fabled huia was last seen on December 28, 1907, by a man named W. W. Smith. It was the only creature known in which the sexes were different in physical form, and habit, for reasons other than sex itself. The male had a short, stout beak, for drilling into wood and digging out grubs. The female had a long, slender beak, for insertion into holes. It was said the male drilled the holes and the female probed them for food, never sharing with him what he had made it possible for her to find.

We moved across the wasteland of the ancient burn which, appropriately perhaps, revealed yellowhammers from Europe, winging from twisted black branches, and the distant form of a white feral cat, which preyed on the imported birds after it had eaten all the easier-to-catch natives. We walked together with the same kind of anticipation, that the past could never be really dead as long as there was a chance of it springing to our eyes in the form of a survivor long thought extinct.

Horace's people had arrived in New Zealand from the central Pacific in 1350 in a small armada of canoes led by a "flagship," the *Tainui*. The Maoris were aggressive, and efficient, as might be expected of a canoe people who had paddled two thousand miles without sighting land. They came across a small-statured race of Polynesians, the dimly perceived and quite mysterious Morioris on the Chatham Islands, enslaved and absorbed them.

The Maoris were a great hunting people, although they also grew some crops, particularly the sweet potato, a South American tuber. Probably, they ventured to South America, found that land unattractive, and returned with the sweet potato, which they loved. Such an energetic people must have meat, and in large quantities, and they had come to a country where there were only birds. This demanded a special culture of hunting.

First, because of the abundance of birds, they concentrated on catching large numbers of the small ones, while they learned the hunting techniques necessary to bring the big ones to their cooking pots.

The zosterops, or silvereye, a greenish, four-inch-long bird, feeds on insects, nectar, and fruit. Because of the great number of nectar-bearing trees in Aotearoa—such as rata, fuchsia, and rewa-rewa—and fruiting plants—such as coprosmas, makomako, and mingimingi—they flourished in the millions. The Maori exploited their natural history to transform them into a big-game hunt.

Two six-foot-high poles were erected anywhere near a feeding place of the silvereyes, joined by a stick, called a rongohua. Beneath this, a length of flax, called a tau maimoa, was strung from pole to pole and from it were hung, by their beaks, the first silvereyes that the Maoris caught alive. It is a feature of New Zealand bird life that the distress of one bird causes immense anxiety and concern amongst all other members of that species' flock.

Once the silvereyes were suspended, and fluttering, the Maori hunter had only to conceal himself nearby, a long flexible rod in his hand, and simply swat down the swarms of silvereyes attempting to come to the "rescue" of their stricken comrades. A pair of zosterops hunters could bring down three to four thousand birds a day.

An early ornithologist, Elsdon Best, who spent years with both birds and Maoris, was witness to the silvereye feasts that followed. "They are not carefully plucked," he said of the birds. "Many feathers are left on and they are not cleaned. But that matters not. The hardy Tuhoean bush-folk crunch up the birds—head, bones, insides, remaining feathers and all—with great zest."

As we walked across the burned area, Horace gestured to a tiny bird that I had noticed flitting from bush to bush, as if keeping up with us.

"Titi-pounamu," he said, as if I did not already know the Maori name for the bird, "will tell us where the deer are hidden."

This was the smallest New Zealand bird, three inches long, and the pakeha knew it as "the rifleman," perhaps because it often seemed to accompany gun-bearing travelers in the bush and then settle on the weapon's barrel when the hunter sought to shoot larger creatures.

The Maori hunt of birds was not merely ingenious; it was catholic in the range of its selection. Looped flax rings lay waiting in the branches of feeding places. The nocturnal brown duck, hiding in kahikatea forests by day, was patiently stalked. The best hunters knew how to catch individual birds alive, and so create the bait for the slaughter of those coming to help them.

No common technique of hunting dominated their food gathering. The sooty shearwater, an ocean-ranging bird, breeds on the third island of the New Zealand group, Stewart, south of the North and South islands. The Maoris hunted them with torches made of the bark of mountain totara. The lights mesmerized the young shearwaters—which later came to be called muttonbirds because they tasted of the flesh of animals not then brought to New Zealand—out of their burrows, when they were killed with sticks. The Maoris then salted them in seawater, packed the bodies in bags made from split thallus segments of bull kelp, the bags collected in flax baskets sheathed in totara bark. The muttonbird "crop" provided meat throughout the year on Stewart Island, and gave a surplus of trade with the "mainland," South Island, to the north.

If birds and men acquired a mystic connection here, it came from the practical realities of red meat, so variously flavored. The songs and the legends filtered through the Maori into the pakeha mind, where the spirit became always free to fly at will, to assume any color it desired, and to create whatever music would make the heart sing too.

Horace's lean form bumped its pack ahead of me up the wooded slopes of yet another mountain, the figure of the hunter intent upon his victim, the satisfaction of blood spilled righteously. In 1350, the Maoris discovered the largest birds on earth, the flightless moas. Had these monsters ever flown? They were about twice the size of an ostrich, and some, of extinct species, had stood fourteen feet high. Originally, they had been birds of the lowlands, but once the Maori learned how to kill them, his pursuit of them for their fine flesh became so enthusiastic that they were soon driven to higher ground. They might have thrived in this kind of country that deer and goats found so agreeable today.

The moa hunters sought animals that could run at fifty miles an hour. Unlike the ostrich or the Australian emu, or the South American cassowary, all of which the moa superficially resembled, the New Zealand bird was aggressive.

Horace liked to tell stories, relayed to him from his grandfather, of how moas would attack the camps of their persecutors, kicking houses to pieces and killing anybody stupid enough to come within range of their powerful legs and long-clawed feet.

The Maoris ambushed their prey along the banks of rivers. They festooned totaras and rimus and kahikateas with liana nets and dropped them on the giant birds. Less willingly, they dug pit traps in which the birds would fall and their heads could be crushed with swift blows of greenstone clubs. The daring moa hunter might make his reputation by raiding the nest of a moa, defended by male and female alike, and coming back to camp with the eggs, each the size of a twelve-pound American turkey.

Primeval New Zealand was, therefore, no simple paradise of chanting birds. It had once held twenty species of the giant moas, roaming the bush like goliaths, and leaving behind them a puzzling question: Why so many species of such big birds in such a small country—a little larger than the British Isles? This said something profound about the country, as a hunting territory, before the arrival of the Maori. There was plenty of food, in the wealth of fern roots, grasses, fruits, all of which the moas ate, and also the freshwater fish, the teeming mussels and the crayfish, which the moas hunted as if they were semiaquatic.

Suddenly, the moas were extinct. They were abundant in 1350. The Maori kitchen middens of the first century of occupation revealed the remains of thousands of the big birds. But this only begged the more substantial question of what had controlled their numbers before the arrival of the Maori. Surely, something hunted them, if only to force evolution toward such a large number of species.

When the bird song was silenced by fire and the forest colors banished by rifle, the voice of the past could be heard only through bones. And the bones of birds do not preserve well. But these were not ordinary bones. A moa leg bone might be four feet long. Giant eagles that flew in the day of the moas stood five feet high on taloned feet two feet long. If such birds flew on wings thirty feet across, they were as big as small airplanes, and strong enough to at least knock down moas. Perhaps eagle talons twenty-four inches long strangled flightless moas fourteen feet high. Perhaps paradise began when the major hunters wiped themselves out.

We passed out of the burned territory and came down into the thickening native vegetation of the valley floor. The rifleman flicked along from tree to tree. It was a little bigger than a hummingbird but no bigger than the .303 shells in my sugar bag. Its cry, a dry percussive ring, like two pieces of wire clicking together, inspired its Maori name. Skimming the peaked wavelets of the rapids, it looked like a flying insect, as we forced the river and set out to climb the other side of the valley.

"Strewth!"

Horace's use of the medieval "God's truth" came from the nineteenth-century English settlement of New Zealand. His finger, trembling and pointing, was aimed at another relict of evolution almost as puzzling as that of giant eagles and huge moas. From out of a gully, shaded almost black by a profusion of dark ferns, a giant parrot had broken into view, trying to half-scamper, half-fly. It must have assumed that we were going to pass through the gully, but its panic led it only more clearly into our view. Its green back, shot with pale yellow, bulked between broad wings, three feet wide. This, I knew without ever having seen one before, was the rare kakapo, a completely flightless parrot which had once been a favorite sporting animal for prospectors, road builders, and sawmillers. Hunting it with dogs, they had pretty much exterminated it except from very remote areas.

Here was another morsel for the great eagles, rushing on spring-steel feet through the rimu forests. Perhaps the eagles were nocturnal too. Eagle, moa, and kakapo were joined, along with the kiwi, to the mystery of flightlessness. Why stop flying after such torturously long preparation to get into the air? No other land had so many flightless birds. Another attack upon life was indicated. The kakapo had abandoned the capability of flight but retained its need, and ability, to climb the highest trees in search of fruit and nectar. As we watched, it scampered, half-lofted itself on those clumsy wings, and banked into disappearance within another gully.

Oddly, the main food of the kakapo, in a country that teemed with native fruits and blossoms, was leaves and grasses, which it masticated with its large and powerful hooked beak. A grazing parrot was strange enough, but it had also become nocturnal and this, surely, must have been in protection against the extinct eagle. It bred only once every two years, and it grunted like a pig when feeding on fruits, at night periodically giving out a harsh scream which sounded more like an eagle than a parrot. It could also, by inflating an air sac in its throat, utter a hollow booming noise, quickly repeated six or seven times, so loud that it hurt a man's ears when heard close up.

"We'll have to wait a long time before we see another of those buggers," said Horace, with satisfaction. "Wasn't she a beaut?"

In the ancient times, the kakapos traveled in packs, like wolves, each under the direction of an autocratic leader who held his sway in much the same way as a lion might over his pride. This gave Horace's people a chance to hunt the birds easily. They caught the leader, tethered him, and his screaming stopped the rest of the band from fleeing, because they could not desert him. Thus, all were killed.

"Kea country ahead," said Horace, as a view of the main spine of the Southern Alps showed through foliage.

The kea was a kind of vulturine parrot, sailing in the mountain updrafts in high scanning of its alpine world. It raided the mountain camps of early shepherds and hunters. Then, in a quick stroke of adaptational genius, it became the only killer parrot on earth.

Somehow, the kea had discovered that the sheep, the

main stock animal of the country from the earliest days, carried a layer of fatty tissue around its liver. This was the morsel that the kea could not resist. Perhaps it had been a killer before the pakeha arrived. The Maoris make no mention of that. Certainly its long curved beak was like a dagger, fine for slashing and chopping. But a meat-eating parrot is surely as sensible as a moa-hunting eagle. Perhaps the eagles hunted the mountain moas, and the kea came to the feast in the role of hyena and jackal.

To grow up in connection with the New Zealand earth meant to be substantially different from other men in nature. It was impossible to think, or feel, in the conventions of biology when I was watching a flock of keas, lined up along the peak of a mountain cabin roof in midwinter, waiting to slide down its icy slope on their undersides. They drew up their legs, and splayed their wings, and screeching with pleasure, came down like tobogganists. Each time a bird misjudged the end of the roof, and fell into a snowdrift, the rest burst into what seemed to be raucous and derisive laughter.

At four o'clock, we reached the crest of the valley wall. The rifleman flicked ahead of us. The main spinal column of the Southern Alps rolled before us, a mountain chain that worked its way to the end of the island, three hundred miles to the south. Like the previous saddle that we had crossed, this ridge, too, was bare, although we could see the canopy of treetops that clothed the descending slope ahead of us. Horace suddenly began to run, his bullets clinking in his sugar bag. His rifle bumped clumsily against his pack. In a moment, I heard a string of delighted obscenities.

The deer of New Zealand are the red deer of Europe. They are nearly omnivorous, in a vegetarian sense. Unlike the moose, which has a strict diet regimen, the red deer eats almost anything—the foliage of ironwood, the blossoms of tea trees, the leaves of young flax. It will root around in shallow waters for aquatic vegetation in one season and then turn, in the next, to giant buttercups in the mountains, bronze forget-me-nots in the valleys, scatterings of plants in high alpine meadows. These deer were like the rabbits of Australia. They had no natural enemies and swarmed everywhere rifles could not easily reach them.

When I ran up behind him and looked down into the third and final valley of our expedition, I understood why he had not shot the goats. And I understood, finally, that the tiny rifleman fitted into some secret scheme of discovery, which Horace understood, but which the pakeha could not know. It was like the honey guide of Africa, which leads honey hunters to bee nests, not because it likes honey but because it must lay its eggs in the wax of bee hives, and can do so only when the hive is disturbed by an intruder.

Geologically, New Zealand is a young country. It has not had time to mature into the softened and eroded outlines of the Adirondacks or Catskills of the eastern United States, which were once as high as the Rockies, and as precipitous as the Southern Alps of New Zealand. Its rivers are turbulent and unpredictable, its rock-walled mountains still falling down into the valleys. A river normally fifty feet wide might fan out over a bed several hundred feet in width, sweeping the gravel into windrows as it changes course, or dropping a cargo of silt in times of flood. Occasionally, a river gouged a deep bend when it was channeled by rock, and so took the first step to becoming a backwater, or billabong, as it was called in Australia.

That is what I saw in the valley below: the river turning westward against a yellow cliff composed of sandstone on a base of harder rock. Where the river changed its course, the deep and tumbling waters did not reach the wall, but exposed a scimitar of manuka-clad flatland. Into this sanctuary the deer had crowded, drawn perhaps by their craving for some mineral in the soil. I looked to either end of the sanctuary, where the river bit close into the base of the cliff. The river could not be swum there. The cliffs could not be scaled.

"About one thousand yards, I'd say." Horace was grinning like a wolf. "She's too far, so we go down a bit, eh, boy?"

We plunged into the bush until we came to a split in the ridge. Horace took the left fork while I went down the right. Firing would begin when he whistled the call of the shining cuckoo. For a moment, I thought that this must be like a prelude to war: comrades in danger, bullets about to fly. Horace had survived the destruction of the New Zealand army at El Agheila in 1942, but had the pleasure of still being in action when only six hundred Germans escaped from North Africa of the seven hundred thousand who had been sent there to capture Egypt.

In such a prelude to action, the functions of the body speed up, as the tiny bipedal man faces the mammoth, or the saber-toothed cat, with only the theory of weaponry to support him and his friends around him. Time slows down. Perceptions sharpen. I found my place on the knoll, a comfortable five hundred yards from the deer. I screwed in the most powerful eyepiece and began lining up the herd. As a rifleman of experience, I knew certain key animals, as Jonah Campbell knew his buffalo, and shot selectively. Shooting was the end result of knowing the animals intimately, and the country in which they lived. Two large stags, whose heads kept coming up, were the prime victims. After them, a large doe, equally watchful, at the right-hand side of the herd.

A shining cuckoo gave its sliding mournful call.

The adrenaline pumped so high I had to force myself to shoot slowly. The recoil of the rifle tore the victims from my telescopic viewing of them, but I would have the weapon down again in a second, the crosshairs lining up on another body even as I saw the first victim crumpling at the corner of my field of vision. The echo within the enclosing curve of the cliffs must have been thunderous, sound pouring in simultaneously from every direction. Immobilized by panic, the animals stood frozen at the hail of bullets coming at them.

The moment of killing is a lean curve of energy being released, which goes back as long as there has been a hunt, here invoking extinct eagles and moa hunters, killer parrots and the thunder of kakapos straining to tell the dusky bush that they were unique and should be preserved at any cost. At last, the deer were streaming away through their two corridors of escape. But our fire was a wall of metal turning them back, into themselves, so that my eyepiece picked up a corporate turmoil of victims. At one point, wondering why I had not found it necessary to reload, although I had fired so many shots, I discovered that only six magazines remained. I had been reloading automatically.

As the deer were cut down, they reassumed individual identity. In the failure of their potential flight, an awful vulnerability filled the air. Here was the pathos of the hunted, here the tragedy of those lives only created, in our sensibility, to feed the meat-eater, to deliver that gift of energy to the carnivorous central nervous system that was also the aggression, and the endurance, and the ingenuity, that drove the hunter a hundred, or a thousand, miles to find them. The last animal's hindquarters collapsed, both rifles slamming it to the ground at once.

Some time passed before I could restore sensible movements to my actions. The scattered magazines eluded my trembling fingers, and the scores of jacketed shell casings that now lay empty, some still smoking from their recent ejection. The barrel of the rifle hissed quietly, lying cradled in the grass.

Moving together, with about a quarter of a mile between us, Horace and I crossed the river together and converged on our victims.

"A clean sweep, boy. Got 'em all!" He was grinning hugely.

Many of the deer were not dead, but either trembled with shock or thrashed about. Some just lay there, flanks heaving, brown eyes wide. If the hunter kills wrongly, he feels remorse; if the killing is right, he feels only regret. Horace stopped smiling, as he saw my face.

"I got no time for these buggers. You shoot 'em. I got to sharpen my knife."

Instead, I watched a rifleman darting through some nearby scrub.

Horace liked to take a couple of skins with him, if the packload was not already too heavy. He turned toward the bubbling edge of the river and started whetting his sheath knife on a pocket oilstone.

"Perchik-perchik," said the rifleman.

When Horace came back from the river, he gestured toward the cliffs, which were now darkening with the swift decay of the mountain afternoon.

"You see that little bugger up there? It's the same feller we picked up in the scrub. Funny. You never see two of them together. They're always alone."

He looked at me.

Usually, I carried a Smith and Wesson automatic in my belt, or back pocket, in case I was surprised by a Captain Cooker, or wild boar, which had become established in Aotearoa in the eighteenth century. They could move too quickly at close quarters for effective rifle work. I drew the pistol and disposed of the surviving deer, before we made camp that night.

4 ○ The Kangaroo

When Big Red stood up, he looked human, his front paws held limp, like man's hands bent at the wrists, his stance quite unlike that of any other animal. He was more than eight feet tall. Lifting himself as high as possible on his spring-coiled jumping legs, curved tail holding him steady, he still could not escape being blinded by the airplane landing light that was directed into his face.

My binoculars revealed the imperious stance of his body, the richness of his red fur, the small head with its large ears canted slightly, to show an almost reflective interest in us. The effect was oddly touching, a manlike creature, well disguised, and also seeming to host a sensibility that was not quite that of any mammal. The marsupial animal may be a step closer to the dinosaur, the egg held within the body just long enough for hatching, and then immediately released, as an embryo, to the external body pouch.

At that second, a high-velocity rifle crashed and a hollow-core .22 magnum bullet hit Big Red in the chest at three thousand feet per second. He went down instantly. When we raced up to him, he was dying. His soft whimpering childlike cries, coupled with the sight of his two front paws reaching forward, intertwining, rubbing each other, anguish in every movement, made me turn my eyes away for a moment. Then I got the ax from the side of the truck and shattered the back of his head.

This was Australia, a remote country of hard landscapes and paradoxical animals. Here, droughts might last one hundred years, to be broken by rains that made lakes as big as Belgium. I had spent an extraordinary year, hunting for its heartland, or some sense of it, and realized, after thirty-one thousand miles of driving around it and through it, that it must always remain the unknown country. It is as big as the United States, as diverse as Europe, its hinterland often as hot and as unapproachable as the Gobi Desert.

Explorers have been hunting for the center of Australia for more than a century. It was inconceivable in the 1800s, that the "center," occupied today by the modern town of Alice Springs, could be the same desert that travelers first began encountering in relatively short inland journeys from the warm seacoasts.

The first paradox of Australia was that many of its rivers, flowing close to the coasts, did not release themselves into the adjacent oceans. They flowed inland. Therefore, it was argued, there must be a very large lake, or an inland sea, somewhere there in the center, surrounded by the verdancy that was missing in so much of the rest of the country. One explorer dragged a longboat more than a thousand miles toward the "center" in attempted proof of this logic. He abandoned it in a dune, where it still lay—in the 1950s, at least—perfectly preserved in the perennial drought.

In 1848, the explorer Ludwig Leichhardt disappeared trying to cross the island from east to west. In 1860, another explorer, John McDouall Stuart, tried to make a north-south crossing, but failed twice, reaching only the "center," where he found salt plains instead of an inland sea. Three other explorers, Robert O'Hara Burke, William John Wills, and George Grey, tried to reveal the country in a bold north-south exploration, from Melbourne to the Gulf of Carpentaria, in the far north. After two thousand miles of desert trekking, they could hear the surf on the shoreline of the gulf, but dense jungle and morasses of swamp prevented them from seeing the ocean. They all died of exhaustion, starvation, or thirst.

My hunting companion for the night, Blue Diamond, who had shot the kangaroo, dealt with the corpse deftly. He gutted it, and with a jerk, heaved the carcass upward to impale one of the legs, between tendon and bone, on sharp hooks which were screwed into the stake sides back of the truck.

"It's a fuggen hard place to know," he had said, in response to my desire to spend a few days, and nights, hunting with him as a means of getting to know the country. "But huntin' roos will teach you a thing or two, I s'pose."

He was a fairly typical "outbacker," the term applied to any man of the land located more than three hundred miles inland, where the sound of the sea never penetrated, and where all life was ruled by periodic and unreliable rains, set against silent hordes of kangaroos, ready to migrate hundreds or thousands of miles to wherever green growth might occur.

His gap-toothed grin, his stocky muscular body, his short sandy hair, were the marks of the British emigrant stock that had colonized the island in the nineteenth century, in large part by felons transported from Britain for offenses ranging from stealing bread to smashing up knitting frames in the Luddite resistance to the industrial revolution. Blue's great-grandfather might have stepped straight out of the pages of Charlotte Brontë, arrested in Yorkshire for attacking a textile mill, sentenced to life transportation to Van Diemen's Land.

We clambered back into the truck to continue the hunt. The kangaroo was as much of a pest in Australia as the red deer was in New Zealand. But since it was the national animal, featured on Australia's coat of arms, along with the ostrichlike emu, shooting the kangaroo was still another paradox in this country where the sea might be near but could not be reached.

"Let's look at it this way," Blue had said, before we set out from southern Queensland, to enter New South Wales on our hunting expedition. "The roo eats about as much grass as a sheep. Every time I shoot a roo, I'm lettin' somebody keep a sheep. With sheep, we get wool, and with wool, we get British quids and Yankee bucks. That way, you can buy your car, wear that jacket."

It was a triple hunt of animal and man. First, the sheep millions, exploring the vast but unreliable pastures for grass to make fleeces; second, the fluid migrations of kangaroos, searching for what the sheep could not, or would not, eat; third, the regulating man and his rifle, seeking extermination or, in Blue's case, meat for pet food, meat for export to Asiatic countries, hides for leather handbags in Sweden, boots in Germany, and belts in California.

Everywhere within the range of our night hunting, the kangaroos competed with the sheep, the national stock of Australia, nibbling the grass down closer than a sheep's teeth could cut, breaking down fences, drinking wells dry. It was as though the American prairies still hosted buffalo, advancing in millions upon cornfields, wheat crops, and domestic stock. Only the size of the country, the diffusion of its populations, permitted the kangaroo its expansive survival.

In the trees, rocketing over our heads now, there were marsupials beyond vision at such speed, and beyond description for anybody not willing to devote a lifetime of study to them. Mouse-size planigales, holding youngsters smaller than grains of wheat in their pouches, caught the flash of our spotlights in their large brown eyes. They, like almost all the other small marsupials that we did not shoot, looked at us blankly. We were very recent visitors to an island of such majestic age, and we were not yet known.

We smashed to the bottom of a gravel bed, an extinct river, and bounced high, to the slam of kangaroo corpses against our sides. The eyes of our victims remained open. It was a parade of innocence. We were slaughtering the origins of the biology itself.

The night is an education in another way of tackling the challenge of existence. There were marsupial anteaters and marsupial moles, marsupial mice and marsupial bears. The bandicoot might appear, and could be described as a groundhog as big as a German shepherd, but with no habit that relates it to either. Some of the opossums are striped like skunks and have long and graceful tails, like small leopards. Stocky wombats look as though they are trying to be beavers, although in fact they hate the water. The rat kangaroo survives in sand dunes, and the wallabies flourish in bogs.

We hunted the highest development of the form, the giant marsupial, or kangaroo, which in fossil form had shown itself to have reached eighteen feet in height—perhaps in the same evolutionary cycle that produced fourteen-foot birds in New Zealand—and to have been capable of taking fifty-foot bounds. We would shoot any big kangaroo, of which Big Red was the largest representative, followed by the wallaroo, or euro, and one of the two species of gray kangaroo. These giant marsupials prowled the expansive grassland forests, drawn here by the slightly more predictable rains, which created the finest grazing country in Australia when they came. This was the country where I hoped to recommence farming.

When the spotlight burns down among thin gatherings of trees, the big eyes of the giant marsupials look like a hundred silver disks, suspended in night space. It took this idea of a jumping animal forty million years to separate itself into a host of subfamilies, tiny kangaroos that can climb trees with the agility of squirrels, kangaroos that can burrow like rabbits, kangaroos that can live in rain forests, kangaroos that can survive in the most hostile of all deserts.

We hunted the giant marsupials, grazing animals which once must have been the victims of the large meat-eating marsupials, mostly now extinct. We would not meet the Tasmanian devil, a striped version of the leopard, or the Tasmanian wolf, which had decimated sheep flocks in the nineteenth century, before near-extermination. There was also a marsupial lion, it was said, which was extinct. More likely we might catch a glimpse of the ferocious phascogale, about the size of a small kitten, with a long and bushy tail, which could not be kept out of farmers' poultry runs until it was shot out.

There was an intimacy about these marsupials that invited immediate nostalgia at their untimely deaths. We rushed through the night, spitting bullets into the trees. Blue put a bullet into the neck of a large euro, which began making insanely high leaps, disappearing into the lower branches of a small grove of wattles.

"Bugger'll tear himself to pieces," he said ruefully. We pulled up nearby just as the euro made a final leap and disappeared into the branches, where it stayed, jammed into a fork and flailing its long back legs. When I climbed up to disentangle the body, I brushed through swarms of closed yellow flowers which, despite the night, released a mist of pollen when I jolted their branches.

"Watch your head," I said, and levered one of the legs free. The euro fell with a glottal crash at Blue's feet and he killed it with his knife.

Australia, like New Zealand, grows into you because it is an anomalous experience. It resembles nothing else. This was hunting, but also torture, like the agonized curves of thick bark peeling from hoary blue gums. The still midday airs of the outback are violent with promise—the sudden shriek of supersonic flies passing; a willy-willy, or whirlwind, waiting to spring out of thin air in a second, and rip the trees to pieces, float barns away in its invisible embrace.

The wattles, through which we now rushed with the beheaded euro, painted the country many colors when in full flower, although yellow predominated, and it was the brilliance of these day colors that made the eyes of the night so haunting in contrast. The brilliant colors were thrown up as shields, behind which gentle browns would be safe. These members of the acacia family reached their climax in Australia as both low shrubs and thick-trunked trees: mulga, myall, brigalow, gidgee, boree, wallowa, and cooba. "Wattle names echo the lost aboriginal tribes of this land, and mark vast tracts of this country," wrote a photographer, Douglass Baglin, who had chronicled them in word and picture all over the island continent.

Their yellow flowers climbed among the unique eucalypts, the predominant trees of the Australian bushland, which have adapted themselves "to the searing red winds of the inland, and the blizzard-swept heights of the Australian Alps," in Baglin's words. The eucalypts look as though they are posing, and waiting, like the eyes of the night: twisted, contorted trunks streaked and mottled with the reds and blues and whites of the red gum. Spires of wood drove skyward to a topknot of leaves, as typified by the spotted gum. The giant gums of Victoria and Tasmania were the tallest hardwoods on earth.

The kangaroos slipped away, like ghosts, from the reaching glow of the spotlight, and Blue did not stop until an animal, or a group, were caught and held by the fire beam blazing into their eyes. Then he pulled up to shoot.

It had seemed to me, in my travels around Australia, that its diverse parts were held together by the marsupial idea. Under the feathering Russell Falls of the south, I had watched marsupial flying squirrels floating through a spider's web of carboniferous ferns. A mauve pyramid of solid rock jutted from mesa-like country in the northwest, where a perfectly preserved Rolls-Royce lay jammed in a canyon and a wallaby drowsed in the shade of its English coachwork.

The night, and every part of its day landscapes, were filled with the spirit of the marsupial, which spoke of a very long dreaming time—before the urgency of the mammal—when there was time to wait for answers. A million termite towers rose from a Queensland plain where antilopine marsupials sailed in graceful leaps. The empty spaces chilled at first, a thousand miles to the next fuel dump, but a parade of pouched animals would entertain along the way.

I came out of a gray mist, into a fragrance that had nothing to do with flowers or foliage. It seemed to come out of the bare earth itself, and there, like an accusation, was the baffling Krichauff Range, an angry tilting of quartzite ridges cut through by antique streams to sculpt the skeleton of a stone giant, sprawled out, miles long, and dead of thirst. But tiny rat kangaroos jumped like mad things and made the dead giant move.

"We got to get water soon," said Blue, eyeing his temperature gauge.

Drought is power to the marsupial, for it has completely adapted to surviving years without rain. The pouched baby waits behind its shield of maternal skin, the teat on which it sucks well shadowed from the unpitying sun.

Kangaroos could smell rain from hundreds of miles away, and reached such greenery when sheep were dying of thirst by the hundreds of thousands. It rained one day before I arrived at Alice Springs on my round-Australia journey, and the country was transforming itself instantly, a flush of green growth and vivid birds spreading away from Ayer's Rock. This mass of matter, which bulks in continuous transformations, is a kind of folding and fading of colors. It is a kaleidoscope of energy, red in the morning, yellow at midday, purple in the afternoon. It is as big as Manhattan, in the middle of a sea of stones.

Blue stopped the truck, and told me to drive. "When I tell you, be ready to floor it," he said. "I need as much speed as this thing's got."

He had modified a Japanese four-wheel-drive vehicle by adding dual wheels at the rear, a beefy Australian-made 400-cubic-inch V-8 engine in front. The truck was a combination of tank and racing car, with railroad track welded front and rear "for rammin' what gets in our way." He could carry fifty kangaroos on his hooks at the back, where they hung and drained as he snarled through the night.

"Hold it here!"

I slewed the truck to a stop under a spidery sagging metal scantling that rose into the darkness above our heads. He shone his searchlight down the length of a long and smoking trough of water that ran out of sight of the beam.

"They don't drink this close to the well," he said, referring to the kangaroos, "or I'd get a shot at 'em right here. Fill up your bottle, mate, but don't drink it till you've shaken some of the fizz out of it. Hot soda water don't taste extra special."

The artesian water came from two thousand feet and was near-boiling. I directed the truck along a double track of wheels that disappeared beyond headlight view beside the trough.

"Move it!"

Soon we were doing seventy, Blue leaning wide out of the passenger window, the rifle cradled. At once, transformed in slow motion, the kangaroos appeared, gray ghosts that flung themselves backward in graceful slow leaps from the water and disappeared into the dusk. Transfixed, I drove into them, hearing the piercing whip of the rifle, seeing one in every fifty animals falling akimbo as we rushed on relentlessly. Eventually, the kangaroos thinned, the trough ended, and we wheeled to make our return.

"Not bad," said Blue. "I got ten, I think."

Some farmers, beset by many thousands of kangaroos, poisoned the water. Whoever controlled the water regulated or cornered the economy. Sir Thomas Mitchell, an early landowner, discovered the "boundless plains" of the Darling region in 1846, a prairie thickly swarded with growth which came to be known as Mitchell Grass, support for millions of sheep. He discovered the Darling River, which flowed west, inland, from the eastern shores of Queensland. Mitchell said the river obviously "led to India."

"It conveys living waters into a dry parched land and thus affords access to open and extensive pastoral regions likely to be soon peopled by civilized inhabitants. It was with sentiments of devotion, zeal, and loyalty, that I thereby give this river the name of my gracious sovereign, Queen Victoria."

Blue's father, Geordie, was on the Darling River in the 1920s when wool prices were high and the rains were ample. The capital of the Darling region, Bourke, swarmed with new millionaires in Rolls-Royces cut down to pickup trucks, driving past warehouses jammed with tight bales of compressed wool. The Darling echoed to the musical whistles of paddle steamers which took the wool fifteen hundred miles south, and west, to the Murray River, and thence to the southern ocean.

"One day, my old man started flyin' a small biplane. He thought he'd try fast freight, havin' been a stagecoach driver for Cobb and Co when he was a young larrikin. The plane took nurses, doctors, sick people, that kinda stuff. He packed in light cargo. He'd deliver urgent mail anywhere. He just never got into the motorcar age. I'll never forget his plane. Aussie-built. A Genaco. I was always dyin' to fly her. But the old man cracked up on the main street of Gulgong. Showin' off. He killed three nags standin' outside the boozer, and bloody near killed himself."

The 250,000-square-mile amphitheater of the North Darling Lowlands has an annual rainfall of about twelve inches. This is ample for good grazing, and Geordie Diamond got his station, or property, there right enough. Blue Diamond was born there. But the twelve inches was an average, and the rain does not necessarily fall evenly.

"The place wasn't big enough," said Blue, after a tucker break. We were back at work, and he guided the truck down a slope into a dried watercourse, overhung with dark green casuarinas. "He needed twenty thousand."

The casuarinas thickened as we bored on through the night, feathery and delicate, really beautiful trees. We entered a parkland of straight-trunked cypresses which condensed into a plantation. Blue turned aside to flank it. For an hour, he shot in this open country, but here the kangaroos were much harder to mesmerize with the spotlight, and usually ran before Blue could get spotlight set and rifle aimed. Soon we entered country tangled with scrub brigalow, another of the acacias, among which sprouted sandalwood and black tea trees.

The atmosphere changed. Red ironbarks, all masculine and brooding, shot into the headlights. Bull oaks, and then gorse, with its knobby hard visages, appeared. Graceful poplar boxes flowed by. If sunlight were added to this nocturnal theater, we would be seeing parrots—yellow rosellas, bluebonnets, regents, superbs, ringnecks—a rainbow of different colors, and the background dominated by ganggang cockatoos, splashed white and yellow on the green sward of this kangaroo and sheep country.

"It is an ancient land," said Thomas Mitchell, "but its promise is young."

The gentle marsupial grazers fly under the moon, rising like dark wingless birds over twelve-foot banks, or scrub, and arcing across streams with a soft thumping of feet and tails striking the red earth.

When we turned out the lights, ghosts rode the night. The aborigines, or "blackfellers," lay as light as pollen upon this land, centered around certain supplies of water, but most minutely adjusted to the possibility of serious drought. They had developed a highly spiritual strategy of survival, which depended upon totemic relationships with the animals useful for food and upon observing the proper rituals to bring rain. The influence of the great droughts passed, dreamlike, through the marsupials, and into the aboriginal mind, where changeless stretches of space and time came to mean a continuity of life that was also a faith to survive anything. But it was an indigenous ethic, particular to that place, and turned upon the finest details of observation, the most delicate remembrances of things past, coupled to that nomadic freedom to move, like kangaroos, when things got too rough.

The settlement of the grasslands ended all nomadic adventures. Nomads cannot be permitted in farming country. They steal horses. They do not work regular hours. They sleep in the heat, and move at night. They have strange, unusable abilities, such as lying on their backs, and tracking flies to water holes.

At first, the ancient skills persisted, such as being able to walk, barefooted, down the near-vertical sides of desert wells. This was not even considered a skill, because everybody could do it. But after a while, the wells became polluted with the bodies of those who could no longer climb out of them. Soon, the blackfellows noticed that they could no longer see the water-guiding flies. They got lost in their own deserts. They started eating the foliage of the many poisonous plants in their ancient country. Then, when they went "walkabout," in nomadic release from evil spirits that afflict all men, they did not return refreshed, but died in the process of escape.

Diamond suddenly began swearing just after he had shot, and was about to process, a gray doe. Both of us saw a shadowy form, just outside the spotlight's glow. He darted into the gloom, and I heard the thunk of his ax. He came back silent.

"What's up?"

He did not reply, and so I went to investigate. Tumbled into a sprawl of limbs was a young kangaroo, not much bigger than a cat. When I got back to the truck, Blue was reviling himself.

"Never saw the fuggen joey!" he raged. "I always see 'em. Aw, fuck it! What the hell, it's just another fuggen kangaroo!" He had a firm policy of never killing any kangaroo which had a youngster, or joey, at foot.

He finished gutting the youngster's mother, hung up the carcass, and slammed back into the driver's seat.

Two things stopped me from following. The first was that something was still moving in that pile of entrails that Blue had flopped down onto the ground. It was moving with convulsive jerks, but steadily, and I had the compelling thought that somehow, in that mass of tubes and organs and membranes, the kangaroo's spirit still pulsed in a heart torn from its body.

The second thing was more visible, and not fanciful at all. A pink hairless form was crawling up the furred pelt of the dead mother. The embryonic kangaroo, which had been born in the last few days, had either been jolted from the pouch or had fled it upon "realizing" that its mother was in trouble. All embryos look alike, of course. The incompleteness of their details suggest almost any kind of ancestry. But this embryo was ageless, and timeless, as it grabbed with invisible nails, and climbed, and climbed, until it must die, in the act of rejoining its mother.

"What's the matter, mate?"

I got back into the truck. We snarled into brigalow, and then among casuarinas, a kaleidoscope of bull oaks, bowed eucalypts, the night brimming with the presence of marsupial. In times of good rainfall, the doe which Diamond had just killed could produce three youngsters every two years, without a break. She had been leading the joey, on foot, and feeding it through one of the two teats inside her pouch.

But she had also been suckling another joey, the embryo I had just seen, inside the pouch, on the other teat. And I knew that inside that mass of entrails had lain a *third* joey, neither egg nor embryo, but an organism that remained dormant, a blastocyst, for as long as it was necessary to await its turn to be born. Then birth would occur at just that moment when the youngster in the pouch left its refuge and became ambulatory.

The pulse I had seen in the entrails may have been the blastocyst, torn from its refuge, and suddenly aroused to be born in the middle of death. But the guts in which it was trapped lay on the ground while the pouch toward which it must crawl lay hanging on the truck. I could feel the bafflement of the blackfellow, slipping back again into the water he must have to live.

Doe kangaroos had progeny in three stages of development both as insurance against hard times and as an aggressive, creative effort to exploit the good times. The youngster on foot suckled on its own special teat, which provided it with ordinary milk. The youngster in the pouch suckled on its special teat, but this gave a separate, elite quality of milk, very high in fat for the fastest possible growth. The blastocyst was the instant backup.

If drought struck, the joey on foot, which was still dependent on large quantities of milk, died first when his teat went dry. The doe's resources were switched to output on the other teat. But if conditions worsened, this milk supply also ended, and the pouch animal died. Now was left the dormant embryo, which could survive months without change. The doe clipped grass so close to the ground that she got food invisible to man's eyes. She could travel a hundred miles for water. Then, as soon as the rains came, the blastocyst surged with growth, the embryo was born, crawled to the pouch, and the cycle was resumed even if all the male kangaroos had died months, or even years, before.

But for drought in the sheep country, no such backup scheme of survival had been evolved. Blue's father was shot in a gun battle on the main street of Milparinka, an outback town now abandoned, over a question of watering some prize merino rams. Without rain, the sheep died by the millions. The Darling River's flow ebbed. Within a few years, the paddle steamers could not even reach the Murray, the waterway to the sea.

The docks were abandoned, the warehouses, empty, collapsed. Bourke came close to abandonment. The paddle steamers settled where they had finally stopped, not for lack of freight but for absence of water. The Darling struggled to keep its meeting with the Murray, but finally gave up, and petered out in the middle of the Great Australian Desert.

As dawn approached, Blue confided in me that he'd had a bit of a "run-in" with a couple of local graziers, which was his way of preparing me for the possibility of an ambush on the way home.

"They know our track pretty well," he said, "but usually, I'm a bit ahead of them."

There had been some hard feelings. Shots had been exchanged. Other kangaroo shooters had put warning shotgun charges through kitchen windows. One grazier had a light tank for use against men like Blue. Horses had been killed. It was the dawn that was dangerous. It was always hard to chase a renegade at night, and graziers liked to sleep then, after the hard slog of daytime.

"I like to have several ways of gettin' home," Blue said, "but that drill isn't perfect. Once it gets light, my tires is the target."

Our headlong movement through the night had been conducted with faultless precision, over many hundreds of square miles of roadless country. Diamond had a map in his mind of the places where the enemy might be likely to mount a roadblock, or an ambush of four-wheel-drive vehicles, or even that light tank that was running around somewhere.

By four o'clock, we had thirty kangaroos on board, about four thousand pounds of meat, or roughly $150 for a night's work. We were then about forty miles from Queensland. At four-thirty, just before dawn, we came to the road to Queensland, ran easily over a mangy fence, and climbed up an embankment to reach the graveled surface, the carcasses behind making the truck sway and groan. Ahead, a light flashed. Blue swore and ground the truck to a stop, peering ahead at a roadblock.

He could leave the road again and run across country. Or he could try and run the roadblock. The decision depended upon his knowing exactly what terrain lay on either side of us, in the dark, and apparently he knew this very well indeed. Viciously, he slammed the truck into gear and we lurched forward.

"We gotta go through," he said. "If I get off into the rough stuff now, they'll run me down with the fuggen tank. You better get your head down, boy."

The lights grew ahead. One bright beam dominated the others, and the dusky profile of vehicles clustered together grew clearer. Blue flipped on the airplane landing light to reveal figures scuttling about. They had guns. I dropped to the level of the dashboard and peered. The truck heeled and skidded, and we seemed to plunge off the road, then to bound and smash forward, only to stop suddenly. A dense tangle of young trees and shrubs blocked our way. Shouts came from the road. Cursing, Blue backed up, his engine howling with rage.

"I'll kill you bastards!" he shouted.

There was an answering roar from the road.

"Come on out, you rotten bugger. We've got you now."

But Blue had the truck half-turned, and pulling at the wheel, he gunned the powerful engine, prudently installed for exactly this moment, and we surged up the slope leading back to the road, all four wheels spinning. The clustered vehicles loomed. I could not believe it and neither could the people in the roadblock. A shot sounded. The roadblock vehicles, I could see, were too closely bunched together, and there was a good chance that we could flank the barrier if the truck did not overturn on the slope. A small British four-wheel-drive vehicle stood at the back of the roadblock and we hit it so hard that it flipped over and disappeared from the road. We did not pause, and surged away.

Later, after I had closed and carefully latched the border gate, Blue said, "I hope you noticed, back there, that

I ducked left, eh? That put me in the firin' side. Made it a bit safer for ya, eh?"

He nudged me in the ribs with an elbow blow which just about caved my side in. But I could not resist his laughter. We both laughed, and punched each other's biceps for several miles down the long straight road into Queensland.

Blue finished his chores in an hour and had all his meat and hides ready for the morning pickup by truck from Brisbane. I walked out of his kitchen into the backyard as the sun came up. Plain, square, corrugated-roofed bungalows stretched to the edge of town, and petered into gidgee country, a scattered infinity of dark-green-foliaged acacias. Oddly, when the life-giving rains fell, these trees smelled of death.

My original arrangement had been to spend a few days with Blue. But I did not feel that I could follow Blue on his course again tomorrow night, and the night after that. I could not face the sheer size of the marsupial facts of drought and rain, of shooting and sheep, of dying rivers and hot soda water wells.

I went back into the kitchen. Blue was grinning. He had the morning tea ready. He took a look at my face, and then brought his fist crashing down on the rickety kitchen table so that the cups and saucers sprang into the air, and a jug of milk shot a plume of white onto the floor.

"All right!" he shouted. "So I'm not going to make it. Who cares? Let's have a cup of char."

But I could not quite join him, even in that, for a moment. I was still back on the downs, thinking about Sir Thomas Mitchell's river, which did not go to India, and did not continue to flow, and to which Queen Victoria's name did not stick. The embryonic kangaroo was struggling through the fur of its dead mother.

In that lonely journey was contained the very essence of the determination necessary to survive the droughts, and to have the patience to wait for the return of the good times, which were all made inseparable in the dreaming time. It was the first act of a hunting animal, to find that mothering pouch and survive by any means.

5 ○ The Leopard

The leader of the baboons, an old and grizzled male, or "dog," usually sat in the highest position in the tree, lordly and disdainful, waited on by underlings. I watched him in trembling close-up, through a modified telescope which, by a scheme of swiveling eyepieces, gave me a series of instant views of the whole animal, his face, his muzzle, his eye, in pictures that filled the binocular viewing glass.

He thus became a series of different personalities, depending upon the magnification of the vision, at once the lordly regent in a complete view of him, and then a gross feeder on nuts, spiders, a handful of wriggling millipedes, centipedes, a fingering of beetles. He drew a snake from the cavity of a tree, and when it coiled around his finger, he nipped it off with his teeth, piece by piece, until only a single band remained on the finger. He relished scorpions and was deft at avoiding their stinging tails, carefully withdrawing the sting between his fingers and then pulling the creature to pieces.

Africa cannot be seen through one lens. Its parts are not joined together by any device as ingenious as the marsupial pouch, or as gentle as Aotearoa's absence of fang and sting. It is not bound by anything. From the air, in the Sudan, or in the central republics, Somalia, some other regions, it is the worst-looking place on earth, neither desert nor forest, jungle nor plain, but instead a vast conglomerate of nothing, stretching like a dried-out wound to a folding horizon. Gavin Candlish said central Africa was a brave attempt by nature to discourage German tourists.

He was a shortish, powerfully built man who had been my companion on an aerial safari through Africa, from Alexandria, in Egypt, to East Africa, seventy hours of flying down half the length of the continent, to reach this place, in Tanganyika. Here we were on the high-altitude, short-grass plains west of Mount Kilimanjaro. Here dwelt a wide-angled view of Africa. Here was concentrated all the spectacle that did not exist elsewhere on the continent. Here was amassed a landscape of action, a gathering of hunters, a flight of victims, on a scale big enough to accommodate a thousand De Mille movies.

Candlish had, from pre–World War II experience, a very long view of Africa. He had spent part of the war as a Beaufighter pilot defending Cairo, and then, after the war, he had been a policeman in a Persian Gulf emirate. Now, possessor of a light airplane, and a year of leisure, he had teamed up with me, after I had finished a British magazine writing assignment in the Middle East. He supplied the plane, the expertise including languages, and I supplied the petrol and the food to make what he called "the last grand safari."

The real stuff of Africa, he said, that which made it tick and hum with menacing energy, lay beyond the camera, not in the elephant wallows or the leopard ranges but in the dust and the dung of "the horrible creatures." By this he meant parasites and maggots, worms and trypanosomes. We had watched the noble beasts of the movies as a convention.

They made stories with which we could identify, and so ignore the larvae that were drilling into elephants' hearts, puncturing them like colanders, the worms that were boring through zebra brains, tunneling through the anuses of wildebeest.

At that time, the 1950s, Africa seemed ready to explode. The Mau Mau might lose, but it was too much fun, gutting Europeans and shooting up the countryside, for the idea not to catch on.

"We'll slip in ahead of Armageddon," said Candlish, "make our safari, and then be gone forever. But make no mistake about it, laddy, we are going to look at animals until we start to think like them."

Our camp was set along the banks of an extinct stream, a place of yellow fever trees, where the leopard lived, and where pallid lemon trunks glowed with an almost ghostly light at midday. "The trees are well named," said Candlish. "They always give me a slight feeling of menace, of unidentified danger, despite their beautiful appearance. Of course, the leopard is here, somewhere, so they may, in fact, be dangerous."

I watched as the moon took its cool light behind a black slab of cloud and then reappeared. The leader of the baboons was visible in a shaft of light that struck through the canopy of the fever trees, splashing onto a yellow-green branch beneath. The baboon looked down this column of light. At once, there was a distortion near the end of its beam, and a leopard's head appeared.

The tree had not trembled, so deft had been the cat's leap into the baboon's tree. But in the next instant, the whole tree vibrated like a plucked instrument as every baboon in its branches wakened. The scent of leopard rose to distill the pure essence of terror. The dog leader did not move, and neither did the leopard. The two animals looked at each other for so long that my eyes watered. I longed for them to be finished.

The strain on my eyes became too much. I blinked. In

that fraction of a second, the leopard's head disappeared. The baboon remained fixed in view. He was still looking down. But now he was trembling.

In the morning, beyond the trees of our camp, in the middle distances, some wildebeest honked. Vultures hovered, looking like black paper airplanes. Almost imperceptibly slowly, a cheetah rose from its sprawled position on a termite mound, and looked down the long range it might run toward some briskly grazing gazelles. Everywhere, nameless expectation. Above me, the baboons were eating, oblivious of us in their concentrated gusto.

Chomp-chomp-chomp-chomp.

The sound of chewing filled the yellow fever trees. A steady fall of debris—broken twigs, dropped fruit, and spiraling seeds—mingled with the spatter of defecation, suggested the beginnings of heavy rain. In fact, rain was falling, but its solid drops were unheard because of this noise of feeding baboons.

The territorial range of the baboons appeared to include a couple of water holes and about a thousand trees, patched along a hunting country that could be made fairly circular by a series of wary dashes through rather open, savanna-like country. The baboons lived in a small and tightly compacted range, and their travel seemed haphazard in direction but steady in movement. They progressed in apparently aimless spurts, staying in one place until they were bored, or until it was eaten out.

The human watcher soon becomes an accepted presence to those in the trees and perhaps is even welcome. The baboons know very well that with a man nearby, the leopard will not be as bold. That is, if the leopard knows the man is there. At evening, a leisurely but structured movement led the troop either higher into a tree, or toward a general distribution of numbers through the spinney, Candlish's term for a grove of acacias. The daylight races from the twilight, and darkness rises from the earth.

"I saw him an hour ago, about a mile down the line," said Candlish. "So perhaps tonight's the night."

I had been watching with daytime eyes, on the assumption that what was clearest seen was best known. Of course, I knew that was an error. If I were more or less helpless at night, then so must be the baboons. That was when their enemy would work to know them. But then I discovered that I could see a great deal, and this lent drama to the watching. The baboons must also see a lot, but be unable to act.

Finally came the moonlit night of arousal. This was, I felt sure, the leopard's scent stealing among the baboons. In a deadly silence, animal after animal jolted awake. In time, I came to believe that this had been contrived by the hidden, scheming cat. It appeared that both the leopard and I understood baboon hysteria.

Certainly, he made no attempt to conceal his aroma. When he had a chance to skirt the sleeping mass of the baboons, he did not take it. Instead, he came downwind. I could almost smell him. His trembling victims, awake, were enveloped in a scent that got progressively stronger. It was, without a doubt, the original Pavlovian reflexive torture. Would he come this night? Would the heavens open and let fall thunderbolts? Where was he?

A suggestion of reality, powerfully conveyed, is the most effective form of propaganda. There must be a skerrick of truth in the lies to achieve the persuasion that is sought. The leopard behaved in the classic manner of the myth-maker, the propagandist. He gave just that suggestion of menace, without supporting action, which would raise all anxiety, and then leave a portentous silence as an unbearable reminder that he was there, he was not there, he had never been there, but that he was there.

The baboon troop and its leader were transformed by the myth-maker. The dull grind, the squabbling camaraderie of daytime routines, gave way to an electric discipline of alerts and alarms. The baboons, although adaptable, had concentrated all their skills into the daylight hours, and so had sacrificed half their lives. The chieftainship of the leader turned upon his handling of the night, and the night was dominated by an animal who lived by the dark and who was at his strongest climbing trees.

The Masai had a song: "The night is here. There is a leopard in it."

The personality of the baboon leader broadened with the watching. His coolness and arrogance, coupled with a lordly indifference to a lion clawing at the base of his tree, gave him his dignity. Then his kindly reception of an old female approaching him for some favor, a humorous recognition of his own foibles, such as barking and then baring his teeth in a terrific "grin" when he dropped a choice piece of food, combined to suggest a sense of humor, a fallibility like my own. We were both primates, all right.

But as night approached, he regressed. He climbed up and down, and hunched, and grumbled, and cuffed the others from their perches, which he then did not occupy himself. The crack of a stick sent him bolting into the treetops, whence he gave his distinctive gasping bark.

The baboon leader had come a great distance to reach his high position. For years, he had seen members of the troop killed by leopards. There were estimates by human watchers that in a year each cat might take as many as half a dozen baboons from an average-sized troop of thirty or forty—an annual mortality of around twenty percent. The leader may have seen the killing of up to one hundred of his comrades, relatives, mates.

In imagining back through the details of the dog leader's history, I was making a piecemeal reconstruction of youthful years combating his superiors, ducking under the disciplinary cuffs, the putdowns, the rejections. He had to survive the high danger of finding himself in the rearguard formations when the troop was fleeing, the youngest adult animals always the first to be sacrificed. He had to dare aggressive action against superiors, thus instigating his rise to power, always striving to displace those above him, so that he might eventually sit at the top of the tree, alone, and tremble in the night.

The daily routines of the baboons were boring. They made dramatic sense only when the nights were known. The visible was rarely important. The baboon leader could be described as the troop leader most fitted to his task. He might also be seen as a survivor in a lifelong nightmare of guerrilla warfare.

The seeing eye was not invented by Kipling. It was the primary weapon, possessed by the first hunter. Success went only to the hunter that had the most information leading to action. Killing could be understood only by another killer. It was not a reflex, or an impulse. It was the terminus of a long process of preparation. But Kipling was original in saying that the seeing eye was not given lightly in the wilderness. It was granted to the animal with intellectual patience to watch, to wait, to move when everything was known.

The long, limpid midday silences screamed for action. The leopard killed a gazelle at night, and left the kill carelessly lodged in a low fork, where the baboons would see it in their passage along the tree line. They paused in a nearby tree, tentatively barking, and baring their teeth. Two of them copulated in slow motion. I grew into the scene, waiting for the arrival of the leopard, my mind teeming with his possible plans.

All at once, I saw him. He had been there all the time, perhaps, but I had looked through him. The gazelle fell out of its notch and landed at my feet. The leopard peered down from his sprawl on a high branch, very sleepy and bored, and then looked directly at me, eyes half-lidded.

"Yes?" he said. "And what was it that *you* wanted?"

I picked up the gazelle and attempted to return it to the crotch. Immediately, he rose on four feet and stretched his neck. This was serious. I was barely back into the truck before he flowed down the tree, headfirst, so fast that he had one paw on the gazelle before I could latch the door.

His lidded eyes looked at me through the truck's side window with complete disdain.

"Don't you ever do that again."

I grew to dislike the dog leader's rough bark, even though I was not always certain that I had identified it. When his cry sounded, I might have my sights on the leopard, and I would see the cat's head come up slightly. The tip of his tail moved in tight, constricted twitches. He had heard something that aroused him.

It seemed increasingly possible that the leopard had a plan, a master strategy of breaking down the wills of the baboons to resist by upsetting the order of their sleeping places. Once, he climbed a tree adjacent to the baboons' tree and I—and the terrified baboons—could hear him sharpening his claws on a branch, like a house cat. When the scratching stopped, I could hear him purring.

The sky paled, and the hysteria of the night subsided. The dog leader appeared, and came to the ground, now that some of the other baboons were already there. He snipped some fresh shoots of grass from their sprouting roots. I began to perceive him as having thrown away too much of his energies in a life of dallying around with one thing or another. There had been too much circling, and beating around the bush, too much squabbling and not enough fighting. He was too bold when the troop was at his back, too craven when he was vulnerable himself.

His arm gripped a branch. He had stopped trembling. He was the leader. His piercing eyes flicked over the troop. Every member was in place. When two juveniles, far down the ladder of power, scuffled noisily, ignoring him, I watched the skin of his scalp pull back, his eyes widen. Then, loosening his grip, he stood up. His whole body was stiff with threat. The mane was erect. His outline, all of it, from knees to head, enlarged. The two juveniles stilled. Discipline returned. Perhaps only a detached and constant watcher would be able to imagine him as the victim of a plan.

Of course, every hunt had to be "planned." It was a

coalition of all the hunter had learned about the tricks of the prey to escape, the devices necessary to avoid as much danger as possible in the act of killing. Clearly, the leopard did not merely waken, and go padding out into the night in the hope of stumbling over a creature that was available for killing. The baboon troop, by itself, represented the marshaling of resources against him which was but a part of the total scheme of existence out there in the dark—animals trying to avoid collectively what he proposed to inflict individually.

The leopard's plan must therefore interlock with whatever "plan" the baboon leader had to protect his troop. It must therefore be a collision of energies in which the baboon was the antagonist of the leopard's plan as well as his most desirable victim. If the dog leader could be killed, then the other baboons would be much more vulnerable. The confrontation between the two animals would be a summation of everything they had ever been, a synthesis of all that they had come to know.

Slowly, the dog leader came down through enclosing foliage. Two strong males followed him, probably number two and number three in the hierarchy.

"Hierarchy!" Candlish scoffed. "Where do you get these words from? Are you a scientist? Are you just swallowing somebody else's interpretations of these fluid, complex, and baffling relationships?"

Nonetheless, the dog leader was at the top. His leadership went back a long way. It was likely that he was a predestined leader, that there had been something in his genes that determined command. This was a common enough observation of animal life, visible in one tiny blind bird in a nest gaping a fraction of an inch higher than its comrades and so getting a disproportionate share of its parents' food. Yet, when the tiny bird is measured, it is the same size as the others.

If leadership was predestined, the young baboon would have taunted the bigger males. He would have endured being bitten on the legs, on the flank or neck, bites intended to deter, and lightly punish. It was "understood" that the superior drive and determination, whether or not to the top, should not be destroyed. But murder might occur if the defender was slipping from his position. Lethal hierarchical fights were rare amongst primates, but leopards might fight to the death over territory or sex. Obviously, such deaths were not the aim of the evolution.

The baboon might feign greater hurt than he felt (which I had observed) and run screaming the pain of a broken limb when he had only been scratched by a fingernail, or pretend an exaggeratedly wounded gait, about to fall, when, in fact, nothing had even touched him. If he perceived that his tormentor's attention had turned elsewhere, he would recover in a jiffy, and race back to taunt again.

Before coming to the high plains, Candlish and I had flown along the coast, south of Dar es Salaam, and he had spotted an inviting beach.

"Let's take a swim," he said.

I turned to make the approach, compensating for the constant soft wind that blows in from the Indian Ocean.

"Watch that turtle."

Later, slumped on pure white sand, drinking bad beer, we looked out toward an ocean colored silver by the slant of the sun, its very small waves sparkling with refracted gleams of precious metals.

"There is a center of power," said Candlish, "which it will be the point of our watching to find. It is individual; it is collective; it is nothing at all and everything at once. You can see it in ants, or in a single elephant walking a thousand miles to find a family that no longer exists. If you do not have the power yourself, you lack the base for right action. I suspect that when an animal lacks it entirely, then it must be killed. It invites being killed.

"The Bedouin live like animals, by our measurements, but they have a power that we can hardly imagine. They live and breathe and think the desert and are extensions of it. When they sit and stare for hours into an empty space of sand dune and a horizon smoking with heat and dust, they appear to be hopeless lazy wogs, when they could be doing something useful, working perhaps. But I've noticed, something always happens! There was this total blackness, but then there is something! Is it induced, an effort of will? They believe that whatever you want will come along eventually, if you have the patience to wait, and of course that must be true. But who has the faith to believe that? We have this notion that by aggressively pursuing our goal, our prey, we will experience a satisfaction of gathering it for ourselves. This is a superficial understanding of the satisfaction of survival. We waste our energies procuring only the death of what we seek."

If there was a center of power, then it probably lay in the genes. But who could measure that? And what was it, anyway? The baboon leader was probably the first of his age to break that bond to his mother which, if allowed to remain intact too long, would impede the "success" of his later life. The relationship to the females, both youngsters and mothers huddled in a nucleus of security, surrounded by males barking at the leopard, was also the energy to move outward, to the defensive perimeter, and become adult looking straight into the eyes of the approaching cat.

He would have been the first of his age to harass the adult females. The rise to power must be through the females. They would have called for help from the adult males. He would have been beaten. Power could never have been easy to acquire. It was unremitting pressure against the power that sought to hold him down. It would have been six years, at least, of clawing and screaming and wrenching his way upward. Finally, he stood under the umbrella of two or three superior males. If he was the youngest, then he might need only to wait for accident or attrition to bring him the top position.

"Very pretty," said Candlish. "But you are using the

English language to describe the sex habits of a carnivorous butterfly on Saturn. It sounds like the executive suite at General Motors. What image can you make for me to work with? Is it not like an Egyptian hieroglyph, which can mean many things, and also have a meaning as a work of art? Perhaps what you are seeing is a poem by Yeats, or a quartet by Brahms."

I remained stubborn. My only reality was the reduction of experience to words. I, too, was that compendium of total history, and if I could not describe what I saw, and felt, then I did not exist here. During his rise to power, the baboon leader maintained a constant testing of the determination and certainty of the baboons above him. His defeat was inevitable, but each setback was an increment of knowledge that would lead to the throne, and so into confrontation with the leopard's teeth.

Young males descended a tree and fanned out. They were the vanguard of the troop and visibly the buffer to cushion the shock of meeting the enemy. The nucleus—juveniles, mothers, females, and the dog leader—must have time to escape. The center of the nucleus was the center of the troop's power, derived from its capability to sustain superficial losses—defeats—in order to preserve the essential center.

The baboons were moving toward a water hole. No scent or sign of leopard impeded them. Hyenas and wild dogs were asleep. A grumble of lions was so distant that grazing gazelles gave it no heed. The troop moved as an entity, slope-bodied and intent, striding toward the next bank of trees, in shadowless midday at the equator.

The process of watching was scarcely begun. The cat revealed himself only in scraps of detail, unlike the chunks of information displayed by the baboons. Each new bit of detail revealed the leopard, not more clearly, but more contradictorily. I cursed myself for not keeping a notebook from the beginning, finally realizing why so many scientists put together dull lists of times, temperatures, dates, weather, which became, it was now understood, vital triggers of memory when the whole picture was put together. I remembered only incompletely how I had felt during each incident, each new tiny truth that came down out of the trees, or up from the mud. I wanted to compare everything, and have it read like a diary of myself.

I could not resist the temptation of presuming the leopard's sense of humor. Watching the baboons, I could now feel the presence of the cat, communicated in two distinct stages. The first was a kind of nagging anxiety in which the baboons uneasily faced the fact that he was there, but that he might not act. The second stage was the stark knowledge that he was about to act.

One typical night, with the moon sliding in and out of layers of clouds, the dog leader had, as was his custom, gone highest of all into the trees. I watched the leopard's silhouette on a branch, gliding, disappearing. Once, I had seen his face in direct moonlight when, with the forehead wrinkled, the cat appeared to have a self-mocking grin.

In the trees, the first stage of cognition was almost telepathic. The silhouettes of some baboons enlarged. No sound had touched the night. The wind was blowing gently from baboon toward leopard. Yet somehow the baboons knew. The thick hair around the necks stiffened, and bushed outward, so that the silhouettes became almost globular.

In the fixed tableau of anticipation, the measurement of distance, scent, proximity, past experience, the state of the hunter, the extent of the fear, the responses of the others, all amalgamated into a scheme for what must be done. The leopard appeared for a second in a shaft of moonlight striking down through the canopy of the trees.

Any attack had to be measured against the severity of the risk. The leopard knew one thing which a non-leopard might not consider: He could fall from the tree. Two hours passed. The outlines of the silhouetted baboons gradually shrunk to normal. When a very distant coughing cry told me that the leopard was now more than a mile away, I reached forward reluctantly to start the truck engine. At that moment, all hell broke loose.

As far as I could reconstruct it, the leopard had indeed left the area, and the baboons had understood the danger to be over. When the screams started—for one tingling moment, I thought they were human; perhaps tourists had blundered into a hunting situation—I did not immediately understand that it came only from the treetops. I switched on the headlights to reveal a sight that was as bizarre as it was unexpected. Everywhere, baboons were falling, crashing to the ground, bouncing, hobbling, scampering.

The leopard had returned, but this time he had a plan. Having reconnoitered in his first visit, he had apparently determined the disposition of the baboons. He came back swiftly, silently, no scent warnings, and immediately fired himself vertically up the trunk of the biggest tree, an acceleration that blasted him through the roosting baboons, past them, and up above the thick canopy of the acacia. Later, I found inch-deep rip marks in the trunk of the tree, where he had climbed.

Now he was tramping around on the top of their sleeping place, his paws splayed out widely so that he would not slip through the feathery foliage. The maneuver was apparently designed to shake the baboons free like so many rotten fruit. Locked in that swaying tangle of darkness, some of them had chosen to drop blindly. Others clung, and screamed. But the shaking just went on and on.

When silence returned, it was complete. I presumed that the cat must come down from the tree. He would bring a baboon with him. At the least, he would become visible. But instead, there was nothing. Perhaps he slipped down the trunk of a tree. But that seemed unlikely. A two-hundred-fifty-pound cat cannot descend a tree that has no horizontal branches without making some noise.

The dawn came. No leopard. Agitated baboons peered about.

The many moods of the baboons, so easily couched in

human identifications, obscured the complexity of the leopard's emotions. I had thought him straight, and direct, and simpleminded, a killer in a spotted coat who had none of the subtleties of primate feeling. But it was he, not the baboons, who was coming closer to me in the interest and meaning of his character. I had seen his Pavlovian blackmail, his aplomb and threats, his dark humor in the treetops. But I had not anticipated his capability for revenge.

The vultures of the great short-grass plains are indicators and guides, the most visible signal system that could be imagined for determining what is going on scores of miles away. The placement of the birds in the sky, which may include, at one time, the Rüppell's griffon, the lappet-faced, the white-backed, and the white-headed vultures, is an almost infallible mirror image in the air of what is occurring on the ground. And the fall of vultures, of course, is the universal signal that sends hyena and lion, wild dog and jackal, into action.

The vultures themselves "home" in on the fall of other vultures, so that the distress of a grazing animal is represented by certain birds circling over it, and then, if it falls, the drop of those birds immediately to the ground. At the same time, a lappet-faced vulture, perhaps three miles away, begins a long fifty-mile-an-hour diagonal glide to earth. Beneath the bird, a hyena is making the same run, but running at only about thirty miles an hour. The vulture reaches the dead or dying animal five minutes earlier than the hyena. If the fallen creature is a gazelle, the hyena will arrive too late to pick up anything except scraps.

The vultures are the spy planes in the high clouds, some of them now preparing, as were the Rüppell's, for nesting on the eastern escarpment of some distant mountains, which would bring them each day, in two-hundred-mile flights, to the plains and back to the mountains. The distances traveled by the vultures, imperceptible to the landbound watcher, became dramatic when we flew, and saw the great flying creatures stretched out for many miles ahead of us, each group circling within its own thermal, abandoning it in a steady stream at the bottoms of cumulus clouds, and gliding down to pick up the elevator of the next available thermal.

The leopard sometimes trembled on his branch at the sight of vultures. His hatred of them sprang from the single flaw in his system of preserving his kills: storing them in the crotches of trees. Even allowing for his natural carelessness (one in five of his victims slipped from their perches and fell among the hyenas and other scavengers), he had justification in becoming upset over the omnipresent vultures. They watched him like eagles, marking his every kill, and were immediately in the area over him, as he ate, dozed, or went off to drink. And once they settled on his cached victim, they had little difficulty in dislodging it to the ground.

The leopard's dilemma was that although he had ample strength to carry his kills as high as he wished—there was one record of a three-hundred-pound giraffe carcass that was wedged into the crotch of a tree at forty feet—the higher he went the more vulnerable his kill to sighting by the vultures. A low-stored kill, of course, was visible to hyenas, and lions. Flying like vultures ourselves, Candlish and I got another level of perception. The leopard ignored lions. He was nimble in his retreats from rhinoceros and buffalo. But vultures drove him mad.

He would watch the big birds sidelong from his branch, as they gathered on the ground to attack the scanty remains of some night foray by the hyenas. He did not appear to be able to see them at great distances in the air. But one time, when they fell to earth near him, he stood up on his branch, and watched with an intensity that spoke of a very great emotion indeed.

Perhaps in response to the leopard, the vultures placed their nests with much care, choosing only the loftiest trees, and constructing great untidy agglomerations of rubbish solely on the canopy itself. These were in essence floating buildings, cloud nests hovering at the fingertips of the yellow fever trees. From the ground, the occupied nests looked the same as an abandoned nest, and there were many of those, a deception the vultures enhanced by the subtlety of their arrivals and departures.

But nestling vultures make a noise, and cats have acute ears. With my powerful glass, I located a nest easily enough, but the leopard made the same deduction by other means. Two young vultures were nearly ready to leave a nest at the southern limit of the leopard's range, and their near-maturity brought both adults to the nest.

From a distance, in the truck parked in the open grasslands, I could see the four birds standing there in the bright sun while, simultaneously, the leopard was visible, working his way quickly through the feverish shade beneath. It was unusual to see such purpose in the cat's movements by day, which was not his time of resolute action ordinarily. But he had it well fixed in his mind what to do.

In a second, he was blazing upward, in ripping grips of the trunk, blasting his way toward the canopy. His speed was so great that he was through the foliage, and beside the nest, and able to take one flailing blow at the nearest adult vulture, before any of the birds could move.

The leopard was too hasty, working at such blinding speed, and the vulture leaned away on protecting wings. The second adult sprawled backward, tumbling, in its surprise. The leopard hooked both youngsters in his claws, and spun them away, broken rubbish spiraling to the ground. He charged the sprawling adult, and almost caught her as she fell through the canopy. She slid down the yellow shaft of the tree until she bounced off a branch, wings outspread, and parachuted for a score of feet that gave her lift, and got away into the sun, heavily.

The leopard smashed the two unhatched eggs that remained. Then with a ferocity and determination that let me briefly into the mind of the hunting cat, he tore the great nest to pieces.

6 ○ The Hyena

"The lion is a scavenger of hyena kills."
HANS KRUUK

The clouds changed. From bulking purity, kapok-thick, and sculpted so white on that breathless African blue that they might have been painted, they were degenerating, sagging like torpedoed leviathans, somber dark colors staining their undersides. With a shock, as when the cathedral bells do not chime on the hour, I saw that the vultures had gone. Storks labored along as though the air had turned to treacle.

At the turn of the seasons in the high upland countries of central south Africa, under Kilimanjaro and Meru, and even on the threshold of the Mountains of the Moon, there is always a quickening of the human pulse at the expectation of the next performance. It is a theatrical place. The landscape is as febrile as the heartbeat of a gazelle.

"A downpour coming, wouldn't you say?"

The hunter is drawn to Africa. Candlish and I had returned, again and again, drawn by the magnetism of an experience that is filled with death. I once made a rough count of the number of times I had reached the majestic continent, and lost the score at around forty. It is not from either the scenery or the people that the place is magnetic, but from the persuasion of its animals. It is where the human hunter is so close to his quarry that he can smell blood in the air and feel mortality in the rumble of lions.

The dry season in these upland plains lasts for a full five months. It is the equivalent of the winter everywhere else, a time of rest and recovery. The rains are the excitement. All other time is anticipation of them. The life of the plains is stretched out very thinly, so that one can witness what lies beneath.

Tension between drought and flood kept us here. We would not have spent so long in a desert, or in the regulated tedium of a southeast Asian jungle, or an Andean cloud forest. All living things, Candlish said, were made vital by the swing of opposites, by stress instead of security, by the constant effort toward equilibrium, rather than by its achievement, which was the death of effort.

There are many ways of dealing with the dry season. Some animals withdraw to burrows, or cavities in trees, or the inner sanctuary of a termite mound, into the shade of undergrowth, or into the banks of shrunken rivers. I flushed a monitor lizard from its shelter in a scummy stream and saw it rocket into the shelter of a bank, as fast as a greyhound. I waited for two days, crouched and hidden, over one small patch of red plains soil, and counted forty species of birds picking over the ground, one behind the other, and each finding something different there.

Waiting for the rains is very frustrating unless you live in Africa, and even then it is annoying. The rains are not to be taken for granted. Yet they must fall for the whole spectacle of migration, feeding, breeding, and killing to take place. As impatience heightens unbearably, suddenly the rain comes in deluges. It may be on schedule, or it may be early, or late, or both, occurring in two episodic fits, causing animals to advance into an embrace of green, only to retreat just as quickly when the grasses themselves retire back into the earth.

A German traveler, Fritz Jaegar, arrived in 1907 just as the rains struck and was overwhelmed by his first view of the Serengeti Plain. "And all this is a sea of grass, grass, grass, and grass," he wrote.

Both Candlish and I had been in Africa long enough to know not to waste time in Kenya or Uganda, Mozambique or Rhodesia, South Africa or Somalia. There is only one place where the breaking of the drought is also the full display of the hunting heart at beat. That is in the Tanganyika territory, later to become Tanzania, later to become celebrated as the home of the Serengeti Plain, upon which we now hoped to see the greatest spectacle of natural history upon the earth.

The clouds darkened to deep mauve, and continued moving, writhing now with an almost frightening internal energy, appearing about ready to burst. In the heaviest of rains, when it is hard to breathe and the ground underfoot seems to tremble, there is a feeling of choking, as if from prairie dust. It is then hard to imagine being out there, in the open, under the lash of such storms.

In the drought, the grasses are quiescent. To preserve themselves, they hide, like the monitor lizard, with the option of racing upward instantly from the base of their leaves rather than by an extension of the leaf tips. The seed of the red oat grass expands with the heat to drive itself into the ground without moisture. Its growth is almost instantaneous with the first touch of moisture. The saw-toothed grass produces its seed on a high stalk but keeps its leaves as flat as possible, just under the nip of the smallest antelope. A careful observer could make out a scheme of survival here, without moving anything except his eyes.

"Oh, well," said Candlish. "Maybe tomorrow. Let's get up there for a while."

The sun was falling into a bloodthirsty collision with the dusty horizon. The clouds disintegrated or sank. A scattered group of hyenas caught our eyes as they crossed a river in the savanna, about fifteen miles to the northwest, and moved toward the dry plains. Grazing animals sometimes unaccountably moved to the plains, the drought still unbroken, when, some observers speculated, they felt a change in the air pressure, or the humidity, or whatever it was, and tried to be under the rain, and on the grass, when the two came together. At once we perceived a distinctive hyena in the pack, which brought Candlish quickly to a lower altitude.

She was clearly an animal well past her prime, probably about ten years old, Candlish said. Few hyenas lived more than seven or eight years in a world so dominated by the need to kill large prey almost every day. The closer we looked, the more ancient this hyena appeared. Then Candlish noticed that she was a nursing female.

"Interesting dilemma," he said. "But if she has cubs, they're almost certainly back in the savanna country and she's on the threshold of losing her game, the moment the antelope and horse pull out of there and go to the plains."

The hunting territory of the Serengeti is composed of two entities: the short-grass plains, which are almost as bare as a table and fully as big as Delaware, and the long-grass savanna, which is an adjacent, undulating country of permanent water in the dry season, a patchwork of trees and swamps, and cut through by rivers. The savanna's long grasses could feed the grazing animals year round. But the short-grass plains grow the food during the rainy season that all the animals seek.

Candlish located the den, or guessed its ownership, near a small river, at the top of a rise, conveniently close to a couple of hundred feet of flat grassland where he could let down. Less conveniently, and perhaps deliberately, the den was near some thickets of growth, which led to a dryish swamp, the territory of the unpredictable water buffalo.

It was not just an old hyena's den, but a complex of dens, a small underground city which may have begun, in the fashion of hyenas, as the result of an exploitation of some other creature's diggings, a jackal perhaps, or even a spring hare. There were about twenty entrances, and there must have been hundreds of feet of tunneling. The cubs belonging to the old hyena might be anywhere beneath my feet. They would likely be crouched at the ends of tunnels dug by themselves, smaller corridors down which adult hyenas could not pass.

The old hyena had trained her cubs to freeze the moment they heard any strange sound. They knew their aloneness. They were a favorite victim of male hyenas, which tried to dig them out when their mother was away. Unlike the wild dogs, which returned to share their food by disgorging it for the den occupants, the hyenas shared nothing. If the old hyena failed to come home, the cubs would die. There was no backup scheme, even though the hyenas appeared to be gregarious, and met in convivial packs, hunting together most days and almost every night.

The hyenas had formed a kind of column, strung out loosely, and left a wake of dust behind their pounding feet. They did not run as dogs, as if it were natural, but heavily, filled with the resistance of their own bodies. Soon we came abreast of them again. I kept my glass on the old female, watching every shake of her sagging sides, the flop and tense of those baggy muscles, the droop and lunge of the heavy, ugly head. A pyramid of rock and shrub showed far ahead. She looked up at us, without sign of fear or interest. Magnified, she appeared even older, her once rounded ears ripped and torn, her right eye canted upward, a scarred white disk, like a human walleye. Her top lip was split so badly that her teeth showed in a perpetual snarl, a warrior of the hunt in defiance.

Females usually led the hyena packs, said Candlish, probably because they were bigger than the males. The skin of her chest and rib cage was scarred with a number of white jagged patches, the marks caused when she herself killed, the scars of her victims' desperate hooves or horns. I had never seen such a smashed-looking body. As we watched, and as she watched us, she tripped and took a long somersaulting fall. The column wheeled, uncertain.

As she got to her feet, it was as if she had been struck by some instant disease. She lurched. She staggered. She could not get her feet in unison. Her back legs collapsed.

"She's dying," said Candlish, with real interest. He turned widely so that we had a full, tilted view of the incident through the side window.

But then she was half-running again, an almost horrible sight, if the fall was connected to it, staggering and lurching and showing every second of her age, but lengthening that clumsy stride, pulling power out of her past, so that soon enough she was bounding along. We were stirred by the recovery, coupled to this streaming energy of the pack behind her.

I had to wonder about the size of her hunting territory. The horizon was empty, and that was from an airplane. The miles fell away, like an elastic band that has been pulled beyond its limit but will not break.

"I'm sorry about this," Candlish said suddenly, pulling up and away, so that the coffee I had poured turned sideways in my cup, "but I can feel it coming, and I don't want to be up here when it falls. Might bring us down with it."

I had noticed nothing, until I looked more carefully, and saw that before the set of the sun, the air had grown dark and striated and seemed to flash with the stroboscopic slashes of trapped electricity. In moments, I was at the camp, and he had disappeared with the plane to make it safe for the rains.

We had put the camp at some distance from a water hole in the savanna which bore reliable water through much of the drought, but which was also a way station, a meeting place, for groups that hunted temporarily on the plains. There, as tribes gathered, we could see the hyenas. Their trails rose like flags, ridiculously short tufts of hair sitting up erect and quivering with tension.

I observed a great deal of coming and going, of mixing

and separating, of individuals and groups, so that the order which was suggested in the running of the pack was negated by the sociality of the groups in meeting.

"Isn't there some scheme to all this powwowing down there?" I asked Candlish.

"Perhaps there is," he said.

"Aren't you interested in knowing?"

"Don't get possessed by Hemingway's ambition," he said, "which was in thinking that if precise enough language can be created, then there will be a truthful description of what is happening. He succeeded, in his terms, but such success blinkers the view, and destroys the capability to enjoy the ambiguous. Language binds us to seeing those fellows in our terms. They're doing their stuff in a totally untranslatable way, where the smell of an arsehole is a five-thousand-word essay in the Burke's Peerage of hyenas."

But it did not rain that evening, or the following day, and our tempers thinned out with the tension of waiting for something that lay hidden only in our imaginations. I did not see the old hyena again until the early evening of two days later, when I came upon a gathering of the animals in a dried streambed, under some yellow fever trees.

There could be no doubt, now, that despite her age, she was dominating the group gathered around her, although to use the word "dominate" does not quite describe the process. She used her sly ways to check the ambitions of other females to take her place, and to exploit the males' obsessive interest in play and sex.

It was clear that before they set out for the hunt, a considerable ritual was necessary. Some of the males bunched together and minced toward her like cats. She acknowledged them with her one good eye, and stood up. Then, in a moment, she crouched, her mouth half open, her teeth showing, and her ears laid flat back against her head. In a rush, the males surrounded her, with their manes expanded like lions', their pathetic little tails erect. They tried to bite her in quick-rushing attacks. They nipped at her hindquarters, danced away, whooped, giggled, and made small-boy concert with their voices. She was not amused. She lunged forward, clomped her terrible teeth down on a leg with such force that the blood rushed and the victim hobbled off three-legged and screaming.

Abruptly, she stood very erect. Immediate purpose was visible in every line of her body. It was said that the identity of the animal to be hunted by the hyenas was indicated by the gait of their running. It was clear that the old female had communicated something to all the others, and that they understood, because they, too, stood, and faced the direction in which she was facing.

Now the tribe bunched together. A sudden unification had occurred. The hyenas' tails rose, an indication of the pack's mood and determination. But a final ritual was needed. The old hyena must mark the place as her own, perhaps to return here after the hunt, perhaps as a warning to all others that this was where she sprang from, and intrusion would not be permitted, though it was a temporary place and might be vacated tomorrow, or even this afternoon.

She approached a stalk of dried grass, invisible to me, and while the others watched solemnly, she contemplated it for a long moment. Then she walked forward, over it, so that it bent under her chest. Then, with her hind legs crouched, her tail arched over her back, she dragged the stalk past her anus. At the same time, she extruded her rectum, touching the stalk and leaving a thin layer of mucus on it.

This was powerful magic. Its smell, carried downwind, could be detected by other hyenas, miles away. It was, in a way, an act of aggression, a warning. She stood there, oddly dignified all at once, keening, and then she was off. The hyenas fell in behind her, and the hunting pack was on its way.

The hunting animal moves great distances, arrives without warning in odd places, is a presence of the unexpected, and so is an image of death in the imagination. This death run, hammer-footing it into an oblivion of dust, reminded me of nothing so much as a battle-worn armored column wheeling from its bivouac, rolling forward.

She was a vulture watcher, on the run, or at rest, after killing, or before. The fall of those dark crosses on detergent-white clouds could turn her pack at right angles on the plains, or send it back into the savanna. She was also a listener to lions, and those ragged ears would cock in a second, at the first rumble in the night, keening for tiny changes in the timbres of the roars. When the right signal was received, away she went, to the certainty of scavenging at the least, and perhaps an opportunistic kill at the best. A scavenging hyena could kill a lion and eat him.

The peculiar combination of airplane and truck gave us a bicameral view of the hunting hyenas. One moment, I would be seeing them from a vulture's viewpoint, thirty miles of the hunting country sprawled beneath, the hyenas a dark clot of movement among the scattered acacias. Moments later, I was bumped to a landing by Candlish, and then into the truck, and circling a herd of wildebeest, grazing the fringes of a river.

Their heads all came up with electric snaps. They were looking toward the hyenas, which were still an hour out of sight. The country was empty in between, except for some impala. What did the wildebeest see in there, in that interposing spirit world of nothingness?

If the approach of death is communicated, then it has many subtle manifestations. Sometimes, the head-lifting animals pause for long seconds, transfixed within the intelligence of the message. If it is reassuring, they all drop their heads at once and grazing resumes. But the next time the emptiness delivers its message, the heads are not raised for a second, but the whole herd wheels as one animal and stampedes away in a boil of dust.

All is still after they have gone, as it was before they ran. The birds are silent; the sky is empty of vultures. There is neither view of elephant nor sound of lion. Because there is nothing superfluous or meaningless in nature, the flight of the wildebeest, or zebra, or gazelle, tells me that the message from the void does more than announce the approach of the killers. Of what use is that? More likely, I sensed, the individual victim is identified. It runs and the rest, ignorant, must follow.

The grip of the hyena's jaws compensates for all the clumsiness of behavior and body. It is powerful enough to smash the leg bones of a horse, and send splinters of bone flying like broken bottles. It is a grip that can kill lions and that no leopard would risk. This, in concert with neck muscles strong enough, some say, to lift a five-hundred-pound weight vertically, made it possible for a tribe of hyenas to reduce a thousand pounds of meat to a scattering of bones in a few minutes.

But this was rarely seen during the day. The daylight hours are when the hyena scavenges. With a rush and a thumping of clumsy feet, the hyenas arrive around my waiting truck. I am parked near the leopard's kill, the gazelle hung carelessly in a low fork. The heaviness and constriction continue in the air.

Mutters of thunder suggested rain. The heads of the grazing animals come up, bovine eyes aglare. "Watch where you park the lorry," said Candlish. "You don't want to be drowned when the waters come."

The leopard wakened with a start, large amber eyes staring with real concern at this scavenging filth that had appeared under his imperial tree. He came down from branch to branch in a liquid flow of movement, carmine lips slightly parted in a silent snarl, his magnificent black whiskers trembling. He clamped his forepaw down on his food, a Thomson's, just as the walleyed hyena, after a dozen leaps, got her teeth to it.

The gazelle's body broke in half. The hyena fell with the haunches, the bulk of the leopard's meal taken with her. I sat there, trembling in the rage of the leopard, while scanning the droop of the hyena's blotched flanks, her hindquarters lower than her shoulders, the heavy, almost brutish head and face, as she bristled at the others for coming close to this morsel she had seized. She cast one eye upward, as I contemplated her, and caught the beginning fall of vultures.

Just then, the skies opened, and a vertical reservoir of water fell. I was blind inside the thundering shell of the truck. Unwisely, I elected to move it, thinking that the windshield wipers would overcome the rain. Instead, I must have collided with a lion, because the noise of the rain was augmented by an exasperated rumble. After the soft resistance of a collision, a huge face appeared at the driver's window, and then fled away, leaving the mark of its lips on the glass.

Within twenty minutes, our tents were leveled and the sun was shining. Fallen branches lay everywhere. A jewelry of refracted water sparkled from the dripping foliage of the fever trees. The plains, first pounded to mud, were now pooled into lakes a fraction of an inch deep. The truck was bogged nearby. Candlish finished his cup of tea, and looked at his watch.

"Let's get going," he said. "We mustn't miss the big show. There are people hurrying to the airport in London, and New York, people who don't care about the Mau Mau, and who will do anything for a chance to see what is going to happen now. The telephone calls have been made."

We dug out the truck, narrowly avoiding a cobra which had climbed up inside the vehicle in search of engine warmth, and which struck at Candlish as he lifted the bonnet. The engine would not start. We needed some ignition parts. Candlish decided to walk to the Masai encampment where he had left the plane, under guard, with its cache of fuel, and fly to Arusha, or Nairobi, for parts and more petrol.

The water was going fast from the plains. Hot, writhing mists announced its departure under a flaming sun. The migration that had now begun, far from our earthbound eyes, was not as big as the buffalo migrations of the nineteenth century, which had involved tens of millions of creatures. But it was the most splendid modern spectacle of animals anywhere.

In *The Rediscovered Country,* a traveler, S. White, tried to describe the scene, leading into the Serengeti, as the animals were gathering, in readiness for the big push.

"Never have I seen anything like that game. It covered every hill, standing in the openings, strolling in and out among the groves, feeding on the bottom lands, singly, or in little groups. It did not matter in what direction I looked, there it was: as abundant in one place as another."

We kept a pistol in the truck, not because it was really dangerous wandering among the animals, but because of chance encounters with poachers, many of whom were now armed as a result of the tribal struggles for independence. We tossed a coin for it and I won, which pleased Candlish, because he said he, with his dialects, could probably talk his way out of trouble. I decided to walk to a nearby inselberg, or kopje, about four miles to the east, whence would come the marching animals.

Before I was a hundred yards from the camp, I found myself walking through, over, and under layers of life. The air in the shade was deliciously fresh, like a spring day in New Zealand. A cool white wine had gone down the throat of the drought. Flappet larks were aroused, rising and falling with the peculiar staccato chatter of beating wing spurs that seems to be an equivalent of song. Thin streams of termites, temporarily equipped with long, fragile-looking wings, were on the move. The ground underfoot was drilled with the highways of ants on the move, their armies more dangerous than any pride of lions, were I immobilized, and relying on eight shots of a gun for defense.

The inselberg was a jutting pyramidal mass of rock, soil, grass, and stunted shrubs and trees. I climbed carefully, watching for snakes and hidden cats. The line of the western horizon was brownish gray. Through the glass I saw dust rising, coiling serpentlike in lazy response to the music of the gentle wind that blows perennially on the plain. At the base of each coil, invisible to magnification, was a horse or antelope herd. Characteristically, the heavy rains had missed the western fringe of the grasslands. The animals were coming forward, in militarylike columns, through the dust to the drying mud, each in conflict with the other to get the best share of the grass that had not yet appeared.

I could almost feel the stretching of the old hyena's hunting territory as the animals upon which she depended for her food moved away from her. The movement of the grazing animals was no halfhearted affair. It was total and complete, and when it was done, the hyena's savanna hunting ground would be practically empty of anything she might be able to eat, except the impala. I had never seen a hyena run down these fastest of all antelope.

The inselberg was occupied by numbers of rodentlike animals—hyraxes—about the size of large guinea pigs, and relatives of the elephant. Their small forms spread from the castle of their refuge to graze the land around it, but never so far that they could not rush home. Watching them was like watching for an air raid that was on its way. In the middle of my attentive musing, however, I was moved to another perception.

A cat had appeared, as if from nowhere, his back to me, erect and intense. He was also watching the coils of dust. The cheetah had been there all the time, of course, but I must have looked through him. At the moment my eyes sought the horizon, I saw that it was green. I could have sworn that it was not green a moment before. But within hours, the green thickened, and slowly "rushed" toward me. My refuge was surrounded by a lapping sea of new grass.

The cheetah was the antithesis of the hyena, dainty instead of gross, daylight-hunting instead of nocturnal, fleet instead of clumsy. He was the delicacy of poetry to the bluntness of prose. His was the solitude of the kill instead of the sociality of group gorging.

Candlish had talked a lot about the mystery of the cheetah, which he recommended as an object of study. The "secret language" was his description of the puzzle he perceived in the animal. The cheetah did not stalk its victims, or ambush them, or panic them with encircling numbers. He was a single blaze of lightning.

Now, in such intent contemplation of a horizon that was empty of anything except dust, I could hear the mutter of a distant kettledrum. The marshaling of the host was begun now, and all the soldiers must hear the calls going out. The cheetah's relatively tiny head was a graceful rounded blossom at the end of a slender curved stem of attention. He was utterly unfrightening in his graceful stance. The columns of dust rose very tall, and curved and coiled together, and with a squeal and a whistle, the hyraxes suddenly all bolted back into the shadows of the inselberg.

The image of the neatly waiting cheetah was soon erased by an uproar of bleating, honking voices, the massed cries of wildebeest and zebra, which sounded regretful, as if coming out onto the plains had been a mistake. We were at the threshold of fifty days of madness, when a million and a half animals tried to cram all their lifetimes into the brief flush of sweet short grasses.

The sense of it is Shakespearean throughout: high tragedy, epic deeds, over a basement of fallibility. It is the survival of the species enacted in full view, with no secrets possible, because there is no cover, no wings in this theater except the night, and no attempt to conceal the vast and inchoate panics, the assassinations and subtle murders, the intrigues of property and sex.

It was as though we were strollers through a dense and teeming city, watching its follies in buildings stripped of their facades and curtains, their shades and pretenses. Or, when we were airborne, it was a city without roofs. Here was the full parade of the most intimate details of the players, their appetites, prejudices, ambitions, and the pathos of illusion, bared in the African sun.

We secured this aerial intimacy at a great cost in petrol, and some worries about the plane, which, after hundreds of thumping landings and cavorting takeoffs, over termite mounds and across bat-eared fox burrows, was starting to complain that the safari had gone on too long. Candlish liked to go up quite high, a couple of thousand feet sometimes, to get a picture of the general placement of the animals, even though this lost the identity of individuals we might be watching. Then he would come down in slow spirals, throttled well back, the motor whispering, to amplify the fine details from the gross picture procured through altitude.

The chessboard of movement could not be followed in all its moves. At only a thousand feet, we could see for perhaps twenty miles, and there would be no break in the animal numbers anywhere. This straggle of zebra was formed into a concentric circle, because they were being sculpted into shape by rushing wild dogs. This long line of wildebeest, a dark shaft of movement, abruptly broke in the middle, a slow-motion, cartoonlike bending of the broken shaft ends where a nomadic lion walked through. The gazelles, in their light-colored, loose agglomerations, were decorations in the mosaic, and their deaths had no substance, occurring without drama. One moment, all was peace, the players in their places; the next instant, a cluster of vultures had formed, and hyenas were running forward to where a gazelle had fallen.

The zebras advanced compactly, with a solid, commonsensical steadiness. They were horses, and they already understood about organization and discipline, which would one day lead other equines to accept riders. The wildebeest, in contrast, showed why they would never be domesticated. They were skittish, incomprehensible in their sudden advances, their panic-stricken retreats, their sudden toils of confusion, all formed from a restless prospecting that made no sense when seen from the air.

The small antelopes, Thomson's gazelles, were also restless. The delicacy of their forms was matched by the precision and economy of their movements. Each gazelle buck had his harem of does, three or four animals, which he guarded as the movement outward on the new grass developed. He "owned" a moving territory. But because of the constant nibbling, and advancing, the interposition of cheetah, the placement of lion, the streaming run of wild dog, this was a territory that changed almost by the second. It existed, not as a fact of earth, but as an idea inside the head of each buck gazelle.

The driving center of the spectacle became the hyenas. There were many groups, or clans, or tribes, whatever the attacking packs might be called. But it was the pack led by the old female hyena that dominated our attention. We came to expect her approach, always from the west, always strung out in a flying column of animals, driving along as if she had an appointment, a secret mission, somewhere among the inselbergs.

From our common training in desert operations at night, Candlish and I understood that most of the important events of war, except the main battles, occurred in darkness. Now, beneath us, we saw the same simultaneity of episode, the same baffling gaps between events, in a great grid of constant confusion. The nights, of course, held all the clues to what we saw by day.

We watched the old hyena, strung out with the others in a feverish run on a zebra herd, being kicked in full gallop, tumbled to the ground, while the others streamed on. She rested for the balance of that day, hunched and alone, in long grasses, before she wobbled to her feet and set out again, miles away from the pack, and all connection with it apparently lost. But the next morning, she was at the head of the group again, and her stomach bulged with food. What had happened during the intervening night?

We were thus put in collision with ourselves, masters of the air, and as fast as the cheetah, but blind to the night. Each day became more irrelevant. It was like going to a football game where you were only allowed to watch the time-outs.

"This is absolutely bloody ridiculous," said Candlish. "We've got to follow that old bag by night."

Immediately, a light of comprehension flooded over the dark grasslands. There may be nocturnal primates somewhere, but we were millions of years away from them. There was a real fear of the dark, which subtly controlled our behavior. We realized we were deliberately ignorant about the night, not because we saw poorly then, but because knowledge of the dark was forbidden to our species.

For quadrupeds, night and day are pretty much the same. Their days are not divided. I felt that fear of the dark was the higher state of consciousness. But knowledge of the dark, whether sensory or conceptual, was the highest state of all.

At first, we were fools in the dark. Candlish made a hilarious attempt to fly at night, but then could not seem to find a place to land that was not full of wildly charging animals. He was so shaken he had to lie down for an hour. On the ground, wild honking came out of the dark. A thunder of hooves sounded. Then screams. Silence.

I ran the truck into a swamp and drove a tooth through my lip. We wanted hyenas, but what we got was the rumbling of lions, which sounded like a ten-thousand-ton freight train rolling over a trestle. The depth of all sounds was a distancing of day creature from night. By flashlight, birds slumbered through the wild honking of wildebeest, fading, in Doppler effect, to the yip of hyenas, the random barking of jackals. In the background, a swarm of sounds which we could never identify: whistles, shrieks, moans, clicks.

Finally, we "ambushed" the hyenas at a meeting place, as they arrived in moonlight. But when we tried to follow them, they moved too quickly, and our vision was too limited, for the tracking to be long effective. Candlish discovered that switching on the headlights had virtually no effect on the hyenas. They ignored the lights, after the initial reaction of looking blindly into them, and continued about their business as though darkness still prevailed.

The headlights of the truck threw light about three hundred feet ahead of the vehicle, within the arc of which the hyena column ran. It seemed, almost, that they used the lights to see deeper into the night. Certainly, a leopard had once dashed ahead of me one night, in lightly treed country, to scoop up a hare dazzled by my headlights. Other animals, caught and blinded in the lights, stood there—like foxes, occasional badgers, many other hares—eye disks gleaming, transfixed until the last second as the hyenas ran toward them. It was silent-movie cinematics, a shallow field of perception, jerky action, Mack Sennett resolutions.

The hyenas loped at about twenty-five miles an hour. Inside the truck, the speed seemed insane. Trees blazed into view so abruptly that Candlish nearly turned over the vehicle avoiding them. We swerved sharply down a slope, the puny English engine screaming in a low gear, and came to the edge of a bank, over which the hyenas had flowed like water. We were airborne and then shaken by the crash of landing, a boggy patch at once ahead, too late to brake, the accelerator floored to get us through. I hit the windshield. We shot into undergrowth. Yellow fever tree trunks flashed. A crash and a judder through a stream, a skip of foliage, and the lights blazed on the low-slung hindquarters of the running column.

The tactics of the hyenas were very simple. They came upon their prey, and they ran after them. When one animal became tired, and slowed, they killed it. They seemed able to run all night, whereas the zebras and wildebeest and gazelles could only run for quite short distances. It was the triumph of brute determination over speed.

But it was the kills themselves that changed all notions of the night. Here, we were touched by some primeval influence, that made death in the dark—no matter how well illuminated—something totally different from the same thing by day. We might lose the hyenas temporarily in the heat of chases, antelope or zebras everywhere flaring from the headlights, stragglers of the hyena clan blundering in pursuit of the action ahead. But we almost always were observers of the aftermath of each hunt, and in detail that drew our senses to very painful points.

The hyenas made no attempt to kill their victims. Their only interest was to bring down the fleeing animal. Once that was achieved, the weight of the hunters kept it from rising. With the victim down, eating began at once. Within seconds, the animal was disemboweled. Each hyena strained upward, with stretched lengths of intestine in their jaws, seeking to pull and break at the same time. Often, their preoccupation with this permitted the animal, usually a wildebeest, to partially rise again, at least the forequarters, which came up out of the swarm of bodies around it like something implausibly conjured in a bad horror movie.

Yet the eyes were serene, or, at least, blank. Once, a wildebeest lost its entire stomach section—all the tubes, liver, kidneys, spleen, and the rest, pulled clear of the body, and being gobbled up by the hyenas. Then the half-risen animal turned its head with a knowing glance. Its jaws began working. Wildebeest, like most ruminant grass-eaters, chew "cud," remasticating grass eaten minutes or hours before. They regurgitate it from their first stomach.

If the wildebeest was indeed chewing cud, then even my strong stomach was turned. Its own stomach was gone, and perhaps the first stomach as well, because the hyenas had reached the rib cage. If this was cud, then the swallowed material would spill from a broken tube into the seething dark of hyena jaws.

The heart, of course, was still intact. We had to presume there was no pain. The animal had lost much of the flesh from its hind legs. Eventually, a large part of one hind leg was ripped off and carried away into the darkness, and it was at about that time that the cumulative shock caught up with the serene and chewing face. The eyes glazed. The front part of the wildebeest fell from the glare of our headlights.

The old female led the long runs of the hunt. She preserved her position, initially, when the pack became convinced—an observable moment—that a kill could be attempted. It was that moment of commitment—landing an airplane, launching a rocket—when it is too late to switch off the power without being consumed by the energy of the movement. The headlights revealed the penalty of her age. The younger, more powerful animals surged forward. She found herself running second, or third or fourth, until, at the moment of the victim's fall, she might be last in the hunting column.

She could dominate, she could lead, she could invoke the years past, when her determination was a steel bond upon the others, and thrust back all efforts to climb into her place. But now, at the kill, she could not maintain her place.

The technique of dealing with the body of the victim was an automatic stratification of pack determination. The hyenas surrounded the fallen, back legs braced and heads plunged forward into the ripped mass of entrails. A hyena which could not get into the front rank might leap on the backs of the others and try to come down to the feast from above. But this risked autodestruction in the jaws of the pack—which happened. Or the animal might try and pull one of the feeders backward. Either way, its position of strength in the group was determined by whether or not it ate.

The chill truth of these nights was that the old female did not eat until the best stuff was gone. Yet she, above all of them, needed extra food.

"Something has to give," said Candlish.

We speculated how the hyena might solve her dilemma, while knowing that solution was impossible. She disappeared from the night gatherings, and for some time we did not reconnect with her. When she reappeared, there had been a major change, and we could only see its simple surface.

We were flying due east, slightly deeper into the plains than usual, when we spotted a hyena, alone, in the tall grasses of some marshy ground. In front of the marsh was a wild dog den, from which the whole pack—the hunting animals, the youngsters, the pups, the nursing females—had quickly come into view. They were extremely excited because a large group of wildebeest had come within sight of the area, and it was clear that the dogs were getting ready to make a hunting run.

When this began, the hyena—which I was sure was the old animal we had been watching—got to her feet and lumbered out after the others. The dogs made their kill very quickly, mainly because they marked an old, sick bull which stumbled and fell almost as soon as the running pressure was put on him.

As the dogs fed, I saw two things. One was the approach of the old hyena, who came within a hundred feet of the feeding dogs, and lay down. Meanwhile, in the distance, I saw a very large group of hyenas approaching at a dead run, apparently having seen the fall of vultures, those birds now gathered in wait for the larger animals to finish eating.

Within a few minutes, the hyenas had arrived, dispersed the dogs, and appropriated the kill for themselves. At the same time, as the squabbling over the kill was in progress, the old hyena darted in and got herself a place at the kill. Candlish made a wide, slow turn, which, for a moment, obscured our clear view of events. When we straightened, I could not pick her from the mass. Once, I saw a hyena rising from the pack, as if lifted by some force beneath, but then it disappeared at once back into the mass.

It took, as usual, about fifteen minutes for the five-hundred-pound animal to be eaten, and dismembered, with only the skull and the backbone remaining as identifiable parts of the bull. But at no time from that point did we see any sign of the old hyena. All the hyenas eating, or resting, or making off, then, were younger animals.

7 ○ The Cheetah

The cheetah aroused himself in the midafternoon when army ants, prospecting the low mound on which he was lying, began climbing into the fur of his paws and body. His long graceful body, lean to the point of boniness, rose slowly, as if propelled upward by hydraulic pressures, a series of angular unfoldings of limbs and elongation of the body.

For some reason, a sunbird was hawking about the cheetah, showing the metallic colors of its wings in bright prismatic reflections of the sun. A locust clattered into the air from a cluster of grasses nearby. The wind, scarcely a wind at all but rather a series of zephyrs, touched the lugubrious faces, the broad splayed ears, the ridiculous short horns, of a herd of hartebeest, which, seen through the now slitted eyes of the cheetah, were silhouetted against banked white clouds on the northern horizon.

The tension was characteristic and familiar to me now. For more than an hour, the hartebeest—well-fed, fat, and free to roam the plains anywhere—had been advancing slowly toward the recumbent cheetah. They looked like mechanical marionettes as they raised and lowered their heads in desultory cropping of the grass. The other animals—the wildebeest, gazelle, and zebra—were well spread across the plains; there was no need for the hartebeest to be in such an obvious collision course with the hunting cat, none that I could understand, anyway.

At the same time, the army ants had been moving steadily north from their last bivouac, located in a mat of fallen grasses near a swampy area, where giraffe liked to collect, displaying crossed necks against the background of honking wildebeest, braying zebra. The ants hunted as an integrated army unit, with scouts running ahead, and to each side, of the main-army advance, and bringing back a constant stream of information as to where possible raid expeditions might be directed. They had just discovered the cheetah. Had he been sick, or injured, unable to move, he would have been attacked while still alive.

"The cheetah," Candlish had said, "holds the key to the hunting process. When we know how he picks his victim, we will understand something so profound it may have little to do with hunting."

We knew that the choice of victim was not random, or accidental. For weeks, we had seen the cheetah, almost from the corners of our eyes, poised like statues in the open landscapes, like porcelain figurines, against backgrounds of the slowly moving host. Yet we had never seen a cheetah make a kill, and only occasionally saw the beginnings of runs, which always petered out before they picked up speed, the cats returning to their observation points, to slump down to sleep, or resume their vigils of watching.

They instilled a background of their own: the suggestion of events about to occur. Every tableau that contained cheetah was alive with a latent and lethal energy. Only the cheetah, of the mammals, hunted by day. Why was it, then, the one we never saw?

"The reason for this may be that the timing of the run is

as significant as the choice of the victim," Candlish said. "The cheetah tolerate us, and they cannot drive us off, but we may upset the obviously delicate balance of concentration that they have invested in their prey."

The preparation of the cheetah for the run often took hours. Within the cheetah's "workup," as Candlish called it, was that infinity of detail which, if understood, would make sense of why the cheetah ran, when the cheetah ran, whom the cheetah intended to kill, and how he made the decision to knock down that one animal and not another.

Since we had come to the plains, the cheetah had been our subtlest guides, indoctrinating us into nuances of the hunt that we might not have understood had we been watching directly. These three cheetah, all rising together, a mother and two half-grown youngsters, then all slowly sinking, as if the air were being let out of their bodies—they had said something to us, but what? This male, who rose suddenly, and then ran clear through a herd of gazelles at three-quarter speed and simply loped out of sight—he had said something too, but in a language that we did not know.

Now, here, the cheetah was rising again, and the metallically bright sunbird flicked away into the northwest sink of the sun. The ants were crushed or scattered in a casual slap of the cat's paw. A run now seemed very likely. I knew this animal well. He tolerated me better than any of the others I had been close to. On one occasion, I had reached out of the truck's window and touched his tail with a stick, and he had looked up at me casually, not with that ferocious concentration of attention that the leopard had displayed but with an easy raising of the head, a flicker of concern in the eyes that I might be capable of mischief.

Now I moved the vehicle from the rear of the risen cat, to one side of him, so that I could watch his face for signs of what he might be intending. His mood was at first as relaxed as the rise of his body, the eyes lidded, a paw licked casually, an immense yawn revealing teeth, tongue, throat. But in facing the hartebeest, which had now lined up, in a kind of phalanx, about one thousand feet away, he slowly came down to the business of their approach to him. They were transmitting information to which he must pay attention. They were telling him, it seemed to me, that they did not want him in their hunting range.

His response was a slow transformation of his face. From being relaxed, almost like a domestic cat's, it gradually sharpened. His eyes, which had been as soft as a kitten's lying before a winter fire, became as hard as golden steel. A slight tremor possessed his shoulders and forelimbs. In some immeasurable way, the fur around his eyes, nostrils, muzzle, cheeks, had changed its configuration and given the face a distinct expression of brutal, lethal concentration. I could feel the transmission of information now, from cat to antelope. He would not flee from their grazing territory now. Instead, he would kill one of them.

The act of killing cannot really be perceived accurately by any observer who is not himself accustomed to killing. Our own soldiers cannot be seen blowing out people's brains unless the people are made guilty. Our own soldiers cannot be seen having their brains blown out unless the foe is portrayed as vicious and cruel. Killing is too serious a business for it to be seen truthfully.

The cheetah displayed the devotional importance of killing both accurately and well. His own life, as an uncrippled running animal, was on the line each time he blazed down the line of attack. Many cheetahs suffered injury in their runs, and we had become accustomed to seeing limping animals. The stopping skid, alone, must give any observer cause to question the safety of the whole business.

How relatively easy it is, I thought, to gather there in the hartebeest crowd, flank to flank, scruffy tails flicking off the biting flies, a uniformity of horns and quick-chewing jaws, a ripple of hooves cutting the turf, a confidence of numbers marshaled against this solitary enemy. Two hundred and fifty pairs of goggle eyes looked across at those slitted windows of observation in the cheetah's tiny head. It was fifteen tons of complacent flesh gathered against perhaps one hundred and twenty pounds of rifling energy.

The decision to kill, as the leopard had revealed, is more interesting than the actual act itself. It is a fragile moment, filled with imponderables, in which the hunter must risk all. The leopard could fall, and be crippled, and eaten alive by hyenas. The hyenas often seemed hysterical at the lethal moment, turned to madness when their jaws filled with flesh.

A week ago, just after I had lost contact with this cheetah when he had made a false run, starting off like a bullet, and then slowing and galloping away to the horizon like a horse, Candlish and I had stood amidst a slaughterhouse of gazelles. A blinding rain had filled the night before and had come, obviously, just as a tribe of hyenas were readying themselves to hunt.

Apparently, the tribe had come upon the gazelles at the height of the rain, when most grazing animals huddle apathetically, waiting for the downpour to stop, and had proceeded to kill the whole herd. About a hundred animals were dead, or crippled, or dying. We had become accustomed to animals being eaten alive, to the screams of stricken zebra in the nights, of vultures removing eyes and tongues from the yet-living. But mass murder gave this scene a human aspect.

Most of the dead had been killed with the characteristic directness of the hyena—a clench of jaws and then a great shaking rip, which tore off a leg, or decapitated the animal. The crippled and dying caught our attention as the work of the hyenas as well as expressing the plight of the gazelles. Partially disemboweled, blinded, tubes protruding, air whistling out of reddened punctured lungs, sheeplike bleats of helplessness—these stricken were the aftermath of a battle with swords.

"One is tempted to ask," the Australian writer Alan Moorehead has written, "whether this is the fate of nature, to be so careless, so wantonly destructive, in the midst of birth and life itself. Surely, there is a better way of doing things."

The hyenas, geared to kill in the pack mood dominated by an animal as authoritative as the old female, had not been prepared for a seemingly unlimited choice of victims. The cheetah's trembling lips, parted in what I surmised was a silent snarl, indicated his readiness to kill but showed also, in the conflict and hesitation of body, that the process of triggering was incomplete. He could not yet run.

The hyenas, launched to kill, had no device of control if they encountered helpless prey. They must massacre all in order to gain their single victim. Here was expressed that fallibility of the hunt which fed backward, toward the victim, as expressive of a kind of control that I suspected the hunted animal often had over its own fate. If the gazelles could have run in the rain, only one would have died. It would become clear that no animal that advanced on a cheetah ever died.

My attention now turned from the shaking cheetah to the apparently blank wall of hartebeest facing him. An hour or more had passed and it was simply not true that the hartebeest were united in confronting their common enemy. In fact, they seemed to be divided into many groups of response, and even into individual sensitivities to the cheetah's concentration upon them.

The wash of rains had brightened the fever trees, made their foliage thicken with new greens, their trunks a richer and deeper yellow. The air itself seemed colored, in its increased clarity, and the faces of the hartebeest seemed tinted pastel pink in sunlight filtering through wisps of clouds. The vanguard hartebeest, blank-eyed as they might appear, were the aggressive members of the herd. They were, I surmised, determined not to die. It was they that had led the herd toward the cheetah. It was they, now, that challenged the cat's authority over them.

At once, I perceived that I must see as the cheetah saw, and it was no longer useful to watch the expression on his face. I returned to my former position, directly behind him, so I could follow the various swivels of his eye and get a rough idea at which animals he was looking. This was the kind of detail that Candlish treasured above all the scientific facts I might deliver to him.

The vanguard hartebeest could not, of course, form a true "wall" in defiance of the cheetah. They bunched, and moved around, and the suggestion of the hunt was gone. But there could be no doubt that somewhere behind the vanguard animals lay the victim. There, the bulk of the herd concealed the identity of that animal which had the least defiance, the weakest will to run, one of the animals which grazed as if nothing much was happening between comrades facing the cheetah and the cat himself. The cheetah watched these hartebeest that did not watch him, often craning his neck at odd angles to get a clear view of an individual.

The cheetah's method of imposing himself was transpsychic as well as physical. The monotony of the watching was as vital as the tedium of army-ant scouting, most of which found nothing, but which by now had reported the activity of the cheetah to the main army, which bent the line of its advance, and the construction of its highways and tunnels, so that it would swing clear of the cat.

It must be as true for the cheetah as it had been for the leopard, that the kill would end at the throat of some animal with which there was a "relationship." It was relationship, then, that the cheetah was seeking among the hartebeest now, if he did not already "know" some of these animals from previous "workups." As the hours slipped away, yet with the expectation of witnessing an extraordinary kill growing almost by the minute, I slipped into a kind of urgent memory of the leopard's showdown with the baboon leader, ten days before, when he had made a kill to give all primates pause.

The baboons had finally interfered with the leopard's prey. In their fooling around, the body of a gazelle had been dislodged and had fallen to the ground. I had seen this, without also knowing the location of the leopard. The baboons considered the gazelle gravely, as if the enormity of what they had done did not have meaning for them.

I happened to be momentarily out of the truck at the time, and my skin crawled that the leopard might be somewhere near me, and take his revenge on the most visible primate. Soon, though, the baboons were headed toward a water hole. Ahead lay a sunlit space. The females started down the trees, cuffing youngsters who were reluctant to move. The leader came down and the group advance across the clearing began. The rear guard of young animals drooped behind. It was clear that the leader would ignore the fallen gazelle and keep his troop heading for the water hole. However, at the crucial moment, a column of spotted fur arose, propelled upward smoothly, out of long grass. For a moment, I had the thought that I would be the first person to see a cheetah ambushing a primate.

Candlish and I had discussed the possibility of hypnosis among animals. Certainly, the cornered rodent may "give up" and cringe, but it may also lunge for the throat of its enemy. The snake does seem to mesmerize the mouse. When the cheetah rises, its gaze is so steady, so unrelenting, that no animal can mistake its intent. Atop an inselberg, I had used my powerful glass to look directly into the face of a cheetah "shaping up" some gazelles, and I had felt the cat's eyes blazing into mine, with the question: Are you the one?

But the spotted fur had belonged to the leopard facing the baboons. Barks ran up and down the line of advance, and from out of the trees. Then vanguard and rearguard baboons howled, barked, and picked up handfuls of grass. All the males showed their teeth. Screaming began. The pressure on the leopard was being variously built up to put the cat to flight. But the leopard did not move. My glass showed that only his whiskers trembled. He was very close to both his revenge and his own death. He had strategically obligated the baboons by rising in their midst, the most audacious act possible. If they closed on him, he was lost. If he kept them separated, he might have their leader.

One by one, the baboons peeled away; those who had once been so vociferous in their expressions of freedom were now unable to take the pressure of defense. The four high-ranking baboons, close to the leader, hesitated longest. They tried to pass on the responsibility by importuning the leader. But when no sign of leadership came from him, they, too, turned and fled, to join the uproar that swelled out of the trees.

Now was the time of the cat. I zeroed in on him, my glass expanding his almost languid stroll forward, so sure of himself that he could pause for a moment and lick the bottom of a paw. This was the payoff for being a leopard, a reward for having to face these hysterical proletarians with their confusing mixture of defenses, the paradox of their helplessness as individuals and their strength in the group. This was the kick for being a specialist, for being so fast, and also so strong, and also fully functional in both the day and the night. There was no old age for him, in the way that baboons arranged their group securities, but there was this moment.

Similarly, there was now the precise moment when the cheetah rose from the mound, having chosen his victim. There was no way of determining how it had been accomplished, only that one of the hartebeest, situated deep in the herd, suddenly began displaying signs of extreme agitation. The animals around him remained calm. The hartebeest tried to run, but only succeeded in making a series of short turns on the grass.

Meanwhile, in passing the cat, the army ants were providing another strand to the tableau. They had found an occupied termite mound. A pause was necessary while its defenses were tested. As the ants advanced, both scouts and foraging parties were scaring up many insects and arthropods in the grass. These were being caught by about a score of different species of birds which habitually followed the army-ant advance.

The birds passed across the tableau, and revealed themselves as being structured into classes of exploitation, so that certain dominant birds had earned the right to take their places at the head of the army's advance. These birds snapped up spiders, beetles, and other creatures scuttling in the grass. Behind them came the flycatchers, which cleared the air of all flying insects. Beneath the birds, at grass level, really, there were several species of flies which were also closely monitoring the ant advance. They were interested not in hunting but in taking advantage of panic, when their natural hosts—cockroaches—were made unwary in escape and so could be implanted with their eggs.

Of course, none of this was without danger. The flies were taken by the flycatchers, and the flycatchers were taken by falcons, hanging well back in the line of march, but all risk was made sensible by the immense amount of booty which the ants scared up in every hour of their advance.

The precision with which the victims were isolated, by the various devices of detection, and then circumspectly attacked was the design of a hunting mosaic that now filled my mind at three different levels. The baboon leader faced the leopard in the tableau of ten days before, his dilemma now associated in my mind with the situation of the cheetah's victim. The hartebeest could not run. The baboon leader could not move. The termites were trapped in their tower.

At the final moment, the baboon had ample time to move. The leopard was a score of feet away. But instead of breaking and running, the primate had drawn himself back on his haunches, his chin downward onto his chest, his back straight, and his arms stretched down tautly before him. He did not even seem to be preparing himself for bluff, or intimidation. He uttered no sound. He was working backward through his own history, and he was mesmerized by so many years of the leopard's passion for him.

This seemed to be the grand tactic of the hunter, to create a condition in which the victim was unable to act for itself. The by now nearly frantic hartebeest, galloping back and forth, and shaking its head, would prove this point, if it was cut down in the cheetah's charge. But the more subtle proof might come from within the termite tower, which, heavily defended, all its entrances thickly plugged with wads of chewed earth, could conceivably resist any frontal assault by the ants.

The trick, then, was to render ineffective the conventional methods of defense or escape. Hypnotism, the apathy of terror, the brainwashing of an individual . . . Why should the ants not possess a technique that was uniquely their own?

The termite queen and her retinue would have been moved to a duplicate set of royal chambers, set higher in the mound. Both the ants and the termites were blind, so the forthcoming battle must depend on senses of smell, perhaps sound, the ability to detect hormones which, in vaporized form, might travel swiftly and far. The termites were densely gathered behind each plugged entrance. To break this standoff, the ants had a separate caste, or race, of their species, tiny creatures less than a twentieth the size of the standard engineer, booty carrier, and warrior. Their secret weapon was that, unlike all the other ants, they carried no smell detectable to the termites.

I was reminded of the story Candlish had told me about being a Beaufighter pilot in the western desert during World War II, when superior British technology enabled him to hunt Germans the way some people hunt ducks. "What we had on our side were some German myths," he had said, "which people believe, even today, about superior technology, weaponry, that kind of thing. What they had was great bravery—or perhaps it was stupidity."

The Germans did not know about radar. They did not seem to understand that the Beaufighter was faster and more heavily armed than their comparable planes. When the junkers were boring through the darkness to bomb Cairo, the pilots and gunners would chat over their intercoms, night after night. They knew it was perfectly safe until they reached the ack-ack of Cairo, and the night fighters rising from Heliopolis.

But Candlish and his fellow Beaufighter pilots were behind them. They had switched off their inboard radars because they could see the flames from the exhaust ports of the German engines.

"Before you pressed the red button," he said, "you had to be very careful about your position. In a second or two, the air would be filled with wreckage tumbling through the dark."

The termites had no way of detecting the tiny ants, once they had slipped into the tower through weather cracks. The invaders had their own separate organization, which was to find the brood chamber, wherein a rich booty of larval and pupal termites was being reared. They raced unsensed beneath the legs of the termites. On their way inward, they laid down a scent that only they could detect, enabling them to "escape" by the corridors by which they had entered. This scent, in turn, would lead the warriors inward, when they were alerted that the brood chamber had been located and the best way to it indicated by the pathfinders.

As the leopard and the baboon had slowly drawn closer together, the uproar of the other baboons, magnified in the natural amphitheater of the clearing, indicated the rage and despair of the troop. Long white teeth, strong enough to rip out a leopard's throat, thrust forward aggressively. Excrement flew through the air as the baboons hurled their only weapon toward the advancing authority of the leopard. Energetic bouts of copulation jerked among the foliage.

The cheetah rose to the full extent of his lean body. His head appeared to get smaller as his body elongated. At the same time, the hind legs bunched with muscles, and trembled with the containment of their power. I could feel the cat's eyes blazing toward the hartebeest, the power of his gaze coming to me through the back of his head. The vanguard hartebeest now fell well back, and were indecisive now as they perceived that their boldness in stepping forward could not now prevent the charge. The bulk of the herd tended to veer away, milling, some running, others turning again and again, to raise their heads high toward the cat. In the turmoil, I lost sight of the nervous hartebeest, but there could be no doubt that the cat had his eyes upon it.

The long slow tensing of the leopard's shoulders had impressed me with strength and speed being held in check. The baboon had impressed me as having drawn his torso back as far as he could without moving his legs, as though his brain were out of touch with the soles of his feet. My eyes watered with the strain of not missing a blink of it. I expected the baboon to run. And so did the cat, apparently.

When the baboon lunged forward, the leopard was as surprised as I was. I got only a brief sense of the primate's arms being flung backward, thus propelling his torso forward, and the thrust of those murderous teeth right into the cat's face. The response was known as stake-all, the risking of life to save it. Rats did it when cornered. If the baboon could strike the face accurately, he would blind the cat. Baboons killed leopards, but rarely without blinding them first.

The teeth came together, millimeters short, and the leopard's counterblow came savaging around. The baboon reeled away, slewing sideways, and then rolling loose. The thing seemed over and done with. Now, I thought, the baboon will be wedged in the crotch of a tree; a leg would be eaten, the liver, perhaps. But I had miscalculated the gravity of the leopard's rage. It was possible that death was too easy for this victim.

Instead of following up his swift blow with a lethal bite, the leopard raised himself again, his head high and his nose pointed down, while the baboon flailed, his spine obviously broken. I could feel his injuries, I could feel the power of the troop in the trees. I could feel the futility of the fallen animal.

The leopard turned away from the baboon and came trudging straight into the magnification of my glass. He walked heavy-footed, in the relaxed manner of all cats, his eyes once again half-lidded, as if the whole thing now bored him. I felt myself yawning. It was not especially hot, but I was drenched in sweat.

The cat became a single half-closed eye in the glass and then jerked out of magnified sight, ascended the tree next to the truck, stretched himself on a limb, and went to sleep. He knew I was in the truck, and he had made my presence a matter of pointed indifference, just as his abandonment of the stricken baboon was also a statement of his attitude. I had been wrong; the cat was not straight-line, direct, and simple. It was the baboon which now appeared simple, without those submerged layers of being that would make him provoke deeper study.

An eerie silence clung to the trees. The baboons had disappeared, or were not moving. The dog leader did not move, but lay still in the sun, a black rounded shape, one clenched fist half-raised. I thought he might be dead: he was topped by clouds of eager flies. But then his leg flexed, and he moved his toes, and I realized that the drama was not yet ended.

When the cheetah left his mound, it was anticlimactic. He loped forward, not directly into the hartebeest herd, but diagonally, almost flanking them, his head up and his body rocking like a cantering horse, no haste in him at all. He seemed deliberately unwilling to even challenge the hartebeest, much less run down one of their number.

A troop baboon had suddenly ventured from the shade and, seizing his courage, scampered into the sunlight. He touched the recumbent figure of his leader. That was when the screaming started.

The screams cleared the birds from the trees, and startled antelope grazing on the grasslands. The fallen baboon did not move but he screamed. He lay with his face in the dust and he screamed at the injustice of it all—screamed at every leopard who had ever treed his troop, and cut off his stragglers, and terrorized his friends, screamed at all the night horrors and day alarms, and perhaps above everything, he screamed at the unfairness of a corporation chief being brought down by a hunter who worked without help.

Candlish had said, "They flew fairly close formation, which was good for us because the Beaufighter had tremendous firepower and might bring down several planes with one burst of fire. In fact, we had to attack one at a time because speed, direction, and stability were all shot to hell the moment you touched that red button."

A termite tower is like an Egyptian tomb, constructed to fool thieves, so that it was possible that the royal brood and the queen had in fact escaped, barricaded in higher levels of the tower. Sometimes, when the original queen was being slaughtered and dismembered in the lower galleries, a young queen would get to the top of the tower, and lead a winged flight to escape over the laboring masses of ants beneath her.

The scene at the ant bivouac was utter confusion. The booty carriers thickened into traffic jams of termite parts, eggs, even the bloated abdomen of the dead queen, carried by two ants. The ants had taken everything, including the beetles and aphids that the termites domesticated for milking of nectarlike substances, and the leaves which had been dragged into the tower to feed them, the fungus crops grown in the subterranean farms that the termites had perfected over the eons.

The leopard had eventually become uncomfortable at the screaming. Grumpily, he got up, and flowed down the trunk of the tree, and trudged over to the baboon. With some savage blows and rips, he killed the dog leader. Then he returned to his tree. This time, he jumped on the hood of the truck, before making a second leap to the lowest branch. He left a smudge of blood on the metal.

The cheetah loped along his peculiar tangent. Then, having come three hundred yards closer to the herd, he stopped abruptly, crouched down, now facing the hartebeest. They did not know quite what to make of it. Some of the vanguard animals stamped their feet, or retreated a few steps, or turned sideways. The animals at the back were increasingly uneasy.

Then, again without haste, the cheetah took off again in another long loping run, still not directly at the prey, but even more widely diagonal to the main mass. The "game"—and suddenly, the word became sensible to me in a new way—simply appeared to be outmaneuvered, incapable of understanding this tactic of deployment when the expectation was the frontal charge, and the survival of those animals bold enough to advance into the enemy's teeth.

The sun was near the horizon now, rimming it with red, and the grasses were dusky in the hollows, a purple haze beginning to form in the grasses. The hartebeest had turned to face the cheetah on a north-south axis, elongated in their mass by the incapability of the rearguard animals to swing around behind the vanguard, and maintain their positions in relation to the cheetah.

It was at that late moment that the cheetah rose to its feet and leaped forward in such a thrilling explosion of movement that the clods of turf kicked up behind him appeared to be the pads of his own feet, abandoned in the savage acceleration. The expansion of his body was in a series of giant elastic leaps in which the release of coiled power created a flying creature only lightly brushing the earth with its feet.

The disorder of the hartebeest retreat now seemed to preclude the choice of any individual victim. They appeared clumsy at their speed of forty miles an hour while the cat drew on at a speed of nearly seventy. Obviously, any one of the animals closest to the flying cheetah could be brought down by the cat.

But the cheetah swerved to avoid the nearest animals, and went past them as though they were statues. Animal after animal was overtaken and left behind. The pumping of the striving shoulders and thighs was also the beating of the hunter's heart. The fabric of the victim's plight was being threaded by a needle.

It was a youngish cow, running straight and hard, who was isolated eventually, at the far side of the disintegrating herd. One paw flipped out deftly and the front legs of the hartebeest tangled so that she was on her nose at forty while the cheetah was a bunched and braking body, front legs splayed before him, hindquarters down and chunks of turf kicked up from the long skid that must keep him close to her tumbling body.

All action now in slow motion, the hartebeest overturned, upside down, and turned again, the cat himself half-twisted in supplication of his victim which he must seize even as she somersaults. Then he is an elegant reach of body, his teeth bared, and the hartebeest's muzzle is clamped in midair between his jaws.

Both animals came to rest in a tangle of limbs. The cheetah's breath whistled from the corners of his mouth. The hartebeest's lung cage pumped desperately as she fought for oxygen through the iron grip over her nostrils and bottom jaw. The grip was not perfect. The gasping and the gurgling went on for as long as the crippled baboon had lain alone in the sun. The hartebeest herd could now relax, in the manner of herbivores knowing it was none of them who was dying now, and crop grass nearby.

The sun was gone, the western sky purple, and hollows all around black with shadows as the precipitous tropical night came rushing in. The sunbirds were in roost and the thermals that supported the vultures had long since collapsed. The ant bivouac choked on the booty of conquest, and somewhere, in a place I would not see again, the leopard was on his Pavlovian rounds, in that relentless process of determining who is ready to die.

8 ○ The Penguin

He stood there, looking at me with an almost speculative intensity, his head angled slightly to one side, both arms held away from his body slightly. He stood about four feet high, smartly dressed in black and white, a kind of establishment formality to it which reminded me of English boarding schools, all of us lined up and ready to walk to choir practice at the church. There was something peculiarly human, even youngsterish, about this emperor penguin.

As recently as 1774, Captain James Cook, the discoverer of New Zealand, had driven his ship at the impassable pack ice, with the mainland still one hundred and fifty miles south of his ship. It was clear, he said then, that the Antarctic continent could never be reached. But should his prediction prove incorrect, he warned the discoverer-to-be, "I shall not envy him the fame of his discovery. I make bold to declare that the world will derive no benefit from it."

Behind the penguin, I could see a conglomeration of ice, about ten times the size of the Pentagon. Squat and insolent, it sat in the middle of McMurdo Sound, the main point of entry into the Antarctic, from early in the century, for New Zealand and the United States. Somewhere to my right, to the east, lay the mist-obscured, smoking volcano of Mount Erebus, pumping a yellow muscle of smoke into the brittle, brilliant air. The emperor yawned, stretched himself luxuriously, and set to work preening his already immaculate plumage.

At once, there was a feeling of power. But it sprang from wonderment, of being in the presence of the impossible. The emperor penguin had defied logic, breasted the flow and sense of evolution. He was against nature and, thereby, apparently closer to the works of man scattered around the sound.

The South Pole, lying beyond the penguin, was protected by a mountain range more than eleven thousand feet high, which would have to be penetrated to gain entry to an upland plateau at an altitude of seven thousand feet. It was swept by winds as strong as typhoons. By foot, the pole was two months away from this relatively benign place by the sea. The world of the emperor was sealed off, guarded from its enemies, on two sides. Or so it seemed.

Why did this bird breed in winter? Why did it not join the millions of other penguins—the kings, the bootstraps, the Adélies, the macaronis, the gentoos—and breed during the summer? Then, at least, there was plenty of food. What could be the purpose of such severe isolation, much of it in twenty-four-hour-a-day darkness, to incubate a solitary egg?

The question hangs unanswered, and behind it lies another, just as puzzling. Why does the female penguin not only lay her egg at the beginning of the winter, but then also abandon it, and return to the sea, and give over the egg entirely to the male?

It was now autumn. The summer had touched these shores with only a hint of warmth, not enough to melt the snow in sheltered places but enough to send rivulets of water into shallow pools, set in basaltic rock, and to rouse ticks, mites, lice, and flies from their eight months' sleep. Their feeding, growth, copulation, egg laying and death were crammed into days rather than the months needed elsewhere.

Already, the Adélie penguins, a fraction of the size of the emperors, had rafted on ice pans and, facing toward the rapidly lowering northern sun, had plunged into the sea, section by section. The seals, which had bred onshore, were leaving in groups. The skuas had gone, after a summer of pirating the eggs and harassing the youngsters in penguin colonies along the coast. The graceful fulmars, the petrels, the sheathbills, and the terns had all gone, to settle in or to wander the shores of South America and Africa, and to reach as far north as the Arctic itself.

But not the emperor penguin. If there was an imperious stance in that tall and elegant body, I fancied it was because he had come upon a natural law and had broken it without penalty. The purplish light descended as I watched and waited for him to move. This was 1947, and little was known about the emperor. There was no way of following him to his breeding place because no man could survive the Antarctic winter without substantial buildings and ample heat. Later, French expeditions would stay with him for the winter. But there was no quick, or single, way of learning about a country where it might cost twenty-five thousand dollars in public money to get one person to the penguin's feet, then a thousand dollars a mile to follow him. It would take many visits to put the emperor's story together, but I will tell it as a single narrative.

He turned his small head to look toward the waters of the sound. A burst of wind whimpered, then died. I felt my ears ring with the purity of the silence. His path lay toward the brooding mountain ranges far south, where I could see a long slit of purple, indicating the buildup of an overcast in which, for sure, a storm awaited.

Evolution should be logical. Perhaps a penguin killer had once ranged these shores, an enemy which could also hunt on land. It would have to have been a bird, but one which was already at the southern limit of its range, or else it could have followed the penguin in its breeding journey closer to the pole. But no bird, with the possible exception of some of the monkey-eating eagles of South America and Africa, or possibly the great eagle of Australia, would tackle an emperor penguin. And these eagles were tropical and subtropical birds, exclusively. Only the extinct eagle of New Zealand was really big enough to feasibly hunt such a large creature. This would have entailed a two-thousand-mile cross-water flight to reach the penguin, which was not logical either. And if such a hunter ever existed, it presumably would have also hunted down the summer-breeding penguins. It remained an oddity in my mind that the emperor moved farther and farther south in its breeding while the giant eagle became extinct in New Zealand, where it had no enemies.

The Antarctic silences encourage fanciful rumination. The emperor had become increasingly committed to winter breeding. It plunged deeper and deeper into the continental wastes, stretching its resources as finely as possible. Each journey south was a little farther from the dangerous edge of the ocean. Eventually, the penguin itself could not turn back. It had become too specialized to utilize the easier path open to it once its enemy had been defeated.

A puff of unaccustomed warmth touched my cheek. Hundreds of miles away, in the Ross Sea, a cyclone was raging. We had that from the weather reports. Distantly, men were grouping about a vehicle. Soon it would be snowing heavily. The penguin also felt the cyclone. He looked toward the direction whence the snow would come. I felt the integrity of his tall frame, packed with fat at this season, the product of summer ocean hunting, and his readiness now to survive for three months without food, brooding an egg that he would hold on his feet, raised an inch or so from the ice, while his female spent the winter swimming free in the Antarctic Ocean.

They were shouting for me now. But I ignored them. My imagination played on, the idea of evolving backward, toward that place from which an animal had come, back toward the sea that no longer held the enemy, back toward summer breeding, and the end of a flight so desperate that it had turned to madness.

Abruptly, the penguin threw himself down and dug his claws into the ice, kicking himself forward like a bobsled. In a few minutes, he had shot himself along a mile or so, to the edge of the ice, towering twenty feet above the water. Orange lights played beyond him. He dived in headfirst, like a man, or a schoolboy, and left a boiling circle of foam in the black water. I returned to the camp.

The southern continent is circled by the Antarctic Convergence, eight thousand miles long and thirty miles wide. It is an amalgam of warm waters from the rest of the globe—the Pacific, the Atlantic, the Indian Ocean, the China Sea, and even the Sargasso—all contributing a wealth of mineral salts. Their waters join the oxygen-drenched flow of the convergence. Therein occurs an almost constant blooming of the phytoplankton, microscopic plants of the sea. Upon these feed the krill, sustainers of whales and many other oceanic animals.

There was a mosaic here, grandiose in the numbers of its chips. Penguins darted through the convergence. A raft of seabirds, thirty miles long, appeared under the wings of my plane. Killer whales slid beside a supply ship and penguins bolted upward like submarine missiles to the safety of pan ice.

"There are about twenty million birds in that raft," said a scientist, as we both peered downward through the bubble of a bomber converted to supply.

The mosaic was a pattern of meaning. A puff of wind held a second meaning. If there was a tiny set of needles in it, then a man might begin running if he was far from shelter. The penguins always knew. They stood boldly together at the edge of an ice floe. Bugling calls rang out to herald the wind needles. The gale that they expected might blow for thirty-six hours, or more.

"When the great winds come," said Sir Robert Falcon Scott, the most distinguished British explorer of Antarctic, "we retire to shelter. There is nothing to be done."

These continental blizzards shake the mind. There appears to be a personal enmity in them. I am threatened personally, and am alone, dozing among a score of comrades, who are as oppressed as I by the challenge to their mortality.

A couple of us managed to spend the night of a blizzard inside the hut that had been Sir Ernest Shackleton's refuge at McMurdo at the beginning of the twentieth century. The ration boxes were still there, with "British Antarctic Expedition, 1906" stenciled on their sides. Pemmican, in cans, was still fresh. I blocked my ears against the storm's raucous voice with old sleeping bags made of reindeer skins. I looked up at the soot of seal blubber that had been burned inside the hut to heat the food. The hut vibrated like a rude musical instrument. Half-century-old hams, still hanging from hooks in the ceiling, swung in pendulum time to the cacophony outside.

The penguins slept, shelterless, their two layers of feathers set at just the right distance from their bodies, like modern synthetic clothing, to keep a protective barrier of warm air in place. The Eskimos wore light and loose clothing, in the same manner, to keep out the cold without also causing sweat, which could kill. Beneath the penguins' feathers was fat, the best insulator, and thanks to the autumnal crop of krill, the penguins were well impregnated with another insulator, oil.

These passive systems of defense were enhanced by the circulatory system, which mingled the vessels carrying the penguins' blood outward with those carrying it from the surface of the body. The chilled blood was warmed by its proximity to the outward-moving stream.

In late autumn, when the heaviest winds begin to blow, a migration of deep-swimming squid takes place. Driven southward by fierce circumcontinental winds from the latitude of the seventies, they travel in search of krill under the forming ice. Krill are tiny red shrimplike crustacea that are eaten by whales first but by almost everything else second. The squid, too, are favorite prey of most Antarctic animals. But they are hard to reach, maybe a quarter of a mile deep, in the darkness of the bottom.

They are within the reach of the emperor. The boiling white circle of the emperor's departure calmed and dissipated, and his sonar system guided him downward. He could stay down for twenty minutes or so, which, allowing for a swimming speed of about five feet per second, meant that he could reach the bottom in three or four minutes. If it took him perhaps three minutes to reach the surface, then he would have between twelve and fifteen minutes to hunt at the thousand-foot depth.

At such distance, under tons of pressure, and in total darkness, he must find his fleet victims and deal with them efficiently. His crop was capacious and could hold a score of squid. The squid inside him was digesting rapidly. No eye would ever see this hunt, but I could imagine him coming to the surface again, up through the dim legions of fish which hunted in the middle depths, upward into the sounds of whistling cries, grunts, and gasps of whales fishing the higher layers of the sea.

Killer whales were the most dangerous animals here, although their menace was swiftly joined near the surface by that of the leopard seal, the most voracious of all the Antarctic hunters. If the penguin surfaced against the wall of an iceberg, where he would not be able to instantly leap out of the water, the leopard would have him. There it was likely waiting, its own equivalent sense of sonar pinging the depths and recording the penguin's rise.

If the emperor's senses registered no hostile bodies, and the light from the surface told him how the pans of ice were disposed, he might be safe in coming on up. He burst out of the water. He stepped forward to the top of a six-foot cliff of ice as his rocketing rise stopped. If a leopard seal's head appeared beneath him, he turned, standing on the lip of the ice, and raged, jumping up and down, flapping his wing stubs in a fury that threatened to topple him back into the water.

In the crystal air, the anger of the penguin was a tiny cyclone of release, which, upon completion, left him visibly relieved, and preening himself. The proximity of ice and blood here seems to make all action more immediate, all motivation more apparent. The Antarctic was a place of great feeling for me. I was almost continuously in the thralldom of its contrasting moods. The savagery of its storms, and the somber echoes of its long, slumbering silences, worked against each other to make a different bite on the truth. Certainly, after the great winds blew themselves out, there was a unique feeling of détente, a silently ticking clock in my mind as I sensed the emptiness storing up another scythe of winds, walls of energy readying themselves in the blasted mountains.

Warmth stole inward, almost in deceit, perhaps five degrees above zero Fahrenheit enough to trigger events as important as a thousand typhoons. The algae, which had preceded all other forms of life in Antarctica, began to grow again in shallow pools, even in declivities of the ice itself. They could flourish in both ice and snow. They grew on rock and on the open ground. Even at the threshold of winter, they responded to the sun. Its warmth was caught and trapped in cracks and crevices.

From a distance, I had seen faint shadows of gray, and, occasionally, pink, flushing distant snowfields. Close up, I had seen them as countless tiny clumps, each one spaced at a uniform distance from its neighbor, algae growing at discreet remove from their nearest competitors. Sometimes, in brief periods of warmth, bright green algae would be flourishing even as the next blizzard came screaming down the glacier.

Swelling, the algae were thieves, stealing minutes of growth from seconds of warmth.

The Wilson Piedmont, the large glacier near McMurdo Sound, is the entranceway to polar Antarctica. It is the end of the earth. There is no imagination beyond this point. My feeling of having "arrived" at Antarctica when landing at McMurdo was always dashed by any glimpse I got thereupon of the vastness that still lay beyond.

"We will establish two bases on the glacier," said Scott, "and it is essential that these be serviced by ponies." Scott's diaries are filled with tiny fillips of optimism to counter the unspoken dread of the emptiness beyond his power to believe.

To know the piedmont, it is necessary to travel upon it extensively, which, in Scott's day, was very difficult indeed. Yet he did it, though without really understanding what he saw, particularly how it told him that his bravery and toughness were not enough for him to reach the pole and return.

Scott suffered from an English difficulty of his time. The empire was slipping but few knew it. The impossible was about to happen: first the *Titanic,* then the war. Meanwhile, the imperialist certainty of control prevailed against the evidence of growing chaos. Scott explored the piedmont thoroughly, but he did not understand the meaning of the dried husks of seals still found up there, thousands of years after their deaths. My old Indian friend Stanley-Robinson would have seen them as an indication of how a summer's day could become deep winter in a second. Scott could not perceive that anything which could so swiftly kill seals in their chosen abode would give his newcomer ponies no chance at all.

The earliest visitors to the continent had been surprised to find that Antarctica contained petrified tree trunks. The imprints of tropical leaves were visible on rocks. Shackleton had stumbled across coal seams showing through the snow and ice. One visitor, Charles Hedley, wrote in 1912 that

Antarctica had been a country of "rippling brooks, of singing birds, of blossoming flowers, and forest glades."

If he had stayed long enough, he would have discovered that the brooks did indeed ripple and the birds sing, and that flowers blossomed. There were no trees but, instead, more ancient forms of plants, lichens. If the algae seemed ingenious in sequestering those seconds of sunlight, the lichens had made a vastly deeper journey into the hostility of the Antarctic wilderness.

All a lichen needed was a millimeter of indentation in rock to get shelter from the wind. It might rouse itself for as little as five minutes a day or as much as fifteen when the sun shone. The rock absorbed a tiny fraction of its heat, and the pulsing plant that responded might be, for all anyone knew, a thousand years old. There was no theoretical limit to the age such a simple life could reach. It was said that lichens had climbed to the tops of the inland peaks, which meant that they could survive at the pole, were it not overlaid by more than a mile of ice. They could live anywhere there was rock, just as the emperor penguin would demonstrate that he could survive any storm as long as he had comrades. The brutality of the weather meant little if the subtlest details in nature were used against it. The emperor penguin drew his strength from meticulous exploitation of almost imperceptible details.

In the autumn, the overcast weather, the quick and treacherous winds, closed down the shoreline to a general dreariness. The male penguins had gathered in a series of groups along the edge of the ice, awaiting that moment when they would strike inland for the breeding rookery. Their upright figures, seen from the air, were insignificant marks near gray-blue banks of mist rising, before a huge glacier.

Each year, they headed toward the same place on the ice-buried land, but each year the ice cover would be different. Sometimes it would be smooth, and the penguins could kick themselves along for hours. Or the road south might be tumbled, and broken, as it was this year, the winds contrary, and snow frequent. Then, even for such well-equipped animals, the journey was hard.

This year, the ice had broken up in early February, the latest part of the summer, and then had refrozen into a jumble of upthrust barriers. The leader penguin led his straggling followers into this tortured wasteland. After a day, he stopped at a barrier and the birds behind him stumbled into each other, squabbling for their secondary places, angry at the usurpation of an inch of space. Once, when I landed nearby in a helicopter, my boots squeaked on the tight-packed snow. Soon, any kind of human existence would be impossible without a house, a solid structure of some sort. A tent would be nothing. Scott and his men had died in a tent at this time of the year, March, with the winter hardly begun.

"When we reached the top of the glacier," he had written, on the outward-bound journey, "we were struck by one of the worst blizzards I have ever experienced. For five days, we were quite unable to move. The effect on the men was considerable. Here it was, early summer, and we were halted by a storm that we thought could only occur in the middle of winter."

The walking penguins dissolve into a spume of wind-driven snow particles, picked up from the ground level and whipped along in swirls and miniature tornadoes. The stuff is as dense as cotton wool. Penguin heads emerge from it, are disembodied, bobbing, to disappear and reappear. Behind me, a bright clear sun blazes down from out of its position over the central Pacific.

The wind dies. A distant door has closed. The leader stops. Though he has walked for five days, he seems to know this place. All the others, perhaps a thousand strong, stumble to a stop behind him. It is no place in particular. The ice is flat. A hummock bulges nearby, but it is pressure ice, and will not be a marker tomorrow. Perhaps a crack in the ice is a marker, except that all ice here is in motion toward the sea.

A ceremony appears to be in order, and it is forthcoming. The lead penguin accepts the eddying plaudits of his colleagues, clashed beaks and beating flippers. Dusk is coming. He looks toward the pole. There, a magnetic field throws up remote radioactive electrons which blossom into a falling blaze of color, folded and curtained in yellow and green and cold, eerily, savagely beautiful. The aurora lives, but it does not connect with these hunched and waiting supplicants.

The lead penguin turns his back on the colored sky and faces north, toward the sea. The marchers are all males. Here they will await the females, coming out of the sea at this moment. Inflating his lungs, the leader begins blasting out a series of cries, the sounds, I have always thought, of an old trumpet, badly played. But in this setting, against the shifting colors of the astral outback, they possess a barbaric quality, indicating there will be no surrender.

During the time of waiting for the females, the temperature drops a few degrees each night. All attention now turns upon the arrival of the first female. Most of the males face north, in expectation. The sun is very low on the northern horizon. A penguin appears in the distance. It is a female and she is alone. But when her long shadow reaches forward to greet the packed and expectant males, no ripple of greeting or recognition passes to her. The fact is that none of the penguins can recognize any female until she sings. She remains mute, and stands near the bunched males, her body now likewise bowed in waiting.

Then, toward dusk, she begins singing. It is a pretty, rather plaintive sound, high-pitched, at times quavering. She moves among the males. She sings here; she sings there. But there is no reaction anywhere. As the dusk rises, other females begin arriving. If there is paradox in my mind as to the migration south to breed in winter, there is even greater contradiction in the fact that these animals are not driven to conquer at the sight of their female. There is no pursuit of the female until she sings.

Most of the arriving females find their mates of the previous year soon enough. But with more than a thousand males packed into this enclave, a female might spend some hours, perhaps days, singing fruitlessly to males who cannot respond to her voice. And there is no information on what happens to females whose mates have been killed during the nonbreeding season, or who are simply not there, for any other number of reasons.

The leader penguin walks slowly among a swelling chorus of sometimes cackling, always singing and—by now—passionately courting birds. Soon, the sun will hardly rise above the northern horizon. It will bring seven hours of pallid daylight, seventeen of night. Already the ice has made a forced march north. The ocean is now sixty miles away.

A buffeting wind arises, and the big penguin comes upon a lone female standing in the lee of the hummock. She does not seem to have made much effort to find any males since her arrival three or four days before. He sings to her. She moves forward slightly and sings her song. They recognize each other. They are mates. They move until they almost touch. The big emperor bows. He expands his neck, and sings again. They stand very close, their breasts pressed together. A shower of gold falls behind them and evening comes.

Robert Falcon Scott had presumed that there was an uninterrupted plain from the edge of the great Antarctica plateau to the South Pole. He and his men would speed along, hour after hour, four men harnessed to the big supplies sledge, one man in reserve bringing up the rear. From glacier to pole was three hundred and sixty miles. At two miles an hour, on skis, traveling ten hours a day, the journey could be completed in between thirty and forty days.

"Once we are on the plateau," said Scott, "I expect no major difficulties."

Instead, however, they blundered forward into gales that deafened them. It is bad enough to listen to the sounds of such winds inside a sturdy building. The voice of nature enters the traveler's skull. The plateau was not flat. Broken ice felled the men. It was incredibly cold.

"But this is summer," said Lieutenant Bowers.

They looked into the opaque blazes of white always confronting them. They wondered what it would be like coming back.

On the night of the leader emperor's reunion with his mate, the temperature went down to forty below. This was the first major test of the collective endurance of the group. The penguins formed themselves into a long oval-shaped mass, a form that French penguin researchers would later call a tortu. The big emperor occupied the center, chest to chest with his mate, as were all the other reunited birds. The penguins, in fact, stood so close together that no wind penetrated the interior of the tortu. It was a building made of blood and flesh and bone.

There could be no haste about the meticulous ritual of preparation for the laying of the penguins' eggs. The courtship could not be shortened without destroying the purpose of it. Throughout April and into early May, the penguins meshed the gears of relationship. A machine of behavior was needed. It must function flawlessly through the worst winter on earth. The preparation for the mating was more important than the act itself.

In this period, some of the most severe storms of early winter struck. The penguins had to continue singing, even though the colony was often obscured in powdered snow. The big emperor mated, and the two birds fell silent, awaiting the arrival of the egg. The pluck of the winds, the eddies of snow dust, touched a mass of hunched, passive, round-shouldered forms, waiting with their backs to the winds.

By the middle of May, the sun appeared above the horizon for only a few minutes. The nights lengthened to twenty-three hours. The inversion of daylight and darkness depressed the capability to think or feel through the medium of sight. The white snow; the white sky; the white sea: they appeared as microflashes in brains dazed by darkness.

Shortly before the brief dawn of a day in mid-May, after more than six weeks of courtship and waiting, the female emperor laid her egg in the middle of a blizzard. The big emperor joined her in a duet delivered into the crash and rant of the wind. The triumph of the egg marked a temporary end to the betrothal of penguin to penguin. The big penguin watched while his female bowed and then revealed the egg by folding back the skin of the incubating pouch between her legs. The big emperor sang brilliantly, and bowed, and touched the egg with his beak. He pushed the female's head. She stepped backward. The egg lay on the ice, exposed.

The emperor shuffled forward and drew the egg back with his beak, so that it lay on top of his flat, webbed feet, the powerful claws doubled beneath so that the egg was both lifted up from the ice and rolled back into layers of thick, insulating feathers. The female sang, and bowed, and turned away. Hobbled by the egg, the male tried to follow. But the female was headed for the north, for the twilight of the horizon. Her work was done. Darkness came with the wind, and other females converged, and joined, and headed for a sea that was now pushed one hundred miles north by the triumphant ice.

Within the tortu, a communal heating system fueled itself. The chilled birds on the outside of it were impelled within by the cold without. They had greater need than those who were warm, and displaced them. Thus, the interior birds were pushed to the outside positions, from which, as they chilled, they pushed their way inward. It was a perfectly graduated scheme of sharing hardship.

But some of the birds were old, or had not stoked enough in the long furnace-fueling dives at the bottom of the Antarctic Ocean. They looked no different from any of the others. But their wills would be expressed in how deeply they would penetrate the tortu, how long they could stay in its inner warmth. The fury of the elements would, for them, be a gradual erosion of will, expressed in a faster deterioration of body than in those around them.

Although it was not possible to stand near the tortu and feel its resistance to the winter, I did fly over it once, by accident, when on a long-distance survey flight in a Lockheed Neptune, a plane that could fly eleven thousand miles without landing. We prowled Antarctica in its winter darkness, green instrumentation glowing in front of hunched, attentive figures. On circling the pole, we flew into the two hours of pale day, when our instruments told us it was eighty degrees below zero, and a steady wind was blowing directly from the pole toward Queen Maud Land, our next survey destination.

I was peering from a tiny square window—none of the crew ever "looked" at what they were "seeing"—when, as we neared the coast, I saw a black mark on the ice, shaped like a Folsom flint, a graceful opening and closing of a leaf, but solid in its placement on the utterly bare white windswept ice country.

I nudged a crew member to look, with my question as to what it was. But after glancing down, he only shrugged. It was nothing of any importance. It did not show on the instruments. Later, when I learned I had seen penguins, my view of nature changed. Nothing, thereafter, could be assumed without question. The elaborate training and technology of our survey flight suddenly became almost irrelevant, in relationship to that mass of huddled figures breeding on the ice.

We landed in Argentina, strong and secure in our aircraft, while "weak" emperors were clutched in the winds, trembling at the edge of the tortu and suddenly unable to force their way inward one more time. They shook, and then were flung away like garbage. Their eggs might shatter at once, and be frozen in midair, or they might spin away intact, and then be rolled a hundred miles in the wind, to end up, abraded as small as a pigeon egg, in a crevice.

Some males simply gave up, and walked away from the

tortu, when there was no danger of their being blown from it. They stood apart from the group, as if in consideration, and then they began walking toward the north, the distant sea. Nobody has ever followed them to see whether it is possible to survive such winter journeys. Their eggs might be swiftly commandeered by those bachelors who had been unable to mate but who had stayed in the tortu.

On a night early in July, the egg of the big emperor stirred. He bent down and opened his incubating pouch to reveal that the egg had cracked and was now jiggling. He closed the pouch and the egg rubbed against his bare skin. At sunrise, the egg broke. The chick kicked itself clear and cried out. Throughout the tortu, other eggs were hatching. The sun drew screams from the emergent chicks. But there was no food.

All the males now became extremely nervous. The tension of incubation was over, but it was also the ending of a phase of determination. Whatever it was that dictated no surrender, it demanded adherence to very old rituals, and these were rigid. The females, who were scheduled to bring the food supplies at this vital time, were already five days late, and then eight days, and finally, ten days. When the big emperor could stand it no longer, he trumpeted, a wild piping scream, and panic shot through the tortu. The birds scattered like shotgunned quail. Their extinct enemy had come upon them invisibly, lurking malign and forever unsleeping in their genes.

As long as the penguins were haunted, as a group, by ancient fear, they were imprisoned at a low sensibility of existence. In there lay immense, if rigid, strength, the capability of the tortu against the winter. But it also held the inability to change anything. They could not, then, refuse to starve themselves near to death in this terrible place.

Despite their exhaustion, Scott and his men tackled the return walk from the pole, after the appalling discovery, first, of Amundsen's dogs' footprints leading toward the pole and, second, of the Norwegian flag hanging limp at the place for which they had already sacrificed everything they had. They had budgeted thirty rapid days to travel back across the ice plateau. It was by an act of will that they kept going for sixty days, pulling their loads, on the return journey alone. The unremitting pressure of distance must have been as severe as any winter blizzard. On February 17, Evans simply collapsed and died. He had walked himself beyond the possible. He had never surrendered.

The will of the others to continue remained untouched. They actually reached the top of the piedmont, from where, had it been clear, they might almost have seen smoke from the McMurdo base camp. Then blizzards, one after the other, gripped them. An emperor is plucked away in such winds. A man cannot function for more than a few minutes in them. Oates got up in the middle of the worst of them, and said, "I am just going outside and may be some time."

Scott wrote in his journal, "It was the act of a brave man and an English gentleman."

The first of the female emperors came out of a blizzard, in the middle of July. The sun, from its low position, threw a blinding horizontal light into the now-fragmenting tortu. The big emperor's shadow stretched for one hundred feet. The females were smug with fat. They walked into a cackling poultry yard of welcome. The big emperor waited, blind to her identity until he could hear her voice, his weight fallen to sixty pounds from the one hundred and ten that he had brought to the rookery one hundred and thirteen days before. He heard a female nearby, singing in front of another unresponding male. He waddled toward her, the complaining chick jiggling on his feet. He sang. She responded. He bowed. She bowed.

By this time, the rookery was within the range of human expedition once again. The details of its function need be no longer imagined but could be seen by average visitors.

The emperor was so bonded to his chick, his burden, however, that he could not let it go. The tortu had been a fixedness of determination. It had represented that absolute refusal to give in, as in walking oneself to death.

The female emperor sought for thirty hours to weaken her mate's bond to the chick by singing and bowing. She then attacked him with powerful flipper blows to his head, and toppled him into the snow. The chick screamed and fell from the incubating pouch. A bachelor emperor waddled forward to kidnap it. When the fighting ended, the female had the chick at her feet, enclosed in the pouch. She fed him with half-digested squid she had brought from the ocean, its reduction slowed by stop-action control of the enzymes which would have given its sustenance to her. The squid, which had migrated from the convergence to feed under the melting ice of the shore, had thus made a thousand-mile journey to reach the squealing throat of the young emperor.

The big emperor hesitated for twenty-four hours. Then, without his burden, he turned north and was soon lost to view in a head-high drift of rushing ice crystals.

The big emperor recovered his lost body weight and energy in the krill-rich waters of the Antarctic Ocean. The shore ice melted backward, south, for more than sixty miles. The sounds of its breakup could soon be heard at the rookery itself, which had become a squalid mess of excrement staining the snow, of dead chicks scattered, and broken and abandoned eggs everywhere. The crash of the breaking ice mingled with the ululations of nine hundred chicks, now forty-nine days of age, downy, bespectacled, plump, and agile. When the big emperor came out of the sea again, and returned to the rookery, he found that his mate had gone again to the sea herself in his absence, and his chick was in the charge of a nursemaid adult, who held sway over a one-hundred-nestling crèche of youngsters.

The slow footsteps of the penguin, when recalled in absentia, are a kind of sliding shuffle, which, when magnified a thousand times, becomes like the hiss of antique winds in winter.

One evening in an Antarctic summer, I strolled the shore ice at McMurdo as dusk was stealing out of the south. Before me, at the edge of the ice, a large emperor penguin stood alone. We were still, watching each other. The northern horizon turned scarlet and then purple.

He raised his flippers, swelled his neck, and uttered his cry, which, to newcomers just off the aircraft squatting on distant ice, was hilarious, a toy trumpet bleating. But to the wanderer who had invested time in him, the voice was filled with meaning.

I had heard that cry before, but I had not well understood what it was saying. His long, graceful body was bowed with the effort of putting everything he possessed into it. Then, it became a sound that could be heard in Asia, in Europe, and the Americas, a cry so wild, so thrilling, that the human heart swelled to embrace it.

9 ○ The Wolf

"The wolf is the beast of waste and desolation."

THEODORE ROOSEVELT
Washington, 1922

From the wind-scoured crest, I looked down into another country—a sprawl of ranges, saber peaks, saw-edged ridges, pyramids, an architecture of the primeval. Stark balconies caught the yellow of the sun, and black pits opened behind them like mouths. Every sign of life had been scraped south by glaciers, long gone, and by winds that had never stopped blowing.

And yet there was life there, and in abundance. It was hard to feel this as wolf country, though. The animal was more a ghost than a presence. His footprint did not show in the rocks. The light plane, riflemen in it, had made him wary of heights, and daylight. He was widely scattered here, across the Brooks Range of Alaska, the Saint Elias Range of the Yukon, the Mackenzie Mountains in the Canadian Northwest Territories. The best view of him was a suggestive flicker, a pack disappearing on tireless legs into white spruce on the floors of valleys.

The Brooks Range spirals southeastward into the Yukon. It is the last barrier before the open sweep of tundra that announces the Arctic. By this time, the early 1960s, the prospectors had been gone for more than half a century. Some uranium hunters might be found occasionally, and rare electronic scanning aircraft passed overhead, looking for minerals or oil. The conservationists and wilderness trackers would not arrive for another dozen years.

In such country, covering perhaps a million square miles, the wolf is the spine of reality. It modulates the landscape, and gives it the dramatic expectation of being momentarily about to materialize. Valerius Geist, an Albertan ethologist, isolated for weeks alone studying mountain sheep, once said that he grew to know when the wolves were coming. It was not because of anything the sheep did, not from clues in the flight of the raven, nor the whistles of rodents in rock outcrops, but simply a sense of anticipation. It was time for the hunters to appear.

To know this country takes a lifetime of living in it. "It is too vast to really understand," said Barry Holstun Lopez, a literary biographer of the wolf. I knew it as I had known the Antarctic, in fragmented visits, airplane trips, hikes between the camps of geologists, trips with documentary-film crews, and, on two occasions, extremely scary lone walks through the mountains.

One fairly certain method of finding the wolf was to follow his victims. These include the mountain sheep. But they, in response to the end of winter, were now moving into as inaccessible country as they could find. A wolf must risk his own life to take them on precipitous slopes, where his victims know the warning signals of avalanche and rock slide much better than he, and can run along ledges inches wide, where he could not be so surefooted.

The march of the caribou is the better guide to the wolf. They move like the mountain sheep, but north, through valleys, on their way to open grassy slopes, the tundra, where they will graze themselves fat, drop their calves, rest up, mate, and then return to either the shelter of mountain valleys or the comparative refuge of the thinly treed taiga.

In marching, the caribou are part of the same phenomenon of nature as the buffalo herds reaching for new prairie grasses, the East African antelope and horse herds pursuing the short sweet grasses of the Serengeti. I knew, from previous visits, that the stalking of the caribou could be watched in the valleys from the balconies of mountains.

This was wolf country of a special kind, the habitat of the Mackenzie wolf, reputedly the biggest animal of the score or so races of wolf that circle the high northern hemisphere. It is legendarily bigger than the Siberian wolf, which does not, in its wanderings of the undulating northern forests of Siberia, have the challenge of such arduous mountains as these. It was the Mackenzie animal that permeated American legends, mountain-ranging shadows which hunted so high that sometimes they died of minor cuts when their blood could not clot in the thin cold air. These were the most energetic movers of the wolf races, creatures who had never been tracked throughout their ranges and whose extent was suspected only by pilots with an interest in hunting. An aircraft was needed, anyway, to follow such tireless feet.

The Mackenzie wolf was larger than life in my mind, because it was a symbol of all wolves in history. Their hold on imagination came, in very large part, from the impossibility of controlling them before the advent of accurate firearms and the development of modern poisons. They infested eighteenth-century Europe, and nineteenth-century America.

When one walks in very high country, there is never very much overt activity visible. But shifting scenes constantly stimulate. The smoking ruins of rock ridges above the Arrigetch Valley in the Brooks do not prepare the walker for the green sprawl of the Noatak River, heading for the

Chukchi Sea. Scores of thousands of caribou compress in travel, heading for the shores of the sea. When the tundra goes green, it is a wash of emerald under bald mountains.

The loneliness in the chill heights is like the stab of an ice knife. The watcher longs for company. Even a fly is welcome. At once, I was half aware that I had been joined. the raven will get scraps. The high-pitched whistles of marmots warned of my approach for those who did not know that the raven had already telegraphed my arrival miles beyond my capability to walk this day.

The loneliness in the chill heights is like the stab of an ice knife. The watcher longs for company. Even a fly is welcome. At once, I was half aware than I had been joined. It was no more than a faint movement in the corner of my eye. The wolf stood about a hundred yards down the cleft, tail astream, his body braced against the steady wind, a coiled spring of readiness to move. Although I was disappointed that this appeared to be a solitary animal, without the pack I would have liked to see following the caribou, it was certainly the Mackenzie animal.

We were at about ten thousand feet, far above any prey that he might hunt. His eyes were directed north, as mine had been, absorbing the smallest details of what he saw. He adjusted his stance slightly, and turned, with a deliberate and graceful movement of his head, and looked directly at me.

"The gaze of the wolf reaches into our souls," wrote Barry Lopez, in *Of Wolves and Men*. I felt my identity being processed, organized, filed.

Of course, he had seen me before he reached the ridge, and noting that I did not possess a gun, and had no comrade, knew it was safe to come forward himself. Wolves in this territory had even learned to recognize which airplanes carried guns that might be used against them. They scattered when they saw the privately chartered Cessnas and Pipers, but held their ground when professional supply and transport planes, like Otters and Beavers, sailed overhead.

Nonetheless, the deliberate exposure of the wolf to my gaze produced a tension of symbolic and historic imagination. The hunter was there, and the warrior, but also the suckler of Romulus and Remus, and the werewolves of European legends with all their associations of abasement, sexual cruelty, depravity, and murder. A hint of bestiality in Little Red Riding Hood, the wolf-man of Freud.

The wolf's gaze continued to search me out. He was dressed in the last phase of his winter pelage, the underfur so dense that if I had come close enough to touch him, I would not have been able to reach the bare skin it sprang from and covered. His feet were enormous, solid pads more than four inches across and five inches long, terminating legs that were more elegantly slender and swift than those of any hunter except the cheetah. These were the ghost legs. They flickered, and appeared to rotate, when seen on that nearby mountain slope.

The feet of the wolf drive the animal along as if on rails, mile upon mile, without observable effort or any sign of fatigue. He can run at the same speed for a dozen hours or more, without stopping, longer than is necessary to exhaust any of his victims. He may weigh a hundred pounds, although some wolves had been known at one hundred and seventy-five, as heavy as a tigress, and measure seven feet from muzzle to tip of tail.

The wolf and I continued to look north, once he had satisfied himself that I would make no threatening move against him. It had been clear, from the moment I saw him, that he was reconnoitering in the manner of the lone wolf. This phenomenon was still not well understood up to the 1960s. It was thought that the lone wolf was a scoundrel who had been kicked out of the pack, or an animal so reprobate that it chose to hunt and kill alone with "bloodthirsty lust," as a sportsmen's magazine has described it. As we have since come to understand, wolves can leave and rejoin packs almost at will, and periods of lone-wolfship are as desirable to some wolves, particularly those that are leaders, as periods of solitude are desirable for creative human beings.

The wolf, now, just watched and watched, never moving. The expansive view from the ridge encompassed a valley into which the wolf looked, along the track of a winding river, a dozen miles of it visible at once, where the snow was stained with fingers of dust, the cargo of the last suddenly warm winter wind, the chinook. The broad wings of the raven paused, very high. The bird was now certain that I was up to something, and the bulky bustling figure of a wolverine scampered among some naked aspens.

A Michigan biologist, David Mech, was one of the first people to understand the connection between wolf and man. In spending years with the wolves in the woods of Isle Royale, in Lake Superior, he found them to be gentle, playful, unaggressive, and also strong, cooperative, and tough. He demonstrated that it was the prejudice of the human watcher that created the animal's ferocious reputation, coupled with an inability to see the two sides of every action in nature. Wolves fought, but they did not kill each other, except when there had been a grievous "offense" against the integrity of the pack, which was something quite different from the insults of one individual upon another. But the genius of Mech's work was its confirmation of the wolf's superlative capabilities as an animal watcher itself.

The wolf turned his head away from me, and I followed its direction. I could see the marmot on the rock, and when I put my glass up, I could see that he was watching us very closely. A family of mice played toylike in a sheltered spasm of broken rock, and these creatures might attend to me too, because they were prey. The wolf saw squirrels standing in shade, and a snowshoe hare statuesque against a white slash of snow, soon to be made refugee by a season moving faster than its change of coat. I felt the pull of the valley and also its network of communication, as the Indians and Eskimos experienced it but could rarely make us understand.

I looked up at the raven, and I knew he was sending messages to the wolf. He reported what was going on miles away. The turn of his wing told of an old bull moose emerging from rumination in the next valley. I had traveled with Eskimos in the high Arctic when the sight of a hovering raven, miles away, brought the exclamation, "Bear!" Or, a week later, "Seal!" Mountain wolves, on the prowl for Dall sheep in the high country of British Columbia and western Alberta, had shown me their intensive sensitivity to eagles, hawks, and even crows, eyeing them with the kind of analytical attention that the wolf on the ridge had bestowed upon me.

The wolf nearby, if he had seen sheep a score of miles away, might devote two or three days to the strategy of the kill. As I had learned in Africa, the hunt is very infrequently an affair of impulse. Rather, it is the culmination of a slow and complex process, in which those thousands of tiny details eventually come together into that pattern that invites, even demands, the kill. At the very least, he would have to descend nine thousand feet into the valley, and then climb nine thousand feet up the adjacent ridge, carefully picking his way among the rock slides and cascading streams, through the deep snow that cloaked ravines and gullies, to place himself on a cliff above his victims.

If the raven were watching, then the sheep might know he was coming, although nobody really knew whether mountain sheep read the raven's signals. Certainly, the wolf could not allow himself to be seen by the sheep, or even the marmot, whose whistle would give him away. Certainly, the sheep looked upward a lot, which might be a quest for feathered intelligence, but was certainly a reflex of expecting wolves to come falling out of the sky.

The fact is that the wolf has been trained to dive from the eye of the sun, like a falcon or eagle, upon his victims, by the elaborate play of his puppyhood. Play, to a wolf, as to many other animals, is not merely important as a training and regulatory device; it also exemplifies the sense of humor that makes it possible for there to be an identification with man, and vice versa.

Adult wolves flip dried, flattish caribou and moose bones to each other, mouth to mouth, as Frisbees. As a puppy, and then as a juvenile, this wolf had gamboled in patches of snow in bitter winds when the temperature dropped to minus forty, and scampered at the tops of low cliffs. He had learned to approach the edge with exaggerated caution, where he peered downward at relatives and friends and pack members in the deep and sloping snow below. They barked at him. In time, his aim became precise, as a result of missing the cushioning snow, or hitting scree too hard in summer play. Such play was a lightness of spirit not possessed by the grazing animals, such as the mountain sheep, which had jellied their brains in skull-crunching charges over the rights to mate and to dominate. Humor was destroyed. This wolf had never been able to take himself seriously. He jumped outward with a puppy yip. Down he came, feet outstretched, and the animals in the snow pretended to scamper away. He hit the snow, exploded like a bomb, and rolled over and over. A yipping chorus of delight snapped back and forth across space empty of all except, perhaps, a silent raven.

Then, one day, he was adult, and a hunter, and standing on a very high ridge looking down on sheep, not wolves, with their lips in the grass, their eyes on the ground. Then he was parawolf, death from the skies.

The steady wind had streamlined the wolf, and had pressed the hair close to his body, so that he looked like a lean etching of an action about to occur. I liked to imagine him as tougher than the buffalo runner, or lobo wolf, which had roamed the American Great Plains during the buffalo times. I thought of him as superior to the Louisiana gray wolf, or the woodlands red wolf which had hunted the eastern United States, or the Rocky Mountain wolf (in its many guises), or the smaller Iranian, European, and Chinese wolves. He was a more formidable animal than the now extinct Newfoundlander. It pleased me to think of him as being a synthesis of all the northern animals, a mix from the Mackenzie Valley, the tundra, the bleak Brooks Range, the Yukon silences, the Siberian vastness.

The mountain wolf works in thin air, rough terrain, and he climbs thousands of feet as a matter of routine. But this close view of the animal was vivid confirmation of his difference from lowland animals. His pelt was marked in many places. A scar ran slantwise across his chest and up to his shoulder. One half of an ear was gone. His left back leg was thickened just below the knee, indicating an old break.

He would have been injured several times before he was five years of age. More than half the members of his pack would have suffered serious injuries, as a result of falls, of being charged by mountain sheep, struck by falling rocks, kicked by caribou, or charged by moose. There were many stories of moose pursuing wolves into the shallows of lakes and attempting to drown them there, or charging into denning places and rooting up the soil in efforts to rid themselves of this pervasive threat that could watch them from the peaks, and kill them in the valleys.

The wolf had now been standing more or less motionless for about half an hour, just as a cheetah watched his grazing animals in search of the details that enabled him to kill correctly. But because the only visible informant to the wolf was the raven, then the wolf must be waiting for the bird to reveal something. It could be inferred that the bird was waiting for us to move, except that when I examined him through the glass, it appeared that he was oriented more to the east, pausing in his circling to take longer views up the valley. With the wind blowing from the west, this was difficult flying for him, gliding with a tail wind. The wolf seemed to get the message, and turned his head to the right more often than he gazed ahead.

A herd of caribou would, in a sense, belong to one pack of wolves, and the pack would likely follow the animals far into the tundra, or perhaps even stay with it during the entire migration cycle. If the wolf on the ridge beside me belonged to a pack, then he would be needing to rejoin it soon, if not immediately, to play his part in the almost incessant harassment of the caribou migration. The alternative was to be a lone wolf through the summer.

The Indians knew these wolves. They watched them closely. "Give me the power of the wolf!" they cried to the Great Spirit. It was an invocation of light against the dark. Their feelings for the wolf were intense. The Cherokee believed that any weapon which killed a wolf became faulty. "Give it to the children, or have it cleansed by the shaman."

When the southern Alaskans killed a wolf, they paraded its body, and shouted, "This is the chief, and he is coming." Instead of hatred and fear, a kind of love linked the two hunting animals.

Neither Indians nor Eskimos attempted to reconcile or integrate the opposites or the conflicts of their hunting lives, because they did not possess the right-or-wrong view of action. Good and evil lay together, just as work and sloth had the same value, which might be because neither had any value, in our terms. So right and wrong switched sides easily, and what was theft today was a moral act tomorrow. Moral value came from result, not theory, and result sprang from action, which made all action moral. The wolf was king. He symbolized the ways things should be done.

The wolf was a friend to the Indian, even though he might also be his greatest enemy. The wolf could be killed and revered at the same time without damaging the structure of the holistic and connected universe that was contained within the hunt. The Indian saw detail with the same eyes as the wolf. All detail, contemplated long enough, yielded the magic of insight. However, once this contact with detail was lost, as with the aboriginals of Australia, then the language became a gabble and the watcher was blind.

The marmot lifted its head toward the raven. I felt much information in the air, very thick and near. Everything became fiercely realistic and concentrated. I almost knew what they knew. The valley was filled with magic.

In the north, the hunter must develop an awareness of spiritual presence in the emptiness of landscape. The Tlingit Indians believed in a unity of spiritual magic which, for them, had a root connection with sex, death, and wolves.

If one had control of death
It would be very easy to die with Wolf Woman
It would be very pleasant

Now the wolf trembled with the strain of leaning forward to perceive the last of the details. His head turned as he looked east, miles distant, to where a thin, double-pronged stream of moving animals had appeared. It was the caribou herd, heading for the Arctic Ocean. The wolf glided forward on his invisible rails and disappeared down a slope clawed by straggling spruces. The raven turned and volplaned downwind.

Tiny dark figures, walking in single file, appeared at the flanks of the caribou. It was like the menace of the executioners in Hemingway's story "The Killers." A wolf pack was in position. The valley lay open.

The march of the caribou stands as a work of its own art, with the spare elegance of the hieroglyph that is also a beautiful picture. Superficially, it is only a large-scale movement of grazing animals from one place to another—that is, if seen in ignorance of the fine details of its performance. To it, however, I had learned to bring the eyes of the African vulture.

A couple of years before, a motion picture friend of

mine had photographed Barren Ground caribou emerging from out of the taiga, that stunted growth of trees lying across northern Canada which eventually gives way to the tundra. The camera people had modified a light plane to make it into an aerial camera platform. The flaps had been extended, the propeller changed to give it an extra-thick b: from the air, the engine exhaust silenced with bigger mufflers. The result was a plane that could move very slowly, and almost silently, on low throttle. Flying into a slight headwind, the aircraft could float as slowly as ten knots. The tundra revolved beneath us as if we were in swivel chairs atop the Eiffel Tower.

Then, morning after morning, when the roseate early sunlight spilled over the moving caribou, I witnessed a wild-drawn geometry of migration. The caribou tracks, etched by the angle of the fresh light, were pounded into circling roadways, like the petals of many white flowers engraved into the snow. I perceived that these flowers, which seemed to mark the involuntary circling of the caribou, were actually the handwriting of wolves accompanying the moving animals. By harassment, ambuscade, and feint, the wolves continually turned back the migration upon itself, not once, but many times. By these means, they compensated for the difference between their top speed of thirty miles an hour and the caribous' forty.

The graceful flowers were not geometry, then, but designs in a ballet of death. The wolves cut across the curving petals and left a series of thinly marked interconnecting lines, like the veins in leaves of a supporting plant. Beyond this map of movement, the patterns might thicken suddenly, as they divided, redivided, and coalesced suddenly into main-stem movements to the north, once the wolves had killed and paused in their pursuit. The flowering plant straightened, and rushed north, until the vein lines caught up again, and the flowers were drawn again by the tracery of the flickering feet of the attendant killers.

Usually, the caribou came through the worst winters in fine condition. They had many methods of resisting the cold. They "yarded" in bad weather, massed to conserve warmth in the same way as did emperor penguins in their tortus. Compared to Antarctica, the Arctic is relatively warm; temperatures rarely go below minus forty degrees.

The hairs of the caribou coats are hollow, efficient insulation, and their splay-toed feet are like shovels one moment, for digging out food in deep snow, like snowshoes the next, for walking on a twenty-foot-deep drift. So flexible are the feet, they click like castanets, and a moving herd is also the metallic muttering of some animate machine. In blizzards, or persistent winds, the caribou dig into snowdrifts and preserve themselves half or completely buried, like snow buntings, or snowshoe hares. Bullocking their ways through miles of snow too deep for the wolves to follow, and finding alder, spruce, and willow tips to browse along the way, they were quintessentially animals who manufactured opportunity from the details of difficulty.

I ran heavily along the ridge, feeling the altitude in my lungs, my pack a burden of lead, shocked that I was so suddenly too old to be up here. If I could reach the middle of a curve of the ridge about two miles ahead, I might be in a position to observe a day's advance by the caribou. I wanted to see all the wolves, including those who did not actually participate in the running. Each caribou herd was different from every other. Some herds, I was told by one of the pilots in the Canadian film crew, refused to run, and gathered like hartebeest challenging a cheetah. They were not hunted. The wolves were bound to their routines. Perhaps only by making the caribou run could they force the kind of response that made killing sensible. But the run could not be merely experimental or the caribou would quickly perceive the game and have no need to reveal themselves. It was a scheme of learning based upon threats of death.

The question was simple enough: What is the response to pressure that continues for months, day and night? What about pressure under moonlight, pressure in the murk of dust storms lashed from ridges of silt on riverbanks, pressure rippling into coteries of fresh-born calves on the tundra, pressure like a hammer poised constantly above the anvil of the summer, pressure that made every second of sleep a risk, every minute of survival a blessing?

The caribou had now spread out, and the wolves had broken the black file of their movement. Some were lying down, in this intermission of the march. It had been said often enough that only the fittest survived in these wars of nature. That was true only insofar as the sick were eaten, the stragglers cut down. The finer detail was what had made them sick, or created straggling, and it was likely that pressure was the cause.

I reached a place where the view down the valley was pretty good, at a dogleg of rock where I could look both up and down the turn in the river flats below. At midday, the caribou began running. The wolves, four of them, had come to their feet, and overtook the fleeing animals, and then turned away. The caribou ran again, and then again. A caribou fell, and the wolves turned away. The victim, if it was indeed there, had not been claimed. Or had not given itself up? The excitement was intense. And yet nothing had happened.

The two leading horns of the caribous' movement had splayed outward, but now they came together slightly, the leftward element responding to the wolves that flanked it. The valley floor was then paved with bright crystalline hard-packed snow, good footing for high-speed running and maneuvering. Each animal would be able to reach its maximum speed on such surface. No ambush was possible. Accordingly, feint would be used.

The most thrilling thing about watching wolves from the air is the variety of detail. In northern Ontario, for instance, I had seen woodland wolves scenting solitary moose, and cutting across frozen lakes, clearings, through dense tree growth, to reach their victim. There was no suggestion of flight there. The moose always stood at bay. Its survival depended on whether it could prevent wolves from reaching its hindquarters, and the vulnerable soft skin at the belly and flank.

The Arctic wolf worked alone, or in small groups, and was never seen to chase its victims, even though, like the Greenland caribou, they traveled in herds or, like the Baffin Island musk-ox, they could not be panicked into flight. The wolf was an actor in many disguises.

One wolf disengaged from the pack and loped at the flank of the caribou. But he was moving wider than before, so as not to turn the line of march prematurely. The caribou stopped and regarded him. But now the wolf seemed to be heading away from them, and eventually he drifted off completely, and then lay down.

At the same moment, the main group of wolves split again. Three of them turned behind the march, bisecting the herd in such a leisurely fashion that those at the rear easily turned left and joined the second line of march. Those in front speeded up slightly. But they did not seem concerned. Two of the wolves in the main body lay down. Two continued their flanking trot.

At this moment, the three wolves who had intersected the caribous' line of march abruptly started forward, in a free-swinging lope that spurred the caribou ahead of them into a gallop. The wolves did not hurry, but allowed the distance between them and the fleeing animals to widen. At the same time, the wolf who had gone ahead turned left, cutting across in front of the leaders of the march. The chase wolves also veered to the left, so that they were running across the shorter diagonal of the movement, and thus catching up rapidly.

It all seemed so casual. The lead wolf stopped, just

when he seemed to be in a position to make that final closing. The chase wolves stopped. They looked at the retreating caribou. One of the wolves sat down and scratched himself. One of them turned and plodded back toward his two comrades, who were still trotting along the flank of the other caribou group. The third wolf remained fixed, motionlessly watching the caribou wheeling around like riderless cavalry. A bunch of them turned toward him in a swift, almost savage rush, and they stood up close, stamping their feet. He sat down, and watched.

I found it necessary to remember that every wolf in a pack is an individual, each capable, like a hunting man, of going it alone. When the pressure was reversed, and put upon the wolf, then its character was revealed. A lone wolf was once trapped by airborne hunters upon the slope of an Alaskan mountain and, being unable to retreat back into the valley, elected to make a run for the summit. It was a high, chunky mountain, half of which had fallen down into an adjacent valley. The wolf dodged the shots, and the low passes, but eventually found himself at the edge of the precipice that marked the fall of the mountain.

He paused at the edge, looking down, then up at the wheeling plane, ready to make its last pass. Far down—the distance depends on the imagination of the hunter telling the story—there was a snowbank, held in shadow and unmelted. The hunters in the plane saw the wolf teetering at the edge. For that moment, he was young again, and playing parawolf, about to fall on his comrades in play.

Then he jumped outward, feet thrust wide to keep his body balanced in the drop (which some men claimed lasted for half a minute) that lay under him. He hit the snowbank like a bomb, throwing up a long gout of white stuff.

Their last view showed him emerging from the snow, and shaking himself like a puppy, before disappearing into the dark spruces nearby, at an altitude too low for their technology to reach.

The day passed in slow motion. The wolves made their passes perfunctorily, so that eventually it seemed as if an experiment was being conducted to illustrate the benefits of failure. The caribou always appeared to be unscathed, untouched by any fear. They might dig their noses into drifts of snow as comrades eddied in flight around them. But then it became clear to me that one animal was always in the group being singled out. My powerful glass focused on his flanks, when, with sudden acceleration, a wolf struck. A flap of skin hung, and there was blood on the snow.

A rip in a caribou's flank was not an injury that could be rested in the shade of summer trees, or bathed in water, so that healing could occur. These animals were on a forced march. All stragglers, whether wolves or caribous, died. The flap of skin jiggled like a flag. It was enormous and demanding. It was tiny and insignificant.

"Help me."

Now there was no lack of purpose. Three wolves wheeled together, tight, and united. Two of them broke up the trailing spine of the caribou movement. The first wolf bisected the herd, in the conventional manner, while the second wolf drove the remaining animals toward the third, who had crouched in a position of open ambush, but so located that he would turn the head of the racing herd. The angle of deflection would be sufficient to give the attackers about a ten-mile-an-hour advantage in speed, critical when only the accuracy of teeth could bring down these charging mad things.

Suddenly, a wolf was among the caribou, dashing through them, toward the hanging skin.

An Oriental serenity descended. All the caribou came to a halt. The victim now knew. The hunters all knew. Distant wolves started to their feet. The raven, who had been joined by two others, spiraled downward, ready to land as the kill was made. The killer's head lowered as he increased his speed. He charged past the statues of the others, suspended in a final tapestry of inaction.

The caribou and its killer were fused together in a circle of chopping jaws and kicking feet. Was it possible that the caribou might still escape? A score of feet away, the snow was deep. The wolves might be mired. The victim was still stronger, faster. The bites came thick and savage, and another wolf curved inward. A lucky kick sent him flying. Had a leg or rib been broken, the wolves might still withdraw. But the wolf was up in a second. The caribou wheeled to deal with this danger as a third wolf came closer, and then there were wolves at his nose, and a wolf at the flank, and a wolf at the hindquarters. The caribou went down, tripped and ripped. In moments, the entrails were being hauled out.

10 ○ The Capelin

Beyond the northern beach, a gray swell rolls in from Greenland and runs softly along the shore. The horizon is lost in a world of gray, and gulls glide, spectral in the livid air. Watching, I am enveloped in the sullen waiting time and feel the silence, drawn out long and thin. I wait for the sea to reveal a part of itself.

A capelin is perhaps the best-hunted creature on earth. It is not more than five inches long, about the size of a young herring, and undistinguished in appearance, except that when it is freshly caught, it is the color of mercury. As the capelin dies, its silvery scales tarnish and the glitter goes out like a light, ending a small allegory about nature, a spectacle of victims, victors, and an imperative of existence. Its death illuminates a dark process of biology in which there are shadows of other, more complex lives.

The capelin are born to be eaten. They transform oceanic plankton into flesh which is then hunted greedily by almost every sea creature that swims or flies. Their only protection is fecundity. One capelin survives to adulthood from every ten thousand eggs laid, and yet a single school may stir square miles of sea.

In mid-June, the capelin gather offshore. They can be seen everywhere and at all times in history, symbols of summer and fertility, of Providence and danger. I see them along the shores of Greenland, Iceland, Norway, and near Spitsbergen. I follow them across the northern coast of Russia. Chill air, gray seas, the northern silences, are the capelin's world in Alaska, in the Aleutians, around Hudson Bay, and along the northeastern shores of North America. But the capelin of the Newfoundland coast are the most visible. Here, they spawn on the beaches rather than in deep water offshore, and I have to see their rush for eternity.

They gather a thousand feet offshore, coalescing into groups of a hundred thousand to break the water's surface with bright chuckling sounds. They gather, and grow. Soon they are in the millions, and with other millions swimming up from the offshore deeps. They gather, now in the billions, so densely packed together in places that the sea shimmers silver for miles and flows, serpentine, with the swelling body of a single, composite creature.

The fish do, in fact, possess a common sense of purpose. Nothing can redirect their imperative to breed. I once swam among them and saw them parting reluctantly ahead of me, felt their bodies flicking against my hands. Looking back, I saw them closing in, filling up the space created by my passage. The passive fish tolerated me, in their anticipation of what they were about to do.

At this time of the year they are so engrossed that they barely react when a host of creatures advances to kill them. Beneath and beyond them, codfish pour up out of the deep. They overtake the capelin, eat them, plunge their sleek dark bodies recklessly into shallow water. Some have swum so rapidly from such depths that their swim bladders are distended by the sudden drop in water pressure. The cod are gigantic by comparison with the capelin. Many weigh one hundred pounds or more, and will not be sated until they have eaten scores of capelin each. The water writhes with movement and foam where cod, headlong in pursuit, drive themselves above the surface and fall back with staccato slaps.

The attack of the codfish is a brutal opening to a ritual, and a contradiction in their character. Normally, they are sedentary feeders on the sea floor. Now, however, they are possessed. Their jaws rip and tear; the water darkens with capelin blood: the shredded pieces of flesh hang suspended or rise to the surface.

Now a group of seabirds, the parrotlike puffins, clumsy in flight, fly above the capelin, their grotesque, axlike beaks probing from side to side as they watch the upper layers of the massacre. They are joined by new formations of birds until several thousand puffins are circling. They are silent, and there is no way of knowing how they were summoned from their nesting burrows on an island that is out of sight. They glide down to the water—stub-winged cargo planes—land awkwardly, taxi with fluttering wings and stamping paddling feet, then dive.

At the same time, the sea view moves with new invasions of seabirds. Each bird pumps forward with an urgency that suggests it has received the same stimulus as the cod. The gulls that breed on cliffs along a southern bay come first, gracefully light of wing, with raucous voice as they cry out their anticipation. Beneath them, flying flat, direct, silent, come murres, black-bodied, short-tailed, close relatives of the puffins. The murres land and dive without ceremony. Well offshore, as though waiting confirmation of the feast, shearwaters from Tristan da Cunha turn long pointed wings across the troughs of waves and cackle like poultry.

The birds converge, and lose their identity in the mass thickening on the water. Small gulls—the kittiwakes, delicate in flight—screech and drop and rise and screech and drop like snowflakes on the sea. They fall among even smaller birds, lighter than they, which dangle their feet and hover at the water's surface, almost walking on water as they seek tiny pieces of shredded flesh. These are the ocean-flying petrels, the Mother Carey's chickens of mariners' legends, which rarely come within sight of land. All order is lost in the shrieking tumult of hundreds of thousands of birds.

Underwater, the hunters meet among their prey. The puffins and murres dive below the capelin and attack, driving for the surface. The cod attack at mid-depth. The gulls smother the surface and press the capelin back among the submarine hunters. The murres and puffins fly underwater, their beating wings turning them rapidly back and forth. They meet the cod, flail their wings in desperate haste, are caught, crushed, and swallowed. Now seabirds as well as capelin become the hunted. Puffin and murre tangle wings. Silver walls of capelin flicker, part, re-form. Some seabirds surface abruptly, broken wings dangling. Others, with a leg or legs torn off, fly frantically, crash, skitter in shock across the water.

I see the capelin hunters spread across the sea, but also remember them in time. Each year, the hunters are different, because many of them depend on a fortuitous meeting with their prey. A group of small whales collides with the capelin, and in a flurry of movement, they eat several tons of them. Salmon throw themselves among the capelin with the same abandon as the codfish, and in the melee become easy victims for a score of seals which kill dozens of them, then turn to the capelin and gorge themselves nearly stuporous. They rise, well beyond the tumult of the seabirds, their black heads jutting like rocks from the swell, to lie with distended bellies and doze away their feast. Capelin boil up around them for a moment but now the animals ignore them.

The capelin are hosts in a ceremony so ancient that a multitude of species have adapted to seeking a separate share of the host's bounty. The riotous collision of cod, seal, whale, and seabird obscures the smaller guests at the feast. Near the shore are small brown fish—the cunner, one of the most voracious species. Soon they will be fighting among themselves for pieces of flesh as the capelin begin their run for the beach, or when the survivors of the spawning reel back into deep water, with the dead and dying falling to the bottom. If the water is calm and the sun bright, the cunner can be seen working in two fathoms, ripping capelin corpses to pieces and scattering translucent scales like silver leaves in a wind of the sea.

Closer inshore, at the wave line, the flounder wait. They know the capelin are coming and their role is also predetermined. They cruise rapidly under the purling water in uncharacteristic excitement. They are not interested in capelin flesh. They want capelin eggs, and they will eat them as soon as spawning starts.

Now the most voracious of all the hunters appears. Fishing vessels come up over the horizon. They brought the Portuguese of the fifteenth century, who anchored offshore, dropped their boats, and rowed ashore to take the capelin with hand nets, on beaches never before walked by white men. They brought Spaniards and Dutchmen, Englishmen and Irish, from the sixteenth to the twentieth centuries. Americans, Nova Scotians, Gloucestermen, schoonermen, bankermen, long-liner captains, have participated in the ritual. All of them knew that fresh capelin is the finest bait when it is skillfully used, and can attract a fortune in codfish flesh, hooked on the submarine banks to the south.

But presently, these hunters are Newfoundlanders. They bring their schooners flying inshore like great brown-and-white birds, a hundred, two hundred, three hundred sail. They heel through the screaming seabirds, luff, anchor, and drop their dories with the same precision of movement of the other figures in the ritual. In an hour, three thousand men are at work from the boats. They work as the codfish work, with a frenzy that knots forearms and sends nets spilling over the sterns to encircle the capelin. They lift a thousand tons of capelin out of the sea, yet they do not measurably diminish the number of fish.

Meanwhile, landbound hunters wait for the fish to come

within range of their lead-weighted hand nets. Women, children, and old people crowd the beach with the ablebodied men. The old people have ancestral memories of capelin bounty. In the seventeenth and eighteenth centuries, when food was often short, only the big capelin harvest stood between the shore people and starvation during the winter.

Many of the shore people are farmers who use the capelin for fertilizer as well as for food. Capelin corpses, spread to rot over thin northern soils, draw obedient crops of potatoes and cabbages out of the ground, and these, mixed with salted capelin flesh, become winter meals.

The children, who remember dried capelin as their candy, share the excitement of waiting. They chase one another up and down the beach and play with their own nets and fishing rods. Some are already asleep because they awoke before dawn to rouse the village, as they do every capelin morning, with the cry: "They've a-come, they've a-come!"

At the top of the beach, old women lie asleep or sit watching the seabirds squabbling and the dorymen rowing. They are Aunt Sadie and Little Nell and Bessie Blue and Mother Taunton, old ladies from several centuries. They know the capelin can save children in hard winters when the inshore cod fishery fails. They get up at two o'clock in the morning when the capelin are running, to walk miles to the nearest capelin beach. They net a barrel of fish, then roll the barrel, which weighs perhaps a hundred pounds, back home. They have finished spreading the fish on their gardens, or salting them, before the first of their grandchildren awakes.

They have clear memories of catching capelin in winter, when the sea freezes close inshore and the tide cracks the ice in places. Then millions of capelin, resting out the winter, rise in the cracks. An old woman with a good net can take tons of passive fish out of the water for as long as her strength lasts and the net can still reach them.

A cry rises from the beach: "Here they come!"

The ritual must be played out, according to habit. The

dorymen and the seabirds, the rampaging cod and cunner, cannot touch or turn the purpose of the capelin. At a moment, its genesis unknown, they start for the shore. From the top of some nearby cliffs I watch and marvel at the precision of their behavior. The capelin cease to be a great, formless mass offshore. They split into groups that the Newfoundlanders call wads—rippling gray lines, five to fifty feet wide—and run for the shore like advancing infantry lines. One by one, they peel away from their surviving comrades and advance, thirty to forty wads at a time.

Each wad has its discipline. The fish prepare to mate. Each male capelin seeks a female, darting from one fish to another. When he finds one, he presses against her side. Another male, perhaps two males, press against her other side. The males urge the female on toward the beach. Some are struck down by diving seabirds but others take their places. Cod dash among them and smash their sexual formations; they re-form immediately. Cunner rise and rip at them; flounder dart beneath them toward the beach.

The first wad runs into beach wavelets, and a hundred nets hit the water together; a silver avalanche of fish spills out on the beach. In each breaking wavelet the capelin maintain their formations, two or three males pressed tightly against their female until they are all flung up on the beach. There, to the whispering sound of tiny fins and tails vibrating, the female convulsively digs into the sand, which is still moving in the wake of the retreating waves. As she goes down, she extrudes up to fifty thousand eggs, and the males expel their milt.

The children shout; their bare feet fly over the spawning fish; sea boots grind down; the fish spill out; gulls run in the shallows under the children's feet; the flounder gorge. A codfish, two feet long, leaps out of the shallows and hits the beach. An old man scoops it up. The wads keep coming. The air is filled with birds. The dorymen shout and laugh.

The flood of eggs becomes visible. The sand glistens, then is greasy with eggs. They pile in drift lines that writhe back and forth in each wave. The female capelin wriggle into masses of eggs. The shallows are permeated with eggs. The capelin breathe eggs. Their mouths fill with eggs. Their stomachs are choked with eggs. The wads keep pouring onward, feeding the disaster on the beach.

Down come the boots and the nets, and the capelin die, mouths open, and oozing eggs. The spawning is a fiasco. The tide has turned. Instead of spawning on the shore with the assurance of rising water behind them, each wad strikes ashore in retreating water. Millions are stranded, but the wads keep coming.

In the background, diminished by the quantity of fish, other players gasp and pant at their nets. Barrels stack high on the beach. Horses whinny, driven hard up the bank at the back of the beach. Carts laden with barrels weave away. Carts bringing empty barrels bounce and roar down. The wads are still coming. Men use shovels to lift dead and dying fish from drift lines that are now two and three feet high. The easterly wind is freshening. The wavelets become waves. The capelin are flung up on the beach without a chance to spawn. They bounce and twist and the water flees beneath them.

It is twilight, then dark; torches now spot the beach, the offshore dories, and the schooners. The waves grow solidly and pile the capelin higher. The men shovel the heaps into pyramids, then reluctantly leave the beach. Heavy rain blots out beach and sea.

I remain to watch the blow piling up the sea. At the lowest point of the tide, it is driving waves high up on the beach, roiling the sand, digging up the partially buried eggs, and carrying them out to sea. By dawn most of the eggs are gone. The capelin have disappeared. The seabirds, the schooners, the cod, flounder, cunner, seals, whales, have gone. Nothing remains except the marks of human feet, the cart tracks on the high part of the beach, the odd pyramid of dead fish. The feast is done.

The empty arena of the beach suggests a riddle. If the

capelin were so perfectly adapted to spawn on a rising tide, to master the task of burying eggs in running sand between the waves, to know when the tide was rising, why did they continue spawning after the tide turned? Was that, by the ancient rules of the ritual, intentional? If it was, then it indicated a lethal error of anticipation that did not jibe with the great numbers of the capelin.

I wonder, then, if the weak died and the strong survived, but dismiss the notion after recalling the indiscriminate nature of all capelin deaths. There was no Darwinian selection for death of the stupid or the inexperienced. Men slaughtered billions, this year and last year and for three hundred years before, but the capelin never felt this pinpricking of their colossal corporate bodies. Their spawning was a disaster for reasons well beyond the influence of man.

A nineteenth-century observer, after seeing a capelin spawning, recorded his amazement at "the astonishing prosperity of these creatures, cast so willfully away." It was in the end, and indeed throughout the entire ritual, the sheer numbers of capelin that scored the memory. The prosperity of the capelin preceded the disaster but then, it seemed, created it. Prosperity was not beneficial or an assurance of survival. The meaning of the ritual was slowly growing into sense. Prosperity unhinges the capelin. It is a madness of nature. Prosperity, abundance, success, drive them on. They become transformed and throw themselves forward blindly. . . .

I turn from the beach, warm and secure, and take a blind step forward.

11 ○ The Lemming

In the hissing darkness of the night, I was kept awake by explosions and the sounds of heavy falls that came out of the wind, entered the trembling tent, and died away. In the background, it sounded as though giant hinges, rusted shut for thousands of years, were being forced open. All this was familiar enough to Jim McLean, who had spent more time in the high Arctic than I had. He slept easily. But my head seemed about to split. I lay there, every sense jumping with discovery and change.

Yesterday, we had seen a raven coming in to shore from the ice pack, bearing a lemming in his beak, a pathetic droop of tiny rodent body, which could not tell us how it had come to be out on the ice or why the raven must bring it back to shore to eat it. It was no use talking to Eskimos about lemmings, which were only useful, it seemed, as children's playthings.

Muktar, our Eskimo friend and sometime guide, could not be persuaded to talk about lemmings, but he was serious about the ice pack. The noise of this spring breakup might be described, in his language, as "Spirit-who-makes-the-earth-move." Muktar's earth was ice. Lying there, listening, I might make my own translation: "Enemy-who-crushes-the-night."

The Eskimos have a bountiful sense of humor, which first of all sees the white man, the kabloona, as a puzzling fellow who is out of touch with the spirits. In a landscape that is swept clear of landmarks, is empty of footprints, and which remains silent for days, the spirits are the only animation of action and reality. However the Eskimo might joke, though, the spirits describe the real world and serious concerns. The ice is a shifting, unstable foundation, upon which they had chosen to spend so much of their time. It is also a world, as asserted by some cynics who did not believe in spirits, to which they had been driven by cultures with a more earthbound grasp of reality. But upon such a shifting base, as demonstrated by the ice pack, who did not listen to the winds?

The blizzard, in blowing itself out, left the freezing air so clear that the stars looked like chips of white fire in the black sky. The rich choke of a snowy owl sounded distantly. Here, on the shores of the Arctic Ocean, I felt a personal preciousness, a value to human life, which I could not remember having felt before. The empty hissing spaces existed in contrast with the last human settlement we had known, a squalid Eskimo village, littered with plastic and metal garbage.

"Did you know," I said to McLean, as we were trudging through the snow-clogged barrens, "that when the universe begins to contract, as some say it must, then the process of creation will be reversed, and we will be rejuvenated from death, grow ever younger, and the sun will absorb light, and our eyes will emit starlight?"

"You have a decent way with words," said McLean, "although I am not sure what you are saying some of the time."

He was my most laconic friend, a Canadian film-maker and the ultimate fatalist, who believed, like Pangloss, that everything was for the best, and that absolutely nothing mattered. "When in doubt," he said occasionally, "do it." His main delight was "escapes," as he called them, to almost anywhere in the vastnesses of the Canadian North, a place he believed to have therapeutic value—a territory so huge, so abstract in its distancing from ordinary perception, that it was another state of reality.

The distances, the silences, combined to create elongations and distortions of the senses. We tramped through a whiteout, a kind of foaming, low-altitude storm of tiny snow particles, almost as fine as dust, through which the sun, invisible as an entity, diffused virginally pure white light. It created the oddest illusion, of being inside a cathedral in which a storm was boiling outward from an altar. When it thickened, I could hardly see my mitts stretched to arms' length, although I fancied, at the same time, that I could see for yards in all directions. A sudden diapason stopped me short. A bleeding wound as big as a soup plate danced and veered in the white air. When I recovered my aplomb, and the compass of sound had diminished to rapid clatters, I realized that we had flushed a willow ptarmigan. The large red mark had been that tiny touch of color of its wattles or its red eyelids.

Both McLean and I were well familiar with the phenomena of northern travel. Detachment from origins proceeds apace. The traveler vaults, in a long somersaulting arc, away from his home. There is a feeling of intense authenticity, a forceful outflow of identity. In the whiteout, it was a feeling of absolute purity, lost in complete whiteness, our senses caressed by whiteness, our eyes blinded by whiteness.

The far northern peoples have a fine-grained sense of humor, I felt, because they must get their laughter from very small situations. This makes them subtle on the one hand, and, because of the emptiness and ice, stoic on the other. Death is closer to laughter than tears.

A Caribou Indian once made quiet fun of a missionary, who probably did not have much humor in him. "My father," he said, "you have told me that Heaven is very beautiful. Is it more beautiful than the country of the musk-ox in summer, when sometimes the wind blows over the lakes, and sometimes the water is so blue and the loons cry very often? That is beautiful, and if Heaven is still more beautiful, my heart will be very glad, and I shall be content to rest there till I am very old."

The northern peoples work with so few details in such sparse landscapes that their perceptions must be focused much finer than ours. There is no such thing as a lost Eskimo. If he does not return, he is presumed to be dead. Or he will be back in the spring. It does not matter. If he were found, close to death, and saved, he would be most irritated, finding himself deprived of that dignifying chance of saving himself.

The really interesting thing about the kabloona was that he could function without being sensitive to the spirits. He was possessed of an emotion which the Eskimos neither understood nor had a word for: anxiety. From this anxiety came a general challenging of all competence that was not his own. He brought experts for each division of the cosmos. There were meteorologists, and social workers, and men who weighed the eggs of owls. In this technology, the raven had no language, and his croak did not indicate the placement of the bear, or the emergence of the seal from its hidden ice-house. The white bear did not come running because the raven had signaled the kill, by an Eskimo, of a seal.

Without a unifying web of meaning, the kabloona's entry into the Arctic, while it brought comfort, disease control, and the outboard engine, was destructive of meaning. The warrior Eskimo, who was revered because he could kill the bear that came running when he harpooned the seal, was made impotent by the rifle. This weapon made all Eskimos equal. The warrior had no significance, because now anybody could kill the bear. In death, the bear used to be revered as the great hunter. His strength and courage merited awe, and his guile invited emulation. But as a rug, on the floor of the kabloona's house, the bear was useless, and transmitted no meaning.

"If our eyes are to emit starlight," said McLean, "what do we do about eating, in this backward journey toward birth?"

Sir Martin Frobisher came to this country of screaming ice pans, and groaning voices in the darkness, thinking he had discovered gold here. He was anxious to please his queen, Elizabeth I. But he was really bothered by this barbaric notion that a bear, just because it was a formidable adversary in the hunt, should also be revered. Bears were bears. They did not have souls, and neither did any of the other animals. Did not the Esquimaun understand that? The Esquimaun kidnapped some of Frobisher's men as he was departing for England with a cargo of broken rocks, dug up from an Arctic island and showing the glint of pyrites.

His huge ships and firearms had told the Esquimaun that the white man must be allied with the gods. Such power was equal only to that of the father over the child. The Eskimos half-understood that they must become children in order to deal with this new spiritual force. Later, the missionaries and the clergymen discovered that the Eskimos did indeed have a childlike quality, expressed, perhaps, in their conviction that spirits lived in stones and that animals had souls.

"Insects and rocks and grasses do not have individual souls," said the kabloona.

The Eskimo looked baffled, if he was not smashed on whiskey, but then he laughed.

"If the bumblebee does not have a soul," he said triumphantly, "then it must be invisible!"

"They are children," said the clergymen, "but they can be taught to repair outboard engines."

This was true, because the Eskimos wanted to find out

how the white man worked. Taking apart his engines was better than being hanged for taking a white man apart. There was nothing of interest inside the kabloona anyway, just the usual tripes and tubes.

"Their magic is a new kind of thing," said the shaman. "It is contained in something that they carry."

Once, I camped with an Eskimo on the ice near Baffin Island, in the northeast. The wind was chill and the skies were clear, and the Eskimo carried his new rifle, a ten-shot Remington. How he loved that rifle! He caressed its burnished barrel and worked the oil-sucking bolt back and forth at our evening camp for so long that in exasperation I had shouted at him to stop.

On this morning, before the spring breakup, when my hands were colored orange in the new light of the sun, we saw that more than one hundred seals had come up on the surface of the ice. I remembered it as a beautiful moment: the adrenaline rush of the hunter in both of us. I could feel a gun in my hands again and see the fall of deer.

The Eskimo fumbled with his magazines (he had only owned a single-shot before) and I looked impatiently at the pale blue horizon, bunched with snow-strewn undulations, angled with planes of ice that had thawed and frozen several times. The Eskimo cursed, and dropped another magazine. Between us and the horizon stretched a sheen of water on a great prairie of ice. A bulk of a solitary iceberg formed a ziggurat of silence with the inevitable observing raven at its peak. The seals were too far from their breathing holes.

The Eskimo needed six seals for his settlement, but the rifle was too exciting. He began firing, hands trembling with eagerness. Strange mouthing noises came out of him as bullets sprayed the icescape shooting gallery. Seals hurled themselves forward in long glissades, and collided, in towering crashes, at the breathing holes. The bullets, badly aimed though they were, could hardly miss. The bodies piled up.

The Eskimo killed ninety-nine seals. He threw down the hot rifle as might a buffalo hunter.

"Why did you kill so many when you needed so few?"

An Oriental silence was the answer.

The rifle lay smoking. We looked at it, but neither of us could speak. This hang-fisted man, who had once talked to animals, had no discourse with his weapon. It was at the tip of my tongue to tell him about the gadget as a servant, or slave, nothing more, but I could not be sure that I believed that myself. The rifle was his only means of escaping from Frobisher's paternal threat: Obey me, or be destroyed.

"The Eskimos," said McLean, when we talked about such things at night, "are a pretty smashed-up people."

The cheerful chatter of snow buntings surrounded our camp. They had advanced into the Arctic on a front thousands of miles across, the first songbirds to attempt a foothold in the snow. Many would die for this presumption. They had been seen falling, with closed wings, frozen in flight during the long winter. A delicate, almost dovelike ivory gull, a wraith in the white sky of his arrival, became visible because of red eyelids and shiny hanging black feet.

There, in a little while, was the raven, awaiting our move. He was a presence, a voice, an intelligence that spoke of the secret life of the tundra, of lemmings drawn from its frozen bulk and carried to an exposed patch of ground, or rock, where deft blows of the beak made the tiny hamster-like bodies little more than an opening of the beak, a jerk of the head, and a swallow.

"I've seen him picking up scraps of krill from around the breathing holes of seals," said McLean. "He follows bears. Last year, off Baffin Island, there were ravens watching killer whales, swimming up Iceberg Alley. When the whales killed, the ravens knew they would eat blubber, from the mangled seals, on the shores of the island."

Ravens attended the bloody aftermath of medieval battles, clouds of carrion seekers at Crécy, Poitiers, Agincourt, where they stirred the disgust of noblemen and commoners alike. The raven flew from Noah's wrist and left Viking ships to find Iceland. The Yukon Indians said, "The raven knows," which tallied with Babylonian inscriptions that called him "the messenger who brings good news, and speaks with kings."

The raven was now very close to the tent. He shuffled his feathers like a deck of cards, and settled on the snow to wait. The lemmings would soon be exposed by the melting snow, swarming, and these tent people would have scraps all summer. Ravens haunted Napoleon in Moscow when he cursed them as birds of "ill omen." His men believed that the ravens were demanding the return of the army to Paris. Perhaps the raven at our tent was the same bird I had seen at the ruins of Carthage, a jaunty thief, stealing an ancient bone from a desert dog.

A newborn Eskimo baby wore a raven's foot fashioned into an amulet, placed around the neck so that the child might one day acquire the bird's toughness and cunning, become a real hunter, and, knowing the original secret, be "satisfied with a little."

A final spring blizzard blew and we dug drifts from the sides of the tent and scraped out tracks to perform our chores. A tiny sacramental bell began ringing in the distance, more a tinkle than a bellbird chime. But soon it was joined by other bells until we were surrounded by a chorus of tinkling voices.

Discolored snow, at first sloshing in helpless rivulets emerging from snowbanks, soon became streams of dirty water which, overnight, turned into torrents of snow and ice and mud. The disintegration of the landscape was so general, and so violent, that not much was to be done except retire to the tent, fasten its entrance, and stay as dry as possible while everything turned to mud.

Outside, night and day, the sea ice cracked and snapped. Frantic lemmings, their snow corridors broken, ran into the tent in flight from the raven, who had been joined by an ermine. An Arctic fox, his tail up like a flag, stood on a ridge, digging into the snow for the squeaking refugees. The snow fell away. He stood naked in his white raiment, bedraggled. The tent fell down.

In the sea, widening leads of water opened up. Floes packed together, upended in briefly savage winds. Strings of snow geese landed in the black and expanding waters. Ducks sped overhead and swans challenged the new season with mute cries. The ermine became a half-weasel as the brown coat of summer came through the white. He ambushed a hare at the shore. The sharp teeth sank into the throat. Blood spurted. Even though the kill was made nearly one hundred yards away, I could hear the rip of teeth.

The clarity of the light made us both aware that this was, indeed, starlight, cosmically revealing. Tiny space travelers disguised as songbirds and shorebirds, navigants by the stars, arrived at night and in the day. They dropped down exhausted; some, landing near the tent, came inside in search of guidance. Cries querying whereabouts echoed above our heads. They were telling us that the journey from one end of the earth to the other was not merely possible; it was obligatory. The voices swelled with the days as birds emptied out of eastern coasts of America, from the Caribbean, South America, Africa, and from the distant shores of the Ross Sea, where cyclones tore at the smoke of a volcano.

The landbirds arrived as a result of the most dangerous journeys, threaded through corridors between cities. They had been lashed by the exhausts of airplanes, cut down impartially by the contrary winds of warring seasons, the spires of skyscrapers, the treacherous appearance of giant towers which had grown in their tracks, like parabolic weeds. Then hawks, eagles, falcons were everywhere, and ambushes by owls awaited every night flier seeking rest in the dusky trees.

The shorebirds, creatures of the beaches, estuaries,

lagoons, and riverbanks, were the greatest travelers, some of whom had vaulted out of the dawns of the Río de la Plata, or from shimmering lagoons in Chile, survivors of starvation flights over paralyzing jungles filled with poisonous enemies. Phalaropes from Africa dropped to shallow ponds and twirled their bodies in tests for mosquito larvae, which would be available later. Graceful curlews, long legs dangling, flew the tundra, while dowitchers mingled their clattering cries with the booming echoes of sandpipers, the twitter of oyster catchers.

The trills and tinkling songs and random tunes made a kind of canon to my own thoughts. I listened to music that empowered memory, and smoothed the passage of great distances, and times, wherein the pain of effort was forgotten in the pleasure of arrival. The birds sang on the ground, in the air, by day and by night, and eventually I turned off my small tape player at night because there was so much music outside. The birds chased and fought each other and their music contained all the essential information in the search for identity in mating, the definitions of territory, the hollowing of faint refuges for the spate of eggs to come. The ice would be gone only briefly, and if the eggs were crushed or pirated by raven or weasel, there would be no second chance.

Before this time, I had always felt a kind of genial contempt for birds. Fine plumage and tiny brains. They were evolutionary refugees who had solved all their problems of survival by running away. I had not seen them as a collective representative of nature, unified in such coordinated purpose, and now, thousands of miles from their main enemies, no longer under such stimulus to flee.

A plover flopped along the ground, feigning a broken wing to draw me away from a nest that she had not yet built. I picked up a purple sandpiper and it sat in my hand as though incubating eggs yet to be laid. A ptarmigan put its chest on my boot, trying to keep me from approaching his mate on her nest.

The rush of spring is also the dash of summer, the two inseparable in the exigent purpose of red meat. This was as relentless as the leopard's stalk, the wolf pack's rush. Lest I mislead that this was a season merely of singing and sex, the insects rose from the earth, a reminder that all the birds were carnivores, consumers of blood-carrying insects. Only insects could sleep through the Arctic winter in numbers sufficiently great to bring creatures from twelve thousand miles away to feed on them. Only insects could slumber as eggs, pupae, adults. Only insects could breed fast enough to hold these space travelers, to transfer the blood from visitor to resident, to female, to egg, to earth, and thence back to the sleep of winter.

There was no place for flycatchers up here because any bird could catch these insects. I watched McLean pour tea from a blackened billy, a hundred mosquitoes fastened to his forearms. The winds came out of the sea and flies and mosquitoes became sluggish, unable to walk, much less fly. Beetles, armored bodies glistening, scurried through the tundra grasses, and made their harvest. They were run down, in turn, by fleet wolf spiders, which stored their victims in silken prisons.

Blood flowed in invisible rivers, and so did nectar. Sleepy bumblebees appeared out of old lemming burrows and droned among the blossoms of Arctic poppy and bog cotton, the flowers of saxifrage, the swarming tiny receptacles of blueberry and cranberry, the catkins of stunted willow trees. Nectar sweetened the blood meals.

I could feel the blood in my own veins, hissing in tube-bound cataracts from the heart to the lungs, driving its way through capillaries, circulating in eyeballs that saw the flowers and eardrums that heard the music—blood that did not remember fear, but felt only love now, most particularly of movement, the urgency to fend off that lack of feeling that is death. Hurry, hurry, before it is too late, and the ice floes come to shore. Life hangs on a spider's strand.

McLean said that the clarity of the air had something to

do with the ability to think more clearly. I said it was also the willingness to feel more accurately, to know the emotions deeper down the slender stem holding us aloft here. I could begin to know the spirits that lay within the stones, and to sense the soul that lay within the nectar of the quivering flowers.

The light grew more brilliant and I walked along the shore, and then deep into the tundra, and followed the paths of bustling streams over which I stepped a thousand times, rivers in miniature, to reach the shores of temporary lakes and ponds, and there was this feeling of having left something behind, of escape occurring, a snap in the elastic of time, broken bonds hurtling dangerously through space, wrestling with a stranger after crossing the dark waters. What if I became lame in such long and solitary walks?

The stunted dwarf willows, a foot high, catkins fluttering a joyous signal, were flowering here five hundred years before Columbus blundered into Hispaniola. I was locked into this place within the steel embrace of millions of years of permanency. What discipline! What control! What subtle regulation! The clarity of the stars at night transformed them truly into separate suns which, just as quickly as they assumed power, slipped toward oblivion when the nights were turned into pallid days.

But we lived under a blaze of starlight. The bumblebees, which were now buzzing all around our feet, did indeed have souls. Had that fact ever been in question?

The lemmings became addicts of the sun. It was impossible to escape them. As I walked, there were lemmings everywhere, emerging from their burrows, forming lustrous carpets with the massing of their bodies. The fox ate them until he was bloated and the raven followed me tirelessly, and dined on the lemming wake of my travel.

The rise of the lemmings was a triumph for the commoner, which overwhelmed such aristocratic statements as the gyrfalcon. He appeared at the campsite one day, a mottled white bullet that rose on a tower of speed and was gone into a cloud. The massed good of the tundra was the fierce growth of plants which could be voted to one species of consumer, only if such selfish election chose to ignore the future. It was something like the springing of a river, fed by rains that cannot be seen or heard. It irrigated all the country, but the fertility must run out.

Family after identical family came out of the earth, one new generation every thirteen or fourteen days. A little more than one hundred days of breeding spewed out seven hundred and fifty descendants from one family. Children were breeding, and grandchildren, and very soon, great-grandchildren approached each other to mate.

Young ducklings flew hesitantly to test their wings and new shorebirds formed flocks in readiness for the migration south, but they were insignificant sideshows to the drilling of the blazing tundra with lemming tunnels. Did such ambition have substance? A bear arrived and stood on a ridged horizon, looking like an old lady in a tatty cream coat. He scooped up lemmings, flung them about, and then rolled on them like a puppy. He came up with his coat decorated with the red explosions of those he had crushed.

After the plowing, the lemmings polluted. What they did not eat down to the roots, which was almost everything, they despoiled with their sewage, changing the flowering earth into a wasteland. This sent them into hasty movement, urgent mini-migrations. But horde met horde. Finally, when all was eaten out for miles, the hordes combined and began mass movements, anywhere, everywhere, nowhere. It was not true that they committed suicide by jumping into the sea. They had to leave the land because they had eaten it bare.

Lemmings in the tent, lemmings in the boots, lemmings dead in ponds, lemmings crazed on their backs, lemmings cringing and atremble in the light of the fire, so weak from hunger that they dropped in the middle of a scamper. "Talk about the tyranny of the weak," said McLean, chuckling.

* * *

We sat in studied silences as the Arctic summer died a subtle death. The feeling of rushing movement had slowed to a gentle crawl, and the sky no longer blazed with revelatory light, but glowed in a softer display. The air is soon touched with a wry and womanly hint of change, a lover's cool hand near the face. Berries ripened and dried, grasses seeded and fell swiftly and insects slipped back into the earth. The sun sat on the tundra, pale gold and as flat as a doubloon; the sea lay under mauve-tinted mist. The lemmings had disappeared. The shorebirds resumed the stage.

These were not the same birds which had arrived here after the last spring blizzard. These were the summer offspring, fresh, virginal, alone. Each slight body was a computer of stored maps, relief models of beaches, headlands, schematics of currents, charts of inlets which threw up plankton at the turn of the Passamaquoddy tide, the location of ponds that harbored minnows, the position of fields folded by diesel plows. Here were the instructions for reaching southern Greenland, finding the staging places in New England, Florida, Surinam, Paraguay. There were hard times ahead, because many of the adults had already slipped away, to eat out the food that these youngsters needed along the way.

One generation had transferred its entire competence to another, without fanfare or propaganda, without the use of guilt or punishment, or fear, or inducement, or anything that we could see or know. The Arctic terns rushed outward at one hundred miles an hour, and their somber nestlings crouched among stones. They knew how to find Antarctica, swing past the volcano, and spend their winter there, in another polar summer. Watching them, I felt the pole at my back, facing the distant echo of the emperor penguin crying welcome from the other side of the earth.

At about that time, the aurora started to move.

The aurora borealis is one of the great phenomena of nature, and, in its variety, more spectacular than the aurora australis. It can be analyzed as a fiery waterfall of electrons, towering hundreds of miles into the stratosphere and illuminating hundreds of thousands of square miles of the northern earth in its eerie glow. It can be described as a brilliant yellow rustling of immense and exotic tapestries, or flaming shafts of crimson boiling into the stars. It may be arcs of smoking gray, or writhing violet, the green glow of an auroral arch, its apex pointed to the magnetic meridian. It is the "merry dancers" of the Shetland Islanders, and the "shimmering curtains" of northern city dwellers, as electrons, thrown out by the sun, make their rushing day-long passage to earth and inflame its magnetic field.

We sat in silence as the colors, limned in orange for a while, turned into a ghostly red, rising in slowing knots of energy. I poured tea while McLean dismantled the fire. He laid aside the charred scraps of wood in readiness for a later fire. We walked inland, and found travelers who would go down the Mississippi and veer and dawdle along the trails of the extinct buffalo, before crossing the Pacific on their way to Australia and New Zealand. The terns, fleet as blown snow, a fork of wings in wait for Africa, had gone to the southern pole.

The sun, which had refused to set, was now reluctant to rise, and in fugitive flights, left spectrally brief twilights. The callow groups of shorebirds gathered around us seemed prepared for sleep, but were gone, delicate footprints left in muddy places, before the twinge of dawn.

The discipline of movement was complete. One long-legged youngster, left behind on a beach, made no resistance when the raven came down and smothered him in a flurry of black wings and jabbing beak. It seemed to be the murder of a small and innocent child, but I felt no pity. We sat on the ruined tundra and looked at the chilling waters.

About the Author

A Canadian citizen, Franklin Russell was born in Christchurch, New Zealand, and received his education in that country and in Australia and England. His early experiences as a farmer in New Zealand provided the base for his lifelong fascination with domestic and wild creatures in their widely varying environments. This interest in human and animal coexistence has been built upon over the years by Russell's international residences in New Zealand, Australia, England, South Africa, India, Canada and the United States, as well as by his travels from the North Pole to the South Pole. He has been a Guggenheim fellow and a fellow of the Canada Council. The author of the bestselling *Watchers at the Pond* as well as a number of other highly original studies of nature, he is now at work on a book on the Arctic.